The RUBBER BRAIN

A toolkit for optimising your study, work, and life!

Sue Morris

Jacquelyn Cranney

Peter Baldwin

Leigh Mellish

Annette Krochmalik

AUSTRALIANACADEMIC**PRESS**

First published 2018 by:
Australian Academic Press Group Pty. Ltd.
18 Victor Russell Drive
Samford Valley QLD 4520, Australia
www.australianacademicpress.com.au

The Rubber Brain:

ISBN   9781925644081 (paperback)
ISBN   9781925644098 (ebook)

Disclaimer
Every effort has been made in preparing this work to provide information based on accepted standards and practice at the time of publication. The publisher and authors, however, makes no warranties of any kind of psychological outcome relating to use of this work and disclaim all responsibility or liability for direct or consequential damages resulting from any use of the material contained in this work.

Publisher & Editor: Stephen May
Cover design: Luke Harris, Working Type Studio
Typesetting: Australian Academic Press
Printing: Lightning Source

This book is dedicated to
Zac and Zoe, Mally and Caillan,
who inspire all that we do. (SM & JC)

Contents

Acknowledgements

Our collective thanks go to:

Stephen May, for his expertise and guidance, and for making our dream a reality.

Our past, present, and future students, who motivate us to leave the world a better place than we found it.

And to our co-authors, for months of earnest creativity, robust debate, meaningful collaboration, and for sharing the passion for optimising student minds and lives!

SM: To David, for your unwavering patience and encouragement; to Zac and Zoe for optimising my world (and for being such an enthusiastic audience for the ideas and jokes in this book); to Lil and Pete, for being my most enduring and vocal fans; and to my broader family, 'framily', and friends, for your love and laughter.

JC: To my immediate and extended family and to my friends for your steadfast support; to many education colleagues for creating cooperative spaces in which we all could grow; to all those who have helped me to constructively challenge my own M_{SUB}'s.

PB: To my incredibly supportive parents for teaching me both compassion and courage; to my amazing mentors who have always shone a light at just the right time; to the truly wonderful people I call my friends; to every client who has trusted me with their mind; and to every person brave enough to try a different way of thinking.

LM: To my family, who have always supported me in pursuing my own interests.

AK: First and foremost: to Eli and our three treasures — Benjamin, Joseph and Lily-Rose — for your unconditional, never-ending love and support and for giving me meaning and true happiness; to the rest of my family for always encouraging and believing in me; to my colleagues for introducing me to the wonderful world of psychological literacy, resilience and wellbeing; and to everyone who has contributed to my own level of wellbeing.

Dr. Sue Morris has a passion for enhancing students' success and wellbeing, with an emphasis on positive psychology and resilience. She completed her undergraduate studies and PhD in Developmental Psychology at the University of New South Wales (UNSW), where she has worked as a lecturer in the School of Psychology, as well as in staff development for educators. Over 20 years of undergraduate teaching, she has focused on developing innovative and engaging learning experiences for students, emphasising collaboration and connectedness. She applies psychological literacy in her teaching, with a goal to 'optimise the world, one student at a time'. Her interest and expertise in enhancing student learning has been recognised through numerous awards, including the UNSW Vice Chancellor's Award for Teaching Excellence, the UNSW Faculty of Science Staff Excellence Award, and an Australian Office of Learning and Teaching Citation for Outstanding Contributions to Student Learning. Sue's university teaching experience has been complemented by serving as a director on the board of Moriah College for the past decade, which has given her extensive insight into the needs of primary and high school students. However, she has learned the most about wellbeing and positivity from her two teenage children.

Associate Professor Jacky Cranney (UNSW Sydney) has extensive undergraduate teaching experience, for which she has won numerous UNSW, national and international awards. She has published research on student learning and motivation, and on psychology education. She has created local, national and international communities of practice for psychology educators, and has also led and contributed to national committees on psychology education. She has attracted several UNSW and national education Fellowships and grants, through which she has driven nation-wide change in terms of undergraduate students learning to apply evidence-based psychological strategies to meet positive personal, professional and societal outcomes. Jacky is a fervent believer in 'giving psychology away', particularly through providing opportunities to undergraduate students and others, to develop psychological literacy (i.e., the intentional application of psychological science to meet personal, professional and societal needs), a part of which is evidence-based self-management (i.e., the capacity to effectively pursue valued goals, and to be flexible in the face of setbacks).

Dr. Peter Baldwin is an academic psychologist and clinician based at Sydney's Black Dog Institute, where he studies digital health interventions. After completing his undergraduate studies in psychology, Peter went on to complete both a Masters and a PhD in clinical psychology, focusing on novel brain-based models of hoarding disorder. Peter has authored several peer-reviewed articles and book chapters in clinical psychology, and has been privileged to use his expertise in hoarding disorder to train allied health practitioners both in Australia and the UK. Peter has also spent over half a decade educating emerging psychologists and understands that mental wellbeing is crucial to the success of his students. He believes that every person (young and old) deserves to understand their own mind using the principles of cognitive and behavioural science, and in doing so, live a more meaningful life. He hopes this book will help young people do both.

Leigh Mellish is a psychologist (Master of Organisational Psychology; UNSW Sydney) working as a career development consultant for university students — focusing on improving their capacity and employability through effective education and practice. At UNSW and USYD he has lectured in psychology, management, and career development across 8 years, and has conducted research and published in psychology and medicine across 12 years. His industry experience has been in organisational development, management consulting, and recruitment. Leigh values scientific thinking, evidence-based decision making, and honest and professional discourse for self-development and global impact.

Dr. Annette Krochmalik obtained her undergraduate degree at UNSW and went on to complete her PhD in the area of anxiety at The University of Sydney. She completed her Post-Doctoral studies at the Center for Psychiatric Rehabilitation at Boston University. She then returned to Sydney where, in the School of Psychology UNSW, she has been focusing on student resilience and wellbeing. She enjoys teaching undergraduate students as well as being involved in research in clinical psychology and psychology education.

CHAPTER 1

What's on Your Mind?

It's a question we are all familiar with. What are our brains thinking about? Your brain is responsible for most of the things you do. It controls your conscious thoughts and behaviours, like deciding whether to study or party, or whether to get two scoops of gelato or six, even whether or not to buy this book. But your brain also controls stuff you might not normally think too much about. Important stuff, like breathing. And while sometimes your brain can be your strongest ally (such as when your lungs are empty), at other times it can be your worst enemy, leading you to behave in ways that aren't exactly as helpful as you might have expected. It might lead you to say things to your friends that you end up regretting or cause you to play computer games all day instead of working on that important assignment or cleaning your house (sound familiar?). We call this **suboptimal thinking**. Essentially, this is when your brain does not deliver the kind of thinking that leads to desired positive outcomes, such as maintaining supportive friendships, and doing well in your work and studies.

The purpose of this book is to provide you with the information, and especially the tools, to check out whether your ways of thinking are suboptimal in relation to what you want to achieve and if they are, then how to change them to **optimal thinking**. We want to help you optimise your thinking so that your mind is clearer, and your life is better.

What is Optimal and Suboptimal Thinking?

When we talk about 'thinking' (whether optimal or suboptimal), what we are really talking about is the activity of the mind, including not just thoughts, but also feelings, beliefs, mindsets, and the capacity to produce behaviour. The mind is the 'software' enabled by the 'hardware' of the brain — the activity of those billions of neurons and associated structures.

Optimal thinking is the kind of thinking that produces behaviour that helps you reach your goals. For example, if your goal is to obtain a pass in your subject and you study enough to 'get you over the line', your thinking is optimal. Suboptimal thinking, on the other hand, might lead you to procrastinate until the night before an assessment is due, and then to pull an all-nighter to produce something that is probably not up to scratch. Moreover, if your goal is to do really well in that subject, then optimal thinking would involve spending much more time (using appropriate thinking) to learn what is required and to prepare more appropriately for assessments.

So you may see that 'optimal' is somewhat dependent on your specific goal, but regardless of the goal, optimal thinking will help you to achieve it. Suboptimal thinking, on the other hand, is decidedly less helpful!

But suboptimal thinking is not simply 'really crappy thinking'. There may be varying degrees of suboptimal, ranging from being so anxious about an exam that you cannot study (highly suboptimal), to only mildly suboptimal, such as spending a decent amount of effort studying in time for an exam, but not using the most effective exam study techniques. Whichever level of 'suboptimal' you are experiencing, this is unhelpful thinking in the sense that it is not optimally moving you closer toward your goals and desired positive outcomes (e.g., passing an exam). Similarly, optimal thinking does not equal 'perfect' thinking (spoiler alert — there is no such thing as 'perfect' thinking). Like suboptimal thinking, optimal thinking lies on a continuum, where we can always decide to strive to optimise or improve our thinking, such that it maximises the likelihood of producing our desired outcome (or, we can decide that our thinking is good enough).

Throughout this book, we give you examples of suboptimal or unhelpful thinking across a range of situations, and then provide the tools to optimise thinking to gain better outcomes. You could just read about these tools (if this is a text book that you are being forced to read) or take things a step further by using some of the tools in your life. That's up to you.

Just to be clear: we are not saying that up to now all of your thinking has been suboptimal — in fact, most of us who are coping okay with life have quite adequate thinking most of the time, and sometimes even excellent thinking (otherwise you would not be reading this book!). The tools in this book can help you to evaluate your thinking and behaviour as you come across the various challenges and goals in your life and then *you* can decide whether or not to use the optimising tools.

Many of the examples we give in this book of suboptimal thinking, and tools to optimise thinking and behaviour, are particularly relevant if you are beginning at university or college with the aim of being successful in your studies and other aspects of your life, including your relationships. Other tools explained throughout the coming chapters will be relevant across a range of life experiences and situations.

As with any tool, practising the right way to use it is important, so we have included lots of short **TRY IT!** exercises to encourage you to actively engage with the tools and concepts we discuss by completing small tasks which usually involve jotting down your thoughts and/or responses.

For those readers who want to find out even more about the topics in each chapter we have included **Diving Deeper** sections that add further explanatory detail.

So let's get started.

Thinking Starts with 'Unthinking'

Some of our behavioural responses in our day-to-day lives are truly 'unthinking' in a biological sense. For example, withdrawing our hand when we touch a hot stove does not involve any thinking, because it does not even involve the mind, just the spinal cord using a neuronal reflex. We can describe this experience using simple shorthand references to represent the event. In this case, the withdrawing of the hand is called the **Response**, represented by the letter **R**, the hot stove we touched is the **Stimulus Situation** represented by the letter **S**, and the **Mind** is represented by the letter **M**.

However, there are many responses that *seem* equally unthinking but actually result from the actions of our mind. Over the course of our experiences, our mind develops **frameworks** — systems for many complex functions, such as driving, eating, forming friendships or reacting to a disappointing outcome (see *Diving Deeper 1.1*). Across most of these situations, much of our behaviour seems unthinking: our mind applies the framework to the given situation, and generally this works fine. However, sometimes this seemingly unthinking type of response is not helpful and causes more harm than good. Sometimes our frameworks are outdated, or unsuitable for the situation, or simply flawed, so when our mind applies them we don't get the outcome we really want.

Applying unsuitable frameworks is at the core of suboptimal thinking. For some of us, our minds tend to keep engaging in suboptimal thinking even though it leads to negative or suboptimal outcomes. In part, this is because our mind prefers to use established frameworks rather than making new ones (after all, it spent a lot of time and resources making the old ones!). But also, sometimes we just don't know any other way of doing things. We might *want* to improve our suboptimal thinking, but we just don't know *how*.

So What is Suboptimal Thinking, Really?

Before we start trying to optimise our thinking, let's illustrate what we mean by 'suboptimal' thinking.

Meet Liam. Liam has a crush on Bec and has finally worked up the courage to ask her out. They met, had dinner, and then Liam dropped Bec off at her house. Later that night, Liam texted Bec to thank her for their great time together. On waking the next morning, Liam reached for his phone, certain that Bec would have sent a cascade of emoji chronicling their perfect evening … but there was nothing! Sad, self-defeating thoughts immediately popped into Liam's mind: 'She doesn't like me! I'm a hopeless failure when it comes to dating! I'm just not lovable'. Liam felt miserable, called in 'sick' to work (again), and spent the rest of the day at home robbing banks (on *Grand Theft Auto*, of course).

Does this reaction sound familiar?

What went wrong for Liam, and how can we help him? To answer those questions, we need to understand how Liam got from 'no text' (S) to 'I'm taking a sickie' (R). We need to examine what is happening in Liam's mind, in particular, the suboptimal thinking that influenced the connection between 'no text' and the maladaptive or suboptimal response of 'taking a sickie'. Again, we can make use of our shorthand: Liam's **suboptimal thinking** is represented by M_{SUB} and his **suboptimal response** by R_{SUB}.

⚑ TRY IT! 1.1

Unthinking Responses

Think about a situation (S) in your life that leads to an *unthinking* response (R) leading to a negative outcome. For example, you arrive home from work/study exhausted, your partner/house-mate/parent asks you to take out the trash, you scream that you 'just need to be left alone' and retreat to your bedroom, slamming the door — all leading to an unhelpful icy relationship for the next 24 hours. What is *your* unthinking response?

In Liam's case we see a fundamental property of human thought — the mind influences the relationship between the situation and our complex responses to it. Often we are not fully aware of this role of the mind, which is one reason why suboptimal thinking and responding can be so difficult to change.

What is likely is that between the situation (S) of 'no return message from Bec' and the response (R) of taking a sickie, Liam's mind was applying some suboptimal thinking. Though understandable, it would be hard to argue that Liam's sad feelings and subsequent behaviour led to good outcomes — the guy is cutting himself off from his social support network and losing money in the process! But are Liam's suboptimal thinking and the subsequent suboptimal responses inevitable? Is this one of those unchangeable S-R systems, like the spinal reflex when you quickly withdraw your hand after you accidently touch a hot stove (see *Diving Deeper 1.1*), or are there things that Liam can do so that the consequences are not so negative? Can we access and optimise the part of Liam's mind that **mediated** (i.e., caused) his unhealthy responses?

Of course we can! Otherwise this book would be much shorter! What we need to do is give Liam ways of optimising his thinking, so that situations (like not receiving a text) elicit healthier, more helpful thoughts and beliefs. We're going to 'fix' suboptimal thinking by getting Liam (and you) to try some optimised thinking.

From Suboptimal Thinking to Optimised Thinking

Because some of the authors of this book are science nerds, we've come up with a model to help illustrate the process of optimising our thinking. We call this the **SMR model** of optimising thinking, and we'll use this model throughout the book. We'd like to introduce it to you here so you know what we're talking about, then in future chapters we will use the same model to tackle different situations you might come across.

Figure 1.1 illustrates what is going on for Liam. There is a strong and inevitable connection between the situation (S) of 'no text' and the responses (R) of feeling 'down' and then skipping work. In the middle you'll notice an M, and this is the 'mediating' thing we mentioned — your mind. In our SMR model, 'Mind' includes your core beliefs and assumptions about the way the world works, which often sit below your conscious awareness, and which influence how you respond to a given situation. The M in our model incorporates your beliefs, frameworks, mindsets, thoughts, and much more. These may be learned or innate and, if learned, they may have developed through your own experience, or through something you have read or heard about happening to someone else, known as **vicarious learning**. They may be beliefs you are already aware of, or those that you need **tools** to help you uncover and understand. Many of these beliefs and assumptions are the reason that your mind sometimes seems to be playing for the other team; these are the beliefs and assumptions that can be part of suboptimal thinking.

Figure 1.1   The situation (S) elicits a suboptimal response (R_{SUB}), mediated by unhelpful beliefs and assumptions situated in the mind (M_{SUB}), which is currently below awareness (indicated by the dashed outline).

Note that, as in Liam's case, there is often is a lack of awareness of the influence of these suboptimal thoughts, indicated by the dashed outline around the M. The first step in examining the causes of suboptimal responses is effortfully becoming aware of these suboptimal thoughts. Reflecting on what is causing these suboptimal responses is a bit like shining a flashlight onto the depths of your mind, to better understand what is going on in there. The solid outline around the M in Figure 1.2 denotes an awareness of suboptimal thinking.

Figure 1.2   Through effortfully examining one's thought processes, it is possible to become aware of the presence of suboptimal thoughts (M_{SUB}), which are driving suboptimal responses (R_{SUB}).

Of course many of your beliefs and assumptions are already very helpful, in that they assist you to respond optimally to a given situation in terms of producing a positive outcome. We call this **optimised thinking** represented by M_{OP}. However, in many cases it is possible to optimise your thinking a little (or a lot) more. The SMR model helps you identify your thinking to decide whether it is optimal thinking (M_{OP}) or suboptimal thinking (M_{SUB}), and if the latter, gives you tools to help you change that suboptimal thinking, so that you're looking less like Figure 1.1, and more like Figure 1.3. Alternatively, you may have fairly good thinking in some areas, but you want to make it even better — again, this is about optimising thinking (M_{OP}).

We are not going to get you to lay down on a couch and cogitate endlessly about how your M_{SUB}'s came about. Instead, we are going to focus on the effect that your M_{SUB}'s have on how you respond to situations in your daily life, and how you can use science-based tools to get your mind from M_{SUB} to M_{OP}. We know from research that as you start optimising your mind, this can lead to more and more optimised responses, which in turn can lead to a life that is healthier, happier and more meaningful than skipping work and bingeing on computer games.

Figure 1.3   Using appropriate tools, it is possible to optimise thinking (M_{OP}) and thus responding (R_{OP}).

DIVING DEEPER 1.1

Unpacking Some Basics About Stimulus–Response (SR) and Stimulus–Mind–Response (SMR)

Let's do a little unpacking of the mind and how it affects our behaviour. The most basic connection is one that just involves stimulus to response (SR) connections. Last night, while baking a lasagne for Bec, clumsy Liam burnt his hand on a baking dish that he forgot was still hot. The stimulus (S) in this case was the hand on the hot baking dish, and the response (R) was a rapid withdrawal of his hand (R). This SR sequence did not require Liam's mind, because this is a spinal reflex — that is, the circuitry that controls the response is in the spinal cord. So no Ms to worry about here.

Now to the next level of complexity. Liam has a YouTube channel that is basically a series of (admittedly hilarious) videos of him scaring his friend Ray. Liam slams a door and Ray jumps. Liam pops a balloon behind Ray's head and Ray screams. Ray gets embarrassed by his reactions (and the million or so people laughing at them), but these behaviours aren't actually under his control. Ray's jumping or screaming responses (R) to the sound stimulus (S) are unthinking. They are an automatic response of Ray's nervous system. These kinds of unthinking responses are innate, and have contributed to our survival, because the startle response allows rapid evasion of a predator (be it a tiger or a balloon) — and this is a good thing. Given the life-saving nature of these responses, we would never want to 'undo' or break that SR connection. But here's the thing — these are not spinal reflexes, but 'subcortical' reflexes. This means that lower parts of the brain control the basic startle response, and so the thoughts and emotions (or our mind, M) have some influence on the nature of the response but cannot really stop the response (as Ray has discovered, much to his chagrin).

However, there are many responses that seem equally unthinking but are not actually innate. Instead, many responses are acquired over the course of our lives. For example, after yet another humiliating scare video, Ray decides to go for a drive. He is driving along a suburban road at a moderate speed, when suddenly a child runs out onto the road in front of him. Ray slams on the brakes, and luckily stops just before the car makes a paediatric pancake.

Ray jumping at the bursting balloon was innate (and hilarious), but his braking was learned. Put simply, Ray's braking is a learned response (R) to a child on the road (S). Over the course of Ray's driving experiences, his mind (M) has developed a framework of how driving should work.

That is, when the child ran out in front of Ray's car, the connection between the situation and the response required little if any 'conscious' thinking. Ray's brain didn't need to think about how to slow the car, instead it applied the driving framework to the current situation, producing the response. This kind of responding is just as important as the innate SR response (especially for the child), and although it might seem unthinking, it is the result of Ray's previously established driving framework and the fact that he was paying attention to the road as he drove. That is, Ray's brain detected the stimulus (S) — the sudden appearance of a child — and engaged the appropriate response (R) of slamming on the brakes. (This is why you need to have a more experienced brain next to you when you are learning to drive!).

Diving Still Deeper: The Driving Framework

Let's unpack this commonly learned driving framework a little more. During your first driving lessons, you are likely all thumbs, high anxiety, and yes, there may be some minor collisions. Driving is a highly complex set of skills, and learning these skills, and integrating them, takes an enormous amount of conscious and effortful brain processing. This puts a heavy load on the high-level 'orchestra conductor' part of your brain, the neocortex of the frontal lobe (just behind your forehead). As you practice over and over the individual skills (e.g., releasing the clutch and applying the accelerator simultaneously with each gear shift upwards) and their integration with other essential skills (e.g., continuous monitoring of traffic), more direct connections between relevant parts of the brain below the frontal lobe neocortex (e.g., parts of the basal ganglia and the cerebellum) are activated and strengthened, forming part of the driving framework or neural network in your brain. As this framework/network is formed (leading to more rapid processing of relevant sensory information, and smoother sensory-motor integration), there is less need for effortful conscious processing and thus less load on the frontal neocortex. Over months of intensive driving experience, the whole driving framework/network is strengthened and improved (assuming you are willing and able to continuously improve your driving skills), such that when a child suddenly runs out on the road in front of you or, more likely, when an imperfect (let's refrain from 'idiot') driver suddenly swerves into the lane in front of you, you automatically slam on your brakes. That is, your very rapid response is the product of months and months of building up and refining your 'driving framework'. The slow, effortful processing that was necessary in the first months of your learning would not produce a good outcome in these situations.

The same framework applies to myriad other situations including exercise, work, study and social activities. With experience, initially effortful mental processing becomes automatic and unthinking. That may work well for you braking as a child runs in front of your car, but it is does not always result in such optimal outcomes.

Optimising Thinking in Practice

Okay, with our SMR model in hand, let's go back and try to help Liam. As Liam begins to understand some types of suboptimal thinking, he may discover that his M_{SUB} (his suboptimal mediating belief) is 'If a date doesn't reply to my text quickly, then she doesn't like me'. Simply by becoming aware of this belief, Liam's understanding of his mind has increased. This is what is going on in Figure 1.2, where you become aware of that aspect of your mind that was producing suboptimal responding. Through developing *self-knowledge*, the M_{SUB} that mediates Liam's stimulus-response connection has been discovered. But now what? Let's assume Liam is motivated to try to change. Luckily, we know from psychological science and practice that this kind of suboptimal thinking *can* be changed; we just need the right research-based tools (and, wisely, Liam has purchased this book which is full of them).

Liam may like to challenge his belief that 'If a date doesn't reply to my text quickly then she doesn't like me', because, well, that is not always true! Maybe Bec was running late for class or work, or hasn't seen the text, or her phone battery died! Or maybe Bec believes that 'If I reply straight away, then I will seem desperate'. Liam might learn to generate alternative and optimal thoughts (M_{OP}) such as 'I would prefer that dates would reply to my message quickly, but they don't have to, and it does not mean they don't like me', and alternative explanations such as 'Bec did say that she may have to work all day today; maybe she just hasn't had time to reply'. By replacing his earlier belief with more helpful alternatives, Liam will likely have a more balanced response to the situation. Liam's optimised thinking (M_{OP}) will then have led to an optimised response (R_{OP}), just like in Figure 1.3. As a result, Liam's response will likely change from cancelling work, to showing up for his shift and earning some cash to help make his next date with Bec even better.

P TRY IT! 1.2

Optimise Your Thinking

What is a more optimal M to replace the one you identified earlier? In the example given, the optimal belief may be 'After a hard day at work/study, I *would prefer not to be* expected to do household chores, but I realise that my partner/house-mate/parent has no idea what kind of day I've had if I don't tell them'! You may wish to come back to this once you have read further and identified ways to optimise your thinking.

So, maybe later Bec *did* text back, apologising for the delay and explaining that she couldn't interrupt her gaming marathon for any man... thus causing an immediately besotted hard core gamer like Liam to propose on the spot, leading to a lovely wedding and the optimised merging of gaming equipment.

Okay, let's insert a little realism. Life doesn't always (ever) go that smoothly. There are very often setbacks in the process of optimising thinking. Liam may occasionally lapse into old ways of (suboptimal) thinking. Also, in a different scenario, Liam's fear that Bec doesn't like him might be confirmed when Bec never responds to his text — in real life, sometimes bad things happen. Thus, Liam will need to use his optimising tools again and again to keep from reverting back to his old ways, and in particular he may need to use different tools to cope with a disappointment in a non-destructive way.

To be honest, optimising thinking can be hard work. So what is the point? Well, it may be that suboptimal thinking is leading you to suboptimal responses, and this is getting in the way of important and meaningful stuff. Suboptimal thinking might be impacting your work, your studies, your relationships, or even your health. The long-term goal of optimising thinking is to increase your wellbeing. There are a number of different ways of defining wellbeing, but in psychological science we think about it as feeling that you are achieving goals that are meaningful to you, that you are cared for by other people, that you are competent in areas valued by yourself and others, and that you have some choice in what you do in your life. So optimising thinking can be hard work, but it's worth it.

We think it will certainly be worth it for Liam. Liam was interested in establishing a new caring relationship, had freely chosen Bec to invite out, and likely felt some competency in negotiating the challenging first date. The lack of response to the text message signalled (for Liam) a lack of success in achieving the goal of maintaining Bec's interest, and thus lack of progress toward his ultimate goal of a meaningful connection with a special someone. As a result, Liam's psychological wellbeing started to suffer. Liam's short-term way of coping was to skip work and spend the day gaming, which only reduced his long-term wellbeing further. By learning to use tools to (a) gain greater knowledge about his mind, and then (b) changing his suboptimal thinking in order to optimise his response, in the future Liam can avoid or at least reduce these drops in his wellbeing. That is, Liam can engage in optimal responses that have more positive outcomes. Liam will be increasing his wellbeing one situation at a time.

So let's dig into this 'optimising' process a little deeper. Figure 1.4 presents an **Optimising Minds Flowchart** of how this might work. We'll briefly describe how it works with Liam's help.

Liam had been responding to 'no text' situations in unhelpful ways for some time, but it was not until Bec contacted him after her gaming marathon that he realised that perhaps his 'sulking at home' reaction was a little extreme (WTF?!), and definitely unhelpful on a number of fronts. He decided to get to the bottom of his sulking behaviour, and so sought out some help to shine the light on what was in his mind that was leading to the suboptimal behaviour. He became aware of his 'If a date doesn't reply to my text quickly, then she doesn't like me' belief, which was leading to the suboptimal responses. He then thought about whether it was worth attempting to change this unhelpful thinking: *Was it something I value?* Yes, because it was important to him not to mess up his developing relationship with Bec. *Do I have time?* Well yes, his work and study situation was not too demanding at the moment. *Is it urgent?* Well not urgent urgent, but he was hoping to see Bec more regularly, and the sooner he got this unhelpful thinking sorted out, the better. Thus, he put in the effort to locate and use the tools to do this (see Chapter 4). Once his new optimised thinking was well established, his level of self-efficacy increased (which did not go unnoticed by Bec).

So, Where do we go From Here?

Now that you know what suboptimal thinking is and how we can help you change it, let's talk about what you can expect from the rest of this book. As you read on, the tools alluded to above will be explained in greater detail, along

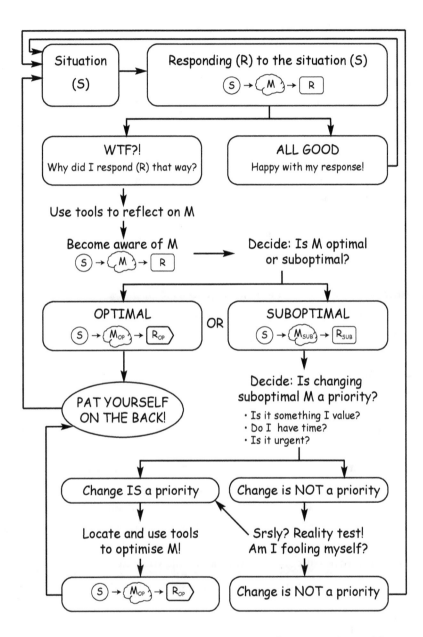

Figure 1.4   Flow-chart for optimising minds. **S** = Stimulus; **M** = Mind; **R** = Response; **OP** = Optimal; **SUB** = Suboptimal. Dashed **M**s indicate 'unaware'; solid **M**s indicate 'aware'.

with many more. You will be given lots of help and practical tips to start optimising your own mind so that you can get the most out of your life, whether it be with your work, your studies, or your personal life. You might even pass this book on to a few 'suboptimal' people in your life on the off-chance that they will learn to live in a way that does not annoy the new optimised perfect you. (We are half joking — people are not 'suboptimal', only some of their thoughts and behaviours.)

In Chapter 2 *The Imperfect Mind*, we consider how suboptimal thinking is a side effect of human brain evolution, and why it is important to take a scientific approach to discovering and changing our suboptimal thinking. In Chapter 3 *Know Thyself*, we focus particularly on tools for increasing self-knowledge. In Chapter 4 *The Flexible Mind*, we introduce psychological flexibility — a core aspect of the optimised mind. After that, we approach some core topics such as stress, motivation and communication. Throughout, we will return to the SMR model to introduce tools to optimise your thinking and behaviour, and thus increase your wellbeing. From time to time, remember to look back at the Optimising Minds Flow Chart (Figure 1.4) to remind yourself of the process.

Each chapter will contain some similar elements. Using the SMR model, we will guide you toward becoming more aware of how your mind influences your responses to situations (we call this *developing self-knowledge*). If you decide that this relationship between your mind and behaviour leads to poor outcomes, we'll help you work out how possible it is to change that relationship (i.e., there *are* some things you cannot change). Where it *is* possible, we'll give you practical, science-based tools to optimise thinking and change your SMR. Making these changes is part of self-development or self-optimisation. You may decide that you do not need to change. Even then, this book should give you greater understanding not only of yourself but of others, which should help improve your relationships and thus your life.

Let us emphasise again that we do not consider that all thinking is suboptimal, and most of it is actually quite good. We invite you to reflect on your current thinking and assess how it can be further optimised, regardless of the current level, in the sense that it helps you better achieve your goals and maintain or improve your wellbeing.

Throughout the book we will be operating on a few assumptions, so let's make them clear now:

1.   *Everyone* (with a reasonably well-functioning brain) can improve their thinking and behaviour, given the right tools and the motivation to do so.

2.   The *best tools* are those based on scientific research indicating that the tools are effective for the majority of people, most of the time.

3.   You are *motivated* to put in the hard (but rewarding) work required to use those tools to optimise various aspects of your mind.

4.   You will have different needs at different times in terms of what aspects of your mind require optimising, so the relevance of the various chapters in this book may change depending on where you're at.

5.   Because everyone is different, even though these tools are scientifically based, some tools will be more appealing to you (and may even work better for you) than other tools.

6.   Sometimes, you will benefit greatly from having experts help you to use these tools — for example, seek out the experts at your local or online psychological service, or if you are a student, your university's student support service.

What About that 'Rubber Brain' Title?

You may have been wondering about the 'Rubber' in the 'Rubber Brain' title of this book. Humble rubber has many laudable properties. Imagine a rubber replica of a brain. If you use your finger to poke the brain, it will bend to the pressure of your finger, and then as you withdraw your finger, the brain will regain its shape. If you throw the rubber brain at the ground or the wall, it will 'bounce back' in good condition. That is, a rubber brain is able to adapt to pressures and stressors in a way that maintains its integrity and good condition (of course, there are limits — brains, whether real or rubber, usually do not survive extreme traumas). Two concepts are relevant here: resilience, and psychological flexibility. Resilience is usually understood to be the capacity to 'bounce back' from an adversity (like a rubber brain being thrown at the ground). Adversities include situations where your goal was not reached (e.g., failing an exam), or where something you had was taken away from you (e.g., your partner broke up with you). Psychological flexibility is the capacity, given different situations (S), to choose ways of thinking (M) and behaving (R) that produce the best outcome for you in that situation. So you may realise that psychological flexibility is very much what we are talking about in terms of the

SMR model of optimising thinking, and we will return to a fuller discussion of that concept in Chapter 4.

Rubberising Your Brain

As we have emphasised in this chapter, this book is also about giving you the tools to optimise your thinking by 'rubberising' your brain to get the most out of your life. Imagine your brain is a car engine. You feel as though the car is not really getting you where you want to go, or it does so in a somewhat inefficient manner. To work out what is happening, the first step is to shine a light on aspects that are difficult to see, so you can identify which parts of the engine are working really well, which could be tweaked a little, and which are seriously malfunctioning. Once you have identified these, you will need different tools to fix those parts, depending on each problem. Sometimes, the problem will be constant, other times it may only emerge under certain circumstances. In terms of this toolkit, we are giving you the best tools we know of to identify what is happening under your bonnet, and then to fix both entrenched problems, and those that happen sporadically, or only in certain circumstances. The tools in our toolkit have passed the 'scientific' test of effectiveness (more on this in Chapter 2). But just like with a car engine, sometimes (as indicated in point 6 above), you may need professional help to fix more serious problems. So, if you have a brain, and you want the tools to make it more flexible and resilient, then read on.

Now you know what the book is about, what suboptimal thinking is, and how we're going to help you to optimise your thinking in order to live the best life you can. Enough talk. It's time to get started.

Summary Points

- Although most of our thinking (M) helps us to achieve positive outcomes, sometimes our thinking is unhelpful, and this leads to responses (R) that are suboptimal for us in that particular situation (S).

- The SMR model of optimising minds assumes that often we are unaware of the role of unhelpful thinking in producing suboptimal responses, which can make it difficult to change those responses. Thus, the first step is to become aware of the suboptimal thinking, and the second step is to use specific tools to help you optimise your thinking.

- This book provides science-based tools that should help you to increase your knowledge of yourself, and to optimise your thinking, if you choose to do so.

More Resources

- Websites with some useful tools:
  www.thefridge.org.au

  www.youtube.com/user/watchwellcast

CHAPTER 2

The Imperfect Mind

Imagine that you owned a watch* that worked perfectly well... most of the time. It was an amazing watch that you inherited from your parents and you couldn't bear to be without it. However, due to a design flaw, every now and then it would just stop for a few minutes at a time. If you were completely unaware of this flaw, it could have significant consequences, like missing the bus, being late for a lecture, or even having the prospective person of your dreams storm away from your first date, assuming you had stood them up (damn watch!).

Now, imagine if this watch still had the same idiosyncrasy, but you were aware of it. Every now and then you would stop to check whether it was working, verify whether its time was accurate, or whether you needed to make a conscious, manual modification to what it was telling you. And imagine if you knew not just that it stopped every now and then, but that there were specific conditions that made these problems worse. You would not only expect that it worked less than perfectly, but you could identify the circumstances in which it was likely to let you down.

---

* For the purpose of this example, lets assume that you do NOT own a smartphone or any alternative means of telling the time. We know that this is an unrealistic assumption, but please indulge us!

Your mind, like the watch, has design flaws, responsible for the occasional lapse in judgment or other unhelpful thinking processes. As you would be aware by now, the goal of this book is to make you aware of these 'lapses', so that instead of constantly playing catch-up (or patch-up), you are able to recognise when your mind is being unhelpful, and then optimise your thinking. In this chapter, we will focus on identifying some of the main types of thinking errors — often called **biases** and **fallacies** — that *everyone's* mind makes, so that you can lessen the nefarious influence of these 'design flaws'. In terms of our SMR model, these flaws represent M_{SUB}'s, which get in the way of optimal responding.

How Biases and Fallacies Limit Our Thinking

The human mind is an incredibly powerful tool, performing thousands of tasks every minute: from interpreting myriad stimuli every millisecond to accessing stored memories of a cherished pet; from making decisions about optimal ice-cream flavour combinations to simultaneously calculating the cost of adding salted caramel sauce. Despite its enormous power, your mind has significant limitations that sometimes cause you to make less-than-optimal decisions (about more important things than ice-cream flavours), to 'recall' memories that didn't really happen, and to reach flawed conclusions based on *very* selective evidence. But ironically, because you rely on your mind to inform you of your reality, biases and fallacies make it difficult for your mind to identify and avoid them! As psychologist Diane Halpern notes, '*Naïve and flawed reasoning practices… are resistant to change because they make sense to the individual, and for the most part, the individual believes that they work*' (p. 449). So, you need to rely on a group of nerdy scientists (like some of us) to help you identify these glitches in your mind, and then optimise the way you think and act.

In general terms, biases and fallacies are limitations in our thinking — that is, they make our thinking suboptimal, as shown in Figure 2.1. These are flaws in our judgment or errors in logic that result from memory errors, mental shortcuts, a false sense of probability, or misattributions. But 'why does the mind make such errors?' you may ask. One reason is that the mind loves to use **heuristics** — mental shortcuts or rules of thumb to solve complex problems and form judgements. This approach helps your brain deal with the incredible amount of information you throw at it every day. Most times, these heuristics help, but other times, they lead to errors of judgment, or the tendency to think in suboptimal ways over and over. Just because a strategy has worked in the past, does not mean it will work in a different context, and relying on an existing heuristic may stop you from thinking of alternative, optimal solutions.

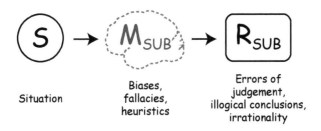

Situation | Biases, fallacies, heuristics | Errors of judgement, illogical conclusions, irrationality

Figure 2.1   Cognitive biases and fallacies, or relying on mental shortcuts (M_{SUB}) can lead to suboptimal responding (R_{SUB}), including errors of judgements and jumping to wrong conclusions.

Stereotypes are a great example of these heuristics. It is very efficient for your mind to assume that all people from a particular group are very similar, and of course sometimes there is truth in this. Then, each time you meet someone from that group your mind doesn't have to think too much; it has a pretty good idea of how this person will think and behave. If your stereotype is overly positive, you might trust individuals who shouldn't be trusted. If your stereotype is overly negative, you might unfairly judge individuals or assume things about them that simply aren't true. If more and more people adopt your negative stereotype, this can lead to prejudice and discrimination.

Another reason for our imperfect minds is evolution (or the lack of it). Natural selection occurs over millions of years, so in some ways your mind is still dealing with problems in the same way as your caveman ancestors did, which is not always appropriate for our modern world (see psychologist Hank Davis' book, cited in the *More Resources* section at the end of this chapter for an entertaining read on this subject). In essence, although throughout our evolutionary history our brain processes have worked well most of the time (otherwise we would be extinct), these brain processes are less than perfect, and these imperfections have become particularly evident as our environments have become increasingly diverse and globalised as a result of advances in technology.

But here is the good news: you are not locked into making these errors forever, nor are you destined to continue to think like a caveman (or woman).

In this chapter, we will help you identify some of the most common biases and fallacies (and poke fun at a gullible mind that is capable of being so easily and repeatedly fooled). In identifying these heuristics and biases, and how they impact your thinking, you can start to consciously overcome these mental errors and optimise your thinking.

1. Confirmation Bias

Confirmation bias is the tendency to notice, seek, and recall information that supports your existing beliefs or hypotheses, while ignoring information that casts doubt on your view. Rather than seeing circumstances or facts objectively, the confirmation bias suggests that when you want something to be true, you end up believing that it is true, by gathering information to support your ideas. If you don't believe us, think about the last time you turned to Google for help to win an argument with a friend. After you found a *Buzzfeed* article that supported your view, did you search for reasons your friend could be correct, just to be balanced? Most of us don't search for information this way. Instead, we specifically look for evidence to support our position, and Google will inevitably find some.

Not only do we tend to seek out confirmatory information, we also tend to avoid individuals, groups, or other information sources that make us feel uncomfortable about our view (like all the *Buzzfeed* articles your friend came up with to support their view). This tendency reflects what psychological scientists call **cognitive dissonance** — the notion that it is psychologically uncomfortable to hold two contradictory beliefs. Many of us deal with cognitive dissonance by acquiring new information that supports one belief, and/or forgetting or reducing the importance of inconsistent beliefs or cognitions. The confirmation bias is in stark contrast to the scientific method, in which we test hypotheses by trying to refute them (see *Diving Deeper 2.2*).

Consider Sam. Sam just met Jennifer at a party. Jennifer abruptly cut their conversation short and went over to chat with the boys from her chemistry lab. How rude! As Sam mentally worked herself up about Jennifer's apparent rudeness, she looked around for people to debrief with. To her right she saw Sarah, who had warned Sam about how flighty Jennifer could be. To her left, she saw Ashley, who played basketball with Jennifer and said she was the nicest person ever (vomit). Sam had formed the belief that Jennifer was awful, so she didn't need Ashley countering this belief with tales of Jennifer's match-winning half-court shots, or how she volunteers at kitten shelters (double vomit). So, Sam chose to talk to Sarah, who told her about how she caught Jennifer flirting with Sarah's ex. This immediately confirmed Sam's belief; Jennifer was a terrible person!

While the previous example may seem trivial, the confirmation bias can have far reaching effects. Many such examples exist in everyday life, including denying global warming, linking vaccinations to autism, or conspiracy theories about why we *really* have fluoride in our water. All of these examples arise because we tend to cling to information that supports our position and ignore those facts that challenge our beliefs. Regardless of which point of view you endorse, in a world where we have unparalleled access to numerous sources of information from every different perspective, the confirmation bias can have an insidious impact on your thinking. This explains why two people can walk away from the same situation, having made completely different interpretations that validates each person's pre-existing perspective. The dangers of a confirmation bias include that:

1. we fail to seek out information that contradicts our belief,

2. we uncritically accept suggestions that align with our belief,

3. we overestimate the likelihood of extreme and improbable events, and

4. our behaviour may further reinforce our belief, leading to a self-fulfilling prophecy (see *Diving Deeper 2.1*).

 DIVING DEEPER 2.1

Confirmation Bias

Imagine a teacher has a belief (a bias) that children with blue eyes are superior in their academic work compared to children with brown eyes. Due to a confirmation bias, the teacher tends to process and remember any information that affirms that belief, in particular, every time a blue-eyed child displayed high academic capability, or a brown-eyed child displayed low academic capability. What this teacher does not process and remember well is any information that contradicts that belief, such as when some blue-eyed children failed an exam, while some brown-eyed children passed easily. This confirmation bias results in disconfirmatory evidence being undervalued, explained-away (the blue-eyed children were just having an 'off' day), or conveniently 'forgotten'.

The presence and consequences of confirmation bias have been experimentally demonstrated. There can be life-long consequences for those on the wrong side of the bias. For example, the teacher may praise and thus motivate the blue-eyed children, leading them to persist and succeed, whereas the teacher's lack of acknowledgement of the brown-eyed children's achievement may de-motivate them, thus leading them to perform poorly in the future. This is the essence of what is called a **self-fulfilling prophecy**, which is where your expectation creates reality. What if instead of eye-colour, the teacher was biased against children from low socioeconomic families who may need the extra support? What if instead of a single teacher, this was the Minister for Education?

A related bias is the **in-group bias**, which makes us overestimate the value and capability of our in-group members, while making us devalue those who are not in our group. We avoid or discount information that would reveal the weaknesses of our in-group, or the positive behaviour of out-group members.

TRY IT! 2.1

Confirmation Bias

Think of an example of confirmation bias that someone in your life has displayed (e.g., when your doctor jumps to the conclusion that you have a certain diagnosis, and only asks questions that provide evidence to support — rather than disconfirm — her belief).

Now consider whether you have displayed confirmation bias in your dealings with other people (e.g., when considering the merits of a potential partner, have you only focused on the positive elements, and neglected to consider (or even notice) those less ideal or more challenging characteristics?).

This can be difficult to do, so you might ask a particularly honest friend to help you (but make sure you have an open mind, otherwise there may be adverse consequences!).

Optionally, consider this question: how does confirmation bias contribute to the strengthening of racist, sexist, or homophobic beliefs?

2. The Availability Heuristic and Vividness

Think quickly: are there more words that start with the letter K, or have K as their third letter? Chances are you said that there are more words beginning with K, and thanks to the **availability heuristic**, you're wrong (there are three times as many words with K as the third letter than K as the first letter). Why do people reliably get this wrong? Because it is easier to recall words that begin with K (e.g., *kind*) than it is to recall words with the third letter as K (e.g., *ask*). Words that begin with K are more *available* to your mind.

The availability heuristic was first noted by psychological scientists Amos Tversky and Daniel Kahneman, who spent many years investigating cognitive biases and heuristics (see *More Resources*). Tversky and Kahneman suggested that people make decisions about the likelihood of an event based on how easily it springs to mind, which is influenced by a number of factors, including how recently they have experienced or heard about the event. The availability heuristic can be a useful aid to decision-making, because when faced with the need to make an immediate choice (i.e., limited time and resources), a rapid mechanism to estimate frequency and probability can help you to arrive at a conclusion (as you probably did, albeit incorrectly, above). But it is easy to see how this mechanism can also interfere with optimal thinking by hijacking your otherwise rational mind with the simplistic notion that any recent or vivid thought that pops into your head must be important or valid. Some events are more available than others simply because they are easier to think about, because they are recent and/or highly 'vivid'. This leads us to overestimate the probability of recent, salient events, or rare but vivid events, and underestimate the probability of remote, less memorable but more frequent events.

When we talk about **vividness**, we mean how emotionally interesting or exciting something is. Not surprisingly, consistent with the availability heuristic, our decisions are more strongly influenced by vivid information than by bland, abstract or statistical information. Imagine that, over the summer, a series of shark attacks were reported in gory detail. You would probably judge the likelihood of shark attacks to be higher than it actually is, based on the availability of these stories in your memory. In fact, you are more likely to be killed by falling plane parts than by a shark attack. Similarly, many people are terrified of flying because they can easily bring to mind news of tragic plane crashes. In fact, plane travel is far safer than car travel — by some accounts, we have a 1 in 114 chance of dying in a car accident, and only a 1 in 9,821 chance of dying in a plane crash. However, as car accidents are not nearly as vivid as a fully loaded jumbo smashing into a mountain (see what we did there?), you would be more likely to judge flying as being a more dangerous mode of travel than driving. For the same reason, more people fear terrorism than global warming. We neglect probability, and overestimate the likelihood of relatively low-frequency yet vivid risks, while underestimating the likelihood of more dangerous yet less obvious ones. Imagine you are eating lunch outdoors during a lightning storm — you might be surprised to know that you are more likely to die from choking on your meatball sub (with odds of 1 in 3,461) than to die from a lightning strike (1 in 161,856).

A related phenomenon is when we suddenly notice things that we hadn't noticed before, but we erroneously attribute this to an increase in frequency, rather than the **selective bias** that is causing it. Imagine that you have just bought a pair of Adidas shoes, and put them on to go for a walk. While walking, you can't help but notice all the cool people who are wearing Adidas running shoes today. Funny, you had never noticed this before, and assume that you are riding some wave of coolness, having just put your finger on the fashion pulse! The same number of people are wearing Adidas sneakers as were wearing them before you bought them, *and* it is highly probable that the same number of people you passed are wearing Nikes as Adidas shoes. However, you are selectively noticing Adidas shoes now because they have become more meaningful to you.

3. The Representativeness Heuristic

Toby loves listening to Bob Dylan and wearing tie-dyed dresses. She reads her horoscope daily. She enjoys yoga and burning aromatic oils. Is Toby more likely to be a holistic healer or a maths teacher?

To answer this question, chances are that you compared Toby's description against your stereotypes of 'holistic healer' and 'maths teacher'. That is, you decide how *representative* Toby is of each category. Tversky and Kahneman explain that people estimate the likelihood of an event by comparing it to an existing mental prototype. In their own research they used a similar example to the one above, of Steve, who is 'very shy and withdrawn, invariably helpful but with little interest in people or in the world of reality. A meek and tidy soul, he has a need for order and structure, and a passion for detail'. They found that people were more likely to suggest that Steve was a librarian than a farmer based on how closely his personality resembled that of a stereotypical librarian. However, they failed to consider relevant statistical facts, such as that there are more than 20 times as many male farmers as male librarians. Instead, *representativeness* was used as a simple way to make a difficult decision. Like other heuristics, the **representativeness heuristic** is designed to provide a mental shortcut, allowing us to make rapid decisions, and these intuitive impressions are often better than just a random guess. However, it can also lead to errors of overestimation, particularly when it supports unlikely outcomes, such as in the librarian example. Just because an event or object is representative does not mean that it is more likely to occur, because in order to determine the latter, we need to take into account base rate information (i.e., how often it occurs in the target population). Perhaps Steve's need for order and structure and passion for detail extended to his award-winning hay bales. Maybe listening to Bob Dylan while burning aromatic oils might simply help Toby to relax while marking calculus questions.

4. The Gambler's Fallacy

Imagine tossing a coin 7 times and getting the following result:

Heads-Heads-Heads-Heads-Heads-Heads-Heads.

What is the likelihood of getting Heads in the next toss? More than, less than, or equal to 50%? And the next toss? And the next toss?

The **gambler's fallacy** is the tendency for people to see links between events in the past and future when those events are actually independent. In the example above, the fallacy is the mistaken belief that because someone has tossed Heads so many times in the past, it will happen less often in the future, as a way to 'balance' nature. But in each toss, there is a 50% chance of getting Heads, regardless of how the previous tosses fell (assuming, of course, that the coin is fair and equally likely to fall either way). It is also known as the Monte Carlo Fallacy, after the most famous example: black occurred in a game of roulette 26 consecutive times, gamblers lost millions betting against black, reasoning that red was now more likely, given the long run of black (even though it was equally likely, regardless of the preceding run). It should be noted that this fallacy only applies when the outcomes are truly independent, that is, when the occurrence of one event in no way impacts the likelihood of the other.

Interestingly, the gambler's fallacy is not restricted to gambling. Notwithstanding the (approximately) 50–50 chance of having a boy or a girl, many parents who have 2 children of the same sex overestimate the likelihood that the third child will be of the opposite sex. Tversky and Kahneman suggest that the gambler's fallacy may be produced by the representativeness heuristic, that is, people establish how likely the next event is based on how similar it is to other instances they have experienced. As we are not used to seeing a coin toss result in the same outcome 6 times in a row, we erroneously assume that a Tails result must be about to happen, because this is more representative of a typical coin toss sequence. The gambler's fallacy is also related to the **just-world hypothesis**, in which people tend to believe in some form of universal justice, karma, or cosmic order, which results in people getting what they deserve, even when the cause is more accurately attributable to chance factors. So when something good happens to someone you like — such as when your friend Josh wins an online contest to meet Beyoncé — you might think he 'deserved' it, as he is a good guy who rescues kittens and helps little old ladies cross the street. However, the same belief in a just world can also lead us to 'blame the victim'. When we pass a homeless person in the street, we might assume that he is lazy, and thus 'deserves' whatever misfortune has befallen him.

5. Halo Effect

It is Sonny's first day of class, and he is asked to choose a partner to work with on a project. There are two possible collaborators: Joseph is a good looking young man, whereas Rick can be generously described as having a face only a mother could love. Whom does Sonny choose? According to the **halo effect**, he is more likely to choose the attractive workmate, as we tend to judge good looking people more favourably with regards to unrelated factors such as personality, intelligence and competence. Put simply, the halo effect refers to the tendency to use one desirable trait (such as physical attractiveness) to make positive judgments of that person on similar or unrelated dimensions. Our first impression of a person has a disproportionate impact on our subsequent judgments. When your grandmother told you that 'first impressions count' she was unwittingly referring to this ubiquitous phenomenon.

However, the halo effect is not just about attractiveness. We might believe that a gifted (yet unattractive) actor is also generous, well-mannered, and kind to small animals and children. Similarly, if you do well in your first presentation to your work team, your line-manager may expect you to do well in subsequent tasks and perhaps unintentionally give you more constructive attention than you would have received otherwise (so—put some effort into that first task!). Yes, we know this may seem unfair to the other workers, but even your line-manager has a human brain with all its failings.

Like many heuristics and biases, the halo effect provides for very powerful marketing approaches. For example, when we see a movie star endorsing a product, our positive impression of the celebrity tends to generalise to our perception of the product they claim to be using. There is also evidence that physically attractive defendants are treated more compassionately by jurors than are less attractive defendants. The halo effect even extends beyond judgments of people. When a snack is labelled as 'healthy' or 'organic', people significantly underestimate the number of calories it contains irrespective of its actual contents.

6. Hindsight Bias

After a long relationship, Ted's partner has just broken up with him. Ted calls a friend to relay the news and ends with the comment 'I knew all along that this would happen'. Ted is demonstrating **hindsight bias,** or the tendency to see events as somehow predictable at the time they are experienced, or more predictable than they are. This can also lead to the mistaken belief that we can predict outcomes that are actually dependent upon chance. This bias with hindsight, or the belief that we 'knew it all along' is fairly common, particularly amongst students faced with poor marks after their first semester, who then claim that they 'just knew' this program would not be good for them, and they should have taken a different program instead. Well, sometimes that could be true, but just as often, it is not! (And there is really no way to tell because we can't do true experimental tests with one person — see *Diving Deeper 2.2*). Similarly, investors, faced with the knowledge of a company's success, are quick to suggest (in hindsight) that they could have predicted this at the outset, despite them having no specialist knowledge that could have contributed to them predicting such an outcome.

There are a number of factors that contribute to the hindsight bias:

1. people tend to misremember or distort their earlier predictions about an event;

2. people tend to assume events are inevitable; and

3. people tend to assume that they could have foreseen certain events. For example, when watching a movie with a surprise ending, how often do you look back and misremember your initial thoughts about the evil-doer, and leave the movie secure in the knowledge that 'I knew it all along' (when you probably didn't!).

7. The Fundamental Attribution Error

Imagine that you are sitting in a lecture theatre, and the lecturer, Eugene, trips over the microphone cable. 'Clumsy oaf', you think to yourself. Just then, you knock your books, which slide to the floor with a thud. 'Stupid lecture theatre desks', you inwardly curse. At the end of the lecture, a fellow student compliments you on your new Adidas sneakers, which you bought because you have cutting edge taste and can sniff out the next trend before it happens. You notice that Eugene is wearing the same shoes as you and laugh to yourself because you are sure that his girlfriend (or his mother!) bought them for him! Congratulations, you have just demonstrated the **fundamental attribution error**.

The fundamental attribution error causes us to attribute someone else's negative behaviour to internal factors (such as their personality), but attribute our own negative behaviour to external factors (such as the adversity of a situation). Similarly, we attribute our own positive behaviour to internal factors, yet believe that another's positive behaviour must be a result of external factors.

A number of reasons have been proposed to explain the tendency to attribute another's negative behaviour to their disposition rather than the situation. Firstly, when watching a situation, the observable actor is more salient than the situational factors. In contrast, when we are the 'actor' we are more aware of the role that external factors play, as they are more noticeable than our own internal context. A second reason may be the just-world hypothesis that we mentioned earlier. Perhaps when bad things happen to others we assume that people are getting what they deserve, but if bad things happen to us they must be due to some unfairness or adversity that we are suffering (as we couldn't possibly *deserve* bad things!).

This tendency to claim more responsibility or agency for success than failure is also known as the **self-serving bias**, as it protects our self-esteem and enhances our confidence. It is linked to optimism, leading to perseverance in the face of adversity (see Chapter 6). Conversely, people suffering from depression may be less likely to exhibit this self-serving attributional style, and more likely to blame internal causes for failure and external ones for success.

One of the dangers of the fundamental attribution error is that it can lead us to judge others harshly while ignoring the difficulties they face. For example, some people may attribute the lack of success of an Indigenous student to internal factors such as laziness, rather than to a measurable lack of access to quality education and healthcare, lower socioeconomic status, or culturally-biased assessments. Conversely, the fundamental attribution error can also lead us to see ourselves as victims of circumstance when in fact we brought about our own downfall, such as assuming that the exam we failed was overly hard, rather than admitting that our study time was overly brief.

8. The Illusory Correlation and the Illusion of Control

Alon has a statistics test, so he makes sure that he wears his lucky blue socks, because he always does well when he wears them. Lara was thinking about her cousin, when out of the blue he called, so she assumes that she must have some kind of psychic power that made him call. Both of these are examples of **illusory correlation**, which refers to the situation in which we perceive a relationship between two variables, where no relationship exists. For example, you might believe that two unrelated events have some type of relationship simply because they occurred at the same time on one or more occasions (like Alon's blue socks and his test success). In other cases, a one-off association between two variables might lead us to assume that the two are somehow connected, and that this relationship is more robust than it actually is. For example, if you have a bad experience with a rude American, you might mistakenly believe that all Americans are rude. Illusory correlations are supported by confirmation bias, in that we readily recall events that support our perceived correlation and ignore events that could disconfirm this relationship. For example, if Alon failed an exam while wearing his blue socks he would be less likely to recall this when choosing socks for his next exam, or may discount that as a one-off.

The desire to explain coincidental events as correlated possibly comes from a desire to believe that we can control uncertain events (of course, Alon can increase the likelihood of success in his stats test, just not by his choice of hosiery!). This is called the **illusion of control**, or the tendency to believe that a personal skill or particular behaviour can influence events that are determined by chance (or by other unperformed behaviours, like studying well in Alon's case). Interestingly, this relates to the just-world hypothesis, such that when something good happens to us by chance, like winning the lottery, we prefer to believe that it resulted from personality, skill, or somehow being deserving of the win.

Illusory correlations are easy to spot by thinking more carefully about the co-occurrence of such events.

If Lara wants to determine whether she is psychic, she should systematically record over a period of time the number of times: (1) her cousin Ari called when she was thinking about him; (2) Ari didn't call when she was thinking about him; (3) Ari called when she was not thinking about him; and (4) Ari didn't call when she was not thinking about him (this one could take a while). Lara will probably find that Ari is just as likely to call when she is thinking about him as when she is not, and that there were many times when she was thinking of him yet he made no contact with her. The weirdness of a call at the precise moment that Lara is thinking of Ari makes it more memorable, and thus more prone to illusory correlation.

A serious downside of the illusory correlation is its role in stereotyping and discrimination. If a member of a minority group performs an unsavoury act, illusory correlation would lead us to assume that all members of that minority group are more likely to behave in that way, compared to those in our majority group. Due to confirmation bias, we will then likely selectively attend to other examples of when members of this minority behaved in the same way. Pretty soon we will form a negative belief about this group of people that is not based on the group's actions, rather it is based on our suboptimal thinking. It is important, therefore, to be aware of the tendency of our mind to see relationships where none exist, and to be more critical in how we go about evaluating such relationships.

 TRY IT! 2.2

Cognitive biases

Identify the cognitive biases in the following situation:

Imagine you see a new politician on TV one night, who you think is attractive. Chances are you will like her political views (_____). Over the next few weeks, you keep hearing her on the radio and reading about her in the news, more so than any other politician (_____). You might also seek out information that endorses your support of her (_____). In doing some research and realising that the seat she is running for has been held by a succession of male politicians, you might decide that the odds are that the next election is hers for the taking (_____), and anyway that's only fair (_____). And when, sadly, she loses, you are

the first to say that you knew that would happen (_____),
as female politicians never win (_____).

See *More Resources* at the end of this chapter for the answers.

9. Logical fallacies

Logical fallacies are errors in reasoning, in which the premise given for a particular conclusion does not adequately support the argument. Logical fallacies can make weak arguments appear more robust than they are, making them very popular with people who want to convince us of their point of view (such as media outlets, advertisers, and politicians). There are too many examples to cover comprehensively in this book, but a brief list includes:

1.   Straw-man — misrepresenting someone's argument and then attacking that misrepresentation, rather than responding to what was truly said. Example: Politician A says that she is in favour of euthanasia. Politician B argues that Politician A should tender her resignation because she is trying to make it legal to kill old people!

2.   Slippery Slope — suggesting that if we let A happen, Z is an inevitable result; therefore A shouldn't happen. Example: Corey argues against marriage equality because if two women can marry each other, what's to stop them also marrying their cars?

3.   False Dichotomy — only two alternatives are presented, when multiple possibilities exist. Example: Aimee tells Jessica that if she won't come to the women's rights rally then she must support misogyny.

4.   Ad Hominem — attacking your opponent's argument on the basis of their (irrelevant) personal traits (the converse of the halo effect). Example: Harry argues that Sheila shouldn't be made treasurer of their club because she's too fat.

5.   Loaded Question — asking a question that contains an assumption, such that it can't be answered without appearing guilty. Example: 'How often do you beat your dog?'

6.   Bandwagon — appealing to popularity as a form of validation. Example: Donald makes it illegal to vaccinate children because thousands of parents wrote to him about their concerns about mercury levels in vaccines.

7. Appeal to Authority — relying on the position of an authority or institution to support an argument. Example: Pauline uses the fact that Deepak Chopra doesn't believe in evolution to argue that it is not true.

8. Circular Argument — an argument where the proposition is supported by the premise, which is supported by the proposition. Example: Pedro argues that the Bible is the word of God because God told us that in the Bible.

9. Affirming the Consequent — this is an error whereby if the consequent (Q) is said to be true, the antecedent (P) is said to be true too. This ignores that there are many causes of the consequent (Q) other than the antecedent (P): Example: if Helen has the flu, then we can probably deduce that she has a sore throat. However, we cannot deduce that if Helen has a sore throat, then she must have the flu, because the flu is not the only cause of a sore throat!

10. Anecdote — extrapolating from personal experience, a case study, or an isolated example, rather than relying on a statistically significant number of instances. Example: Sean tells you that smoking isn't harmful because his Uncle Mick smoked a pack a day and lived to be 100.

11. The Fallacy Fallacy — arguing that because a fallacy has been made or an assertion has been poorly argued, it must be untrue. Example: Just because Sharon argued that we should eat healthy food because her nutritionist said so (Appeal to Authority) doesn't mean that we should not eat healthy food!

10. Faulty Memory

There is a fallacy that our memory is like a video-recorder, such that what you remember accurately reflects past reality. This has long been shown to be incorrect. In *TRY IT!* 2.3, we invite you to examine aspects of your own memory that may be faulty (and that may also affect your sense of self).

TRY IT! 2.3

Memory, Self-knowledge, and Identity

Our self-knowledge, identity, sense of self, are all predicated on memories. But how good is our memory?

Write down what you think were some key positive and negative incidents in your life, and why you think these key incidents were positive/negative for you. In particular, you might want to focus on those negative incidents that still 'haunt' you in the sense that they negatively impact your self-perception, your current relationships, or your aspirations. In your recounting, attempt to distinguish between remembered 'facts' (e.g., behaviours) and your interpretation or reactions to these facts. For example, you may consider that in your family, you were the neglected one, in contrast to your big sister, who was the favourite. The genesis of this self-perception revolves around a key historical 'fact' (as recalled by you): 'Mum was sick and had to go to hospital for several months. My big sister was allowed to visit her, and I was not.' The associated 'reaction' might be: 'I felt abandoned, lonely, devalued.' This reaction still negatively affects how you interact with your older sister. You could colour code the 'facts' vs. the 'reactions' in your own recounted memory.

Now, approach some key people who were part of this episode. Ask them factual questions, for example: 'Was Mum in hospital when I was young? If so, for how long? Did my sister visit her? If so, how many times? Did I visit her? If so, how many times?' Write down your questions, and their responses.

Try to take their responses, no matter how different from yours, at 'face value', that is, as 'true for them' — no matter how different their stories may be from yours. If there are extreme differences, you might attempt to obtain some more objective sources of information (e.g., a more independent third party). Write down what you are going to do, and the results.

You should then re-evaluate the validity of your 'factual' memories and their relevance to your current relationships and other aspects of your life. Write down your conclusions.

If this process is very upsetting for you, you might want to ask for help from a professional such as a psychologist.

The value of this exercise is that you may realise that: (a) memories are often inaccurate (there is extensive research showing this to be the case), and (b) regardless of the accuracy of memories, they may be having an unnecessarily negative impact on your current life — determine whether you want to try to change this, and if you do, seek expert help to do so (e.g., a psychologist). (Of course, you may enjoy the 'whining hard-done-by baby sister/brother' identity, and so don't want to change; thus you discount any disconfirmatory evidence.)

11. Correlation Proves Causation

Put simply, this is the assumption that because two things are related in some manner, that one must have caused the other. Consider this: several years ago, a large-scale study of the factors related to the use of contraceptive devices was conducted by social scientists in Taiwan. The research team was interested in identifying the behavioural and environmental variables that best predicted the use of birth control methods. After collecting a huge amount of data, they found that the variable most strongly correlated with contraceptive use was the number of electrical appliances (toaster, fans, etc.) in the home. Can they conclude that owning a toaster causes contraceptive use?

Even the most gullible reader (you know who you are — your picture is on page 49 of this book) would not suggest that there is a causal relationship between these variables. However, we are constantly being bombarded with spurious yet seemingly compelling claims of relationships between variables, and our mind often leads us astray in believing these relationships.

In the example above, the implied causal relationship is so unlikely that we immediately try to come up with alternative explanations. One alternative explanation is that the relationship is caused by a **third variable** that impacts both variables separately. For example, higher socioeconomic status might enable an individual to afford to procure both electrical appliances and contraception.

Another alternative explanation is **reverse causality** — that is, sometimes it is not the proposed variable that causes the other, but the reverse. In the above example, we might propose that using contraception enables one to afford more appliances (kids are expensive little… angels), but perhaps a different example will make our argument more compellingly. A correlation exists between reading capability and eye movements, such that poorer readers make more erratic movements, more movements from right to left, and more stops, than do good readers. Educators assumed that these additional eye movements were impairing reading ability, so they implemented programs to train the eye movement of poor readers. Unfortunately, it was subsequently determined that the relationship was actually in the opposite direction — poor reading ability leads to erratic eye movements! Training eye movements, therefore, did absolutely nothing to improve reading.

Another example of reverse causality is the myth of the swimmer's body. Many of us think that swimmers have those broad shoulders, long sinewy limbs and tiny waists because they train certain muscles in certain ways as part of their sport. We conclude that professional swimming *causes* the swimmers body, so we exercise in similar ways to try and achieve their body shape. In truth, the opposite is true! Successful swimmers are born with the type of body that enables them to swim faster and for longer than most other people. As a result, they excel at their sport and end up on the Olympic dais where we all envy their lithe physiques.

Just to make things even more confusing, causal relationships can be **bi-directional,** as in the case of happiness and altruism, with for example, people doing volunteer work reporting higher levels of happiness. Once the possibility of a third variable was eliminated, it was found that being happy makes people more altruistic, *and* being altruistic makes people happier.

How, then, do we ever determine true causality? There is a simple answer: the controlled experiment, which is the foundation of science. In a nutshell, a controlled experiment enables us to isolate a potential causal variable and eliminate alternative explanations. Two groups of people who are as comparable as possible in every way are given experiences that differ only with respect to the variable of interest, and the outcome is compared (see *Diving Deeper 2.2*). If the groups experience different outcomes, we can reliably conclude that our variable of interest caused the difference, rather than toasters or swimming or anything else.

 DIVING DEEPER 2.2

Scientific Thinking and Research Design

One of the *key advantages of a scientific way of thinking* is making you aware of possible *alternative explanations* of a particular phenomenon. You can then gather evidence to test the various explanations against each other.

Keith Stanovich (2013) describes three characteristics or principles of science:

1. Science employs **systematic empiricism,** which means observing phenomena in a methodical and controlled way, usually driven by previous relevant theory and findings.

2. Scientific knowledge is **publicly verifiable**. This involves peer review of scientific reports and being able to replicate the findings of scientific studies.

3. Science seeks problems that are **empirically solvable** and that yield **testable theories**. This means that questions that we cannot answer experimentally (or which we do not currently have the methods to answer) are not the province of science, for example, 'Does heaven exist?'

The scientific method usually involves testing **hypotheses** about **relationships between variables**.

A Sample Experimental Design

There's a strong link between being a hipster and having a beard, but all the research to date has been correlational. You might deduce that becoming a hipster causes beard acquisition, but how do you know that beards aren't causing an as-yet-unclassified condition known as Hipsteritis? You might think to yourself, 'My Dad has a beard and he's no hipster', but without experimental studies, who can say for sure? Given your father's love of plaid and hiking boots, how can you be sure he isn't simply in the early stages of the condition? For the sake of your father and society at large, we need to determine what causes the hipster-beard correlation. Your mission is to design an experiment that can test the hypothesis that *becoming a hipster causes beard growth* (for this mission you can pretend that there are no ethical or resource barriers).

To be able to make strong causal inferences regarding our findings, and to rule out as many alternative explanations of our findings as possible, we need to choose a methodology that fairly and rigorously tests our hypothesis. This methodology is called a **true experiment**, and there are two key components to this kind of rigorous experimentation: (1) we must **manipulate** the variable we assume is a causal factor while keeping all other variables constant; and (2) we must **randomly assign** members of our sample to each level of the manipulated variable.

First, we would need to identify a sample from a population that we are interested in. We might choose to focus on beard growth in young, urban, middle-class men, so we would need to choose a sample that is representative of that entire population in terms of socioeconomic and cultural backgrounds. Because we are interested in 'hipsterisation' as a possible causal factor in said beard growth, we would need to have a way of manipulating the level of hipsterisation across our groups (our **independent variable**), and have some way of measuring beard growth across time — in this case, the Facial Fur Coefficient or FFC (our **dependent variable**). We will also need to make sure all participants are of beard-growing age but do not presently exhibit facial fur, to ensure that we are measuring both groups from an equivalent baseline. To rule out potential alternative explanations for our hypothesised effect, we will attempt to keep all other potential confounding variables constant (e.g., age, general hirsuteness).

Next, how will we influence each group's level of hipsterisation? To do this, we will need to manipulate the major factor that contributes to the hipsterisation process. The vast (and imaginary) hipster literature tells us that the key factor of hipsterisation is 'level of exposure to hipster culture', so we need to find a way to vary this between our groups. To do this, we create two dwellings: one is an unremarkable apartment in a middle-class neighbourhood surrounded by a mix of local businesses (our 'control' apartment); and the other is a converted warehouse apartment with exposed brick walls, next to a plaid shirt factory, above a vintage camera store, and across the road from an organic, bespoke, fair-trade coffeehouse (our 'experimental' apartment).

At the beginning of the experiment, each of the young men in our sample is randomly assigned to live in either the experimental apartment, or the control apartment. Random assignment ensures that other variables that may influence hipsterisation — such as access to old bicycles — are equally distributed across both groups. Each group will live in one of these apartments for six months, to ensure the 'dosage' is equal in each group.

At the end of their stay in their assigned apartment, the Facial Fur Coefficient (FFC) of each participant is measured, and the average FFC for each group is computed. What we are expecting to find, of course, is that our experimental group will report a higher average FFC than our control group. If we do find this, then we can be reasonably confident in our causal inference that increased hipsterisation leads to higher levels of facial fur.

Although we have proposed an experiment which is likely not feasible on ethical and resource grounds, it is possible even in complex situations to implement highly controlled experiments, including the 'gold standard' RCTs (randomised control trials) in health research. Even then, it is generally accepted that no one experiment can control all potentially confounding variables. Wherever there is an uncontrolled variable, there is the possibility of an alternative explanation for the findings. Any one experiment with its particular methodology cannot usually control all potential confounding variables, and in that sense is 'flawed'. Thus, it is necessary to conduct a number of experiments, each controlling for a subset of such potentially confounding variables through its unique methodology. Across this set of experiments, all potential confounding variables should be addressed — this approach is called the **logic of flawed experimentation**. Why is this important? Firstly, it is good science to address all alternative explanations. Secondly, it is often the case that people who don't 'like' a particular finding (i.e., variable X causes variable Y) from a particular experiment will point to a flaw in methodology (which is likely there, because no one experiment can usually address all alternative explanations). Hence, it is important to be able to point to the converging evidence in support of the predicted outcome from multiple experiments with multiple methodologies, which together address all alternative explanations based on potential confounding variables (that is, the **principle of converging evidence**).

Moving Forward With our Imperfect Mind

So yes, our reasoning capacities can be far from reasonable. Hopefully this chapter has helped you recognise where fallacies and errors (M_{SUB}'s) are getting in the way of your optimal thinking. Identifying these errors is the first step to understanding why there are suboptimal responses and outcomes (R_{SUB}'s), just like knowing your watch isn't working can help you seek out more accurate sources of time. It is only through practice that we can recognise these fallacies in our everyday lives, and slowly but surely minimise the effect they have on how we think and act. The more we do this, the more we can optimise our minds, as shown in Figure 2.2.

It is worth noting that the strategies presented in this book derive from a scientific approach to knowledge. The claims that we make and the approaches

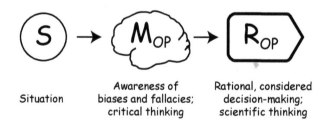

| Situation | Awareness of biases and fallacies; critical thinking | Rational, considered decision-making; scientific thinking |

Figure 2.2   Being aware of these cognitive biases and fallacies (M_{OP}) can lead to more optimal decision making, including applying the scientific method (R_{OP}).

we suggest emerge from controlled experimental studies, and many are based on converging evidence from several different studies. Where we refer to researchers we are not simply making an appeal to authority, rather we are using their evidence to inform how we help you help yourself. As scientists, we have attempted to employ our critical thinking skills to (a) guard against our own cognitive biases in information processing, (b) examine the logic of the arguments and evidence, (c) gather information that would constitute evidence for and against the various explanations, and (d) critically analyse the assumptions and methodology underlying that information. Unlike with some self-help books, therefore, you can be confident that the contents of this book are not merely wisdom imparted by our mothers, or cunningly crafted arguments written by those who 'talk their book'. Our recommendations are evidence-based, and therefore this book itself reflects the scientific way of thinking applied to our often less-than-scientific everyday way of thinking about the world around us.

Summary Points

- We may assume that our thinking processes are reasonable and rational, but unfortunately they are prone to biases and fallacies, due to imperfect evolutionary processes.

- One of the most important biases is the confirmation bias, which is the tendency to overweight information that supports our existing beliefs. This bias can lead to prejudice and discrimination.

- One of the most important logical fallacies is that correlation equals causation, that is, the assumption that because two things are related, one must have caused the other. This can lead to erroneous conclusions about the direction of the relationship between variables, or to ignoring the impact of a third variable.

- With our knowledge of these biases and fallacies, we can better identify and correct suboptimal thinking in ourselves and others.

More Resources

- The evolution (or lack thereof) of your mind:
  Read *Caveman Logic: The persistence of primitive thinking in a modern world*, by Hank Davis (2009).

- Availability Heuristic and Vividness:
  Read *Thinking, Fast and Slow* by Daniel Kahneman (2011) for an overview of this work.

- Answers to *TRY IT! 2.2*: halo effect, availability heuristic, confirmation bias, gamblers fallacy, just-world hypothesis, hindsight bias, illusory correlation.

CHAPTER 3

Know Thyself

How well do you know yourself? How important is it to know yourself? Given what you have read in the last chapter about the fallibility of the brain, you might not be surprised to learn that most of us are also less knowledgeable than we think about ourselves, including our beliefs, strengths, values, personality, interests, and capabilities. And knowing who we are and what we want *is* important, as it enables us to set realistic and meaningful goals, and to make deliberate choices based on what we value. Part of knowing oneself is also knowing all of the ways our human minds can let us down, as outlined in the previous chapter, as well as becoming aware of our specific thoughts, beliefs, and mindsets — the M_{SUB}'s — that might lead to suboptimal or unhelpful responses (R_{SUB}'s) to situations that we encounter. While this entire book is in some sense about knowing thyself, this chapter provides you with specific tools to better understand what makes *you* tick.

What is Self-knowledge?

Self-knowledge sounds a bit new-aged, but the study of self-knowledge has quite a long history in Western society. Self-knowledge was a particular focus of the Classical Greek scholars, with the Temple of Apollo at Delphi bearing the inscription 'Know thyself and thou shall know all the mysteries of the gods and of the universe'*. While explaining *all* universal mysteries might be beyond the scope of this book, our message in this chapter is more along the lines of 'Know thyself and thou shall better understand others and be able to live a more meaningful life'.

In more recent times, psychological science has tried to understand what we mean by 'self' and 'self-knowledge'. Self-knowledge encompasses many constructs, including knowledge about your past, present, and predicted future attitudes, beliefs, values, motives, aspirations, and goals, as well as ways of thinking and feeling, personality traits, character strengths, capabilities, interests, and behaviours.

Self-knowledge is a key component of what we call **psychological literacy**, in particular when we intentionally apply psychological principles to understanding ourselves. It is particularly helpful for young people to understand who they are in order to determine what they want to do with their lives. When some of the authors went to university (in about the late Palaeolithic period), most people went there to become a noun — such as a lawyer, scientist, engineer, teacher, or psychologist. There were significantly fewer pathways to significantly fewer careers. Now, however, the number of university programs has skyrocketed, and each of those programs can lead to multiple career paths. Given this complexity, the best way to determine what you want to do with your life is to 'know thyself' — to learn more about your thoughts, emotions, and behaviour, as well as your personality, your capabilities, your values, your character strengths, and your interests. The more you do, the more you will understand what truly matters to you, and how you can pursue a life so meaningful that Netflix eventually turns it into a mini-series.

Metacognition

Self-knowledge is one aspect of **metacognitive knowledge**, which incorporates knowledge about thinking in general (i.e., the activities of thinking, under-

---

* Nick Sikotis (Greek-Australian Electromechanical/Electronics Engineer/Scientist), indicates that Γ Ν Ω Θ Ι Σ Ε Α Υ Τ Ο Ν means, in a dynamic way, 'Get to know' thyself, or 'Start to discover' thyself or 'Evaluate' thyself. However, in the full context of its placement — where people entered the Temple with the aim to PRAY FOR JUSTICE or STRENGTH, BEG FOR HELP, WISH-GOOD, WISH-ILL, PLACE a CURSE, CONFESS, ASK FOR FORGIVENESS, this inscription had the obvious connotation/suffix (not inscribed) of .. 'before you are critical of others', 'before you measure up to others', 'before you blame others', 'before you feel sorry for yourself', 'before you proceed with something terminal and irreversible '— know thyself!

standing, learning, and remembering), as well as higher order thinking which enables understanding of your own cognition and cognitive processes, especially as they relate to learning. It has been described as 'knowing what you know', or 'thinking about thinking', but it is far broader than that, as it encompasses strategic and reflective knowledge about how to go about solving a problem. It includes activities such as planning how to tackle a learning task, monitoring your understanding, and evaluating your progress toward completion of the task; thus, metacognition is critical to being a successful learner.

Central to understanding how best to approach a problem is knowledge of self, which is the highest level of metacognition. As such, self-knowledge is a highly advanced form of knowledge, so it is not surprising that it can be somewhat difficult to acquire!

There are also many different components of self-knowledge. We store lots of different information about ourselves, including a global self-concept, autobiographical memories, and our conscious here-and-now self, all of which contribute to self-knowledge. And to make things more complicated, self-knowledge includes becoming aware both of our general tendencies (e.g., 'I am generally quiet') as well as our context-specific behaviours (e.g., 'I am talkative at parties'). So self-knowledge seems to comprise a vast array of information about ourselves, accrued over time and contexts, which needs to be melded into a single coherent identity.

Accuracy and Sources of Self-knowledge

But how accurate is your self-knowledge?

Jack the researcher wants to examine exactly that question — the accuracy of some of your mental constructs. First, to examine the accuracy of your memory, Jack gives you a list of items to remember, then tests the accuracy of your recall against those items — easy! Similarly, if Jack wants to see how accurate your **predicted attitudes** are (e.g., what you will think about paying tax when you graduate from university in 3 years' time), he could ask you what you *predict* you will think, then 3 years later he could ask you what you *actually* think and determine your accuracy — simple! But things get a lot more complicated when trying to assess the accuracy of your self-knowledge, as people have internal states and mental processes which sit below their awareness. As a result, knowing oneself is not just a simple matter of navel gazing, or introspection, you also need to rely on alternative and possibly more objective measures to assist you in the task of getting to know yourself.

Social psychologist Timothy Wilson suggests 3 strategies to know thyself:

1. seeing ourselves through the eyes of other people (and we suggest that this can include social comparison and social observation);

2. utilising findings from psychological science (central to psychological literacy); and

3. becoming objective observers of our own behaviour (which we encourage in this book).

To elaborate on the first point, we may come to a better understanding of ourselves through others' appraisals of us, and through social comparison. For example, one way that we might come to better know ourselves is through considering others' responses to us.

Meet Sienna, who considers herself to be quite boring, unattractive, and generally uninteresting to others. After her first psychology class, in which she adeptly answered the lecturer's tricky question, she is approached by Nathan, who asks her out on a date. She agrees (although is confused by the attention, and wonders whether this is one of those psychology experiments she has heard about, where they deceive you with all sorts of sneaky tricks). The next week, Jamie asks her out on a date, mentioning that he saw her talking to Nathan last week and hopes she is available. She says yes, and goes out that night with him. The next day, Eddie, having seen the attention Sienna was getting from both Nathan and Jamie, asks her out on a date. Notwithstanding the challenge Sienna is having in finishing her assignments with all this dating (she should probably read Chapter 7 — in her spare time!), Sienna's belief about herself as boring, unattractive, and uninteresting to others is being challenged as a result of seeing herself through their eyes.

Of course, there can be a downside to this phenomenon as well. Meet Mai, who in her home country was considered a successful business woman. After immigrating to her new country however, she finds that her gender and skin colour is suddenly a barrier to finding support for the business she is attempting to develop. That is, she would not be served well by accepting others' misogynistic and racist perceptions that she does not 'have what it takes' to be a success in the business world.

Others can also influence our self-knowledge through social comparison, which entails learning about oneself through comparison to others. For example, if you want to know whether you are kind, or fast, or intelligent, you could compare your behaviour to that of others. Although the best person to compare yourself to, in order to get an accurate comparison, is someone fairly similar to you (comparing your running speed to that of Usain Bolt, or your kindness to the Dalai Lama is probably not the most accurate benchmark), we are often driven by more than just a desire for accuracy. For that reason, we tend to compare ourselves to those who are better off than we are (upward comparison), to inspire us to improve. Conversely, we may also compare ourselves to those who are worse off than we are (downward comparison), in a desire for self-enhancement, or to reassure ourselves that we could be worse. Unfortunately, social comparison can have negative effects, for example with women judging themselves more negatively after viewing images of attractive female models, and children as young as 5 years old showing an increase in body dissatisfaction after exposure to Barbie dolls.

 DIVING DEEPER 3.1

How Well do People Know Themselves?

Surprisingly, there are only moderate relationships between the average person's ratings of their abilities and characteristics and more objective measures of such things. Moreover, other people seem to know more about some of our personality traits and behaviour than we do ourselves. So why are we sometimes less aware of ourselves than are others? What are the barriers to self-knowledge? There are two categories of barriers: *informational* and *motivational*.

Informational barriers are where the poor quantity or quality of available information negatively impacts self-knowledge. Our brains have evolved in such a way that most of the mental processing underlying our behaviour is unconscious, and processing information in this unconscious way is actually highly adaptive in most circumstances. However, self-knowledge is by definition conscious, so we cannot rely on unconscious processes to understand ourselves (let's put aside for the moment the controversies regarding the value of 'intuition'). Homo sapiens have the most advanced capacity for conscious or explicit processing, so we can choose to use these cognitive tools to deduce or extract information about ourselves, and in particular, to test our beliefs about ourselves that develop over our lifetime.

Note that information is also about the contents of our memory, and *TRY IT! 2.3* addresses the impact of memory on self-knowledge and identity.

Motivational barriers are where self-knowledge is negatively influenced by self-enhancement motives (i.e., the desire to perceive oneself positively) and self-verification motives (i.e., the desire to confirm one's identity). These types of motives may lead you to only seek out self-knowledge that paints you in a positive light, or confirms only nice things about who you are (remember 'confirmation bias' in Chapter 2).

Finally, there may be other barriers to better self-knowledge that relate to cognitive capacity, which may be developmentally immature or compromised in some way (i.e., brain structure and function cannot support the complex processing required).

How can we acquire more accurate information about ourselves? As mentioned above, there are three routes, which overcome the different types of barriers to varying extents:

1. Attempt to be objective observers of our own behaviour (i.e., the focus is on the self as a better information gatherer; this would involve applying some of the tools in Chapters 2 and 4);

2. see ourselves through the eyes of other people (i.e., the focus is on what information others can give us — but we need to be both open to and critical consumers of this information);

3. apply findings from psychological science to ourselves (i.e., the focus is on what research can tell us about ourselves — e.g., taking an introductory psychology unit that emphasises application). Note that in this book, we explicitly emphasise tools that have a strong evidence base in psychological science.

Self-knowledge and the SMR Model

Other than utilising others as a lens to know ourselves, self-knowledge requires us to become objective observers of our own behaviour. This is particularly relevant to our SMR model, because when we talk about your mind (M), we are referring to what makes you 'you' — your core beliefs and assumptions, your attitudes, values, character strengths, capacities, and goals. Some of these sit below your conscious awareness, and others are more accessible, but they are all able to influence how you respond (R) to a given situation (S). Moreover, there are some aspects of the self that require advanced tools to fully unearth, even though you have some inkling of what lies beneath. These include your personality, interests, and capabilities, for which psychologists have developed robust measurement tools to help you better understand yourself ... but more on this later.

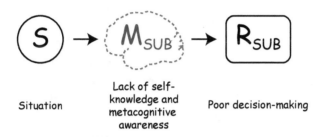

Situation   Lack of self-knowledge and metacognitive awareness   Poor decision-making

Figure 3.1   Lacking self-knowledge (M_{SUB}) — that is, being unaware of your beliefs, personality, capabilities, values, character strengths, and your interests — results in suboptimal responding such as poor decision-making.

Becoming more self-aware, therefore, whether through introspection or psychological testing, is the first step in optimising thinking, as you can better determine those aspects of your mind (M_{SUB}) which are producing a less than optimal response (R_{SUB}). In this chapter, we hope to convince you that, in comparison to rational ignorance (Google it), such self-knowledge is worth the effort. By better understanding your strengths and weaknesses, you can adjust to situations, acquire extra knowledge or capabilities when needed, and make optimal decisions.

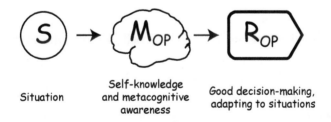

Situation   Self-knowledge and metacognitive awareness   Good decision-making, adapting to situations

Figure 3.2   Gaining greater self-knowledge (M_{OP}) about what is important to you, including your core beliefs, strengths, weaknesses, personality, and values, enables better adjustment to situations and optimal decision-making (R_{OP}).

To help illustrate the various aspects of self-knowledge covered in this chapter we are going to follow the journey of Chris, as he gets to know himself better. To most casual observers, Chris has everything going for him. Chris grew up in a great home, attended a quality high school, and landed a spot in a highly competitive law program at a top university. Chris is living in a fancy new residential college where he is loved for his razor-sharp wit. Moreover, his personal style certainly doesn't go unnoticed by the ladies. But Chris has been struggling lately. The pressure for high grades is stifling, as few jobs await numerous graduates. The resulting competitiveness has led some students to denigrate others in class in order to psych them out, or to exclude some people from social groups because they are not 'smart enough'. If that doesn't sound bad enough, Chris has caught friends he respects cheating outright. They hide smart phones to allow them to search for information during exams, and even buy essays online, all in the pursuit of future financial success and social status. Chris himself even cheated on an essay last semester just to stay in the game. This culture of denigration and dishonesty has really made Chris start to despair. If this was law school, he didn't want to do it anymore. But what *did* he want to do?

To help Chris make some decisions about his future, he needs to develop his self-knowledge: about his beliefs, values, character and capability strengths, personality, and interests. Chris will be able to identify some of these through observing his own behaviour, and doing a bit of looking inward. However, he will also need some help from the careers advisor, Eva, to help him to reflect on what is truly important to him, and that in turn can help to guide his career decisions.

Knowing Your Core Beliefs and Icebergs

A belief is a premise that we hold to be true, into which we place trust and confidence. **Core beliefs** are our fundamental beliefs about who we are and want to be, about other people, and about how the world around us should operate. They are an intrinsic part of who we are. Core beliefs can be formed during our childhood, based on our interpretation of our experiences, or transmitted from those important to us. They may be positive or negative, and broad (e.g., people matter) or specific to a particular context (e.g., a 51% mark is 1% wasted effort, or 'Ps get degrees'). Core beliefs are so fundamental that they often sit below our awareness, yet they impact the way we see and engage with the world around us. In some ways, they are like a window through which we see the world — we are so used to looking *through* it that we don't often look *at* it. We also refer to them as icebergs, as often they float below our awareness, and all we notice is the tip of the iceberg — the response that results from a tightly held, deep-seated, core belief. Yes, core beliefs are part of the M in our SMR model. Sometimes these core beliefs guide us to behave in optimal ways that are aligned with our values (see later in this chapter), however sometimes they produce suboptimal responses, and often result in an overreaction to a situation (like jumping down your flatmate's throat when he leaves the milk out… again).

These beliefs or icebergs may reveal themselves as a thought that pops into your head while you are experiencing a situation, but other times they are harder to identify. One way to identify these beliefs is to try to find patterns in your thinking and/or responses, to help you identify the broader category or theme to which your core belief relates. Positive core beliefs may be about appreciation of what you have received, positivity about the future, contribution, excellence, or wonder. Negative categories include fear of loss of something you care about ('he might leave me'), danger of something bad happening ('the world is not a safe place'), violation of rights ('people should always do the right thing'), causing harm or offense ('I must never say 'no' or she'll think I don't like her'), or negative self-worth ('I am not good enough'). Each theme of suboptimal thinking (M_{SUB}) leads to a *set of* specific responses (R_{SUB}) — for example, beliefs about danger might lead to an anxious response, whereas a belief about others violating your rights could lead to anger and aggressive behaviour. Noticing such themes in your thinking and/or your responses may help you to identify the icebergs that underpin them.

There are many, many different core beliefs or icebergs (many of which may lead to optimal thinking some or most of the time). Which of these you adhere to will impact how you respond to a given situation, and sometimes our core beliefs may actually be inconsistent, rendering decision-making extremely difficult. Examples include:

People should always do the right thing.

People can't be trusted.

Others will take advantage of me if I let them.

The world is a dangerous place.

People should be treated with respect.

I should put other people's needs before mine.

I am capable and competent.

You should respect your elders.

The world is a fair place, where good things happen to good people.

Good guys finish last.

Asking for help is a sign of weakness.

Asking for help is wise, not weak.

I can only rely on myself to get things done.

None of us is as smart as all of us.

I am better than most other people, and so I deserve more.

Family comes first.

Hard work should be rewarded.

Failure is a sign of weakness.

FAIL = "First Attempt In Learning"

Anything less than perfect is failure.

I can do anything but not everything.

Every day is a blessing.

Real men don't cry.

Women can be as successful as men.

If someone doesn't like me, there must be something wrong with me.

It is my job to make others happy.

Do unto others as you would have them do unto you.

Other people matter.

You should always try your best.

Being honest matters to me.

People should act with integrity.

I will persevere when things get tough.

I deserve to be acknowledged for my effort.

Some of Chris' core beliefs may include that he is capable and competent, that being honest matters, that people should always do the right thing, and that people should act with integrity — these core beliefs are likely to be the reasons that he decided to study law in the first place. He may also believe that the world is a fair place, where good things happen to good people, and that hard work should be rewarded. Such beliefs would possibly cause the distress he is feeling, as he sees that this is not the case when his cheating friends seem to be reaping the rewards, and his hard work seems to be getting him nowhere. These beliefs could lead Chris to feel angry and/or despondent — both clearly suboptimal ways of responding! However, his belief in persevering when things get tough makes it hard for him to decide whether to stay in law, or to change careers.

 TRY IT! 3.1

Identify Your Core Beliefs and Icebergs

Start by choosing some core beliefs and icebergs from the list provided on pages 51-52, then think of others that you might hold. Try to include both positive and negative ones, as well as general beliefs, and more specific beliefs pertaining to your study, career, and/or relationships.

Once you have identified your icebergs, it is interesting to notice the different situations in which they rear their (sometimes ugly) heads. While core beliefs are not, in and of themselves, evil things, they can cause suboptimal responses in a number of ways. They can become activated at unexpected times, leading to disproportionate emotions and reactions, or reactions that are misaligned to the situation. Watch what happens when Chris's icebergs get in his way. He is driving to uni, and waiting for the traffic light to turn green. As it turns green, the car in front of him indicates to turn across oncoming traffic. Chris bangs his hands on the steering wheel in fury, and describes the driver using a colourful stream of adjectives that would make his grandmother blush. He is ropable! This overreaction (R_{SUB}) results from Chris' core belief that 'people should always do the right thing' — in this case, follow the road rules. He feels angry as his rights have been violated. Chris finally gets to university, decides to get some food, but then someone cuts in front of him in the café queue and buys the last cinnamon scroll. Not surprisingly, he is furious — see that iceberg again! Once activated, iceberg beliefs may also cause you to subconsciously scan your world for other instances of violations.

Conflicting icebergs can adversely influence decision-making. For example, Lil believes that women can be as successful as men, but also that family comes first. When offered a promotion into her dream job as the first female partner at her firm, which entails being relocated away from her disabled mother, her clash of icebergs makes her choice a difficult one. Finally, iceberg beliefs can be too rigid, resulting in the same suboptimal responding patterns emerging time after time.

 **TRY IT! 3.2**

Identify Your Iceberg Beliefs

Think of a situation (S) in your life that caused a suboptimal response (R$_{SUB}$), particularly one that may have been out of proportion to the situation (you could use your example from Chapter 1, or think of a new one). Can you identify the iceberg that may mediate that S-R relationship? What is the theme that underpins that belief (e.g., loss, danger, rights, harm, self-worth)? Can you think of a different situation where the same theme or a similar iceberg also caused a suboptimal response?

While a key to knowing thyself (and to using the SMR model) is to identify those icebergs or core beliefs that are resulting in suboptimal responding, the next step is to know what to do to manage those beliefs. Chapter 4 will provide numerous strategies to help you to further unearth suboptimal ways of thinking (M$_{SUB}$'s), and should you choose to, either change them to more optimal thinking, or manage them so that they don't lead to suboptimal responding (R$_{SUB}$). Fortunately, one of Chris's core beliefs is that it is wise (not weak) to ask for help, so the next step was to ask Eva, the careers advisor, for help in getting to know his values, to help him understand what jobs might make him feel happy and fulfilled.

Know Thy Values

We all have things that we value, but our **values** can be tricky to identify. Values aren't goals or things. Rather, values are deeply held and relatively constant beliefs about what we consider to be important, that guide what we aspire to, and how we live out those aspirations. Or, in the inimitable words of Elvis Presley: 'Values are like fingerprints. Nobody's are the same, but you leave them all over everything you do'.

For example, you might say that you 'value' your friends, but what this means is that your friends are important to you because you value *friendship*. When you think about people you admire, you might stumble across your own values, such as integrity, bravery, kindness.

Even if you are not at the point of despair like Chris was, knowing your values helps you think and act in ways that are consistent with who you really want to be. We call this **valued living**, and this can help you to set and achieve meaningful goals, stay well, and develop a sense of purpose and identity. Some of your values may change throughout your life, but many will remain the same. The key point is that knowing what is important to you in the long term can help you make good decisions in the short term. Knowing what you value can also help you in times of stress, so that as you face the inevitable ups-and-downs of life you don't lose sight of the things that really, truly matter to you (part of 'psychological flexibility' — see Chapter 4).

To further illustrate the role and importance of values, let's meet Chris's high school friend, Zac. Zac really values helping others, which has led him to want to study clinical psychology so that he can work with refugees suffering trauma. As you can immediately see, Zac's value of helping others is not a goal with a specific end-point (there will always be someone to help). Instead, the value of helping others is a guiding principle: it inspires Zac to do his best work, and to persist when things get difficult. Zac reminds himself of this value as he faces the drudgery of studying for a statistics exam, which he needs to pass to progress in his psychology degree. Even if Zac fails, he won't give up, because how Zac responds to this setback also will be driven by his value of helping others. He may try again using better study strategies, or he may decide to modify his career goal and study something else that will still enable him to help others, but does not involve studying statistics. As you can see, values have helped Zac to identify career options that are meaningful to him, and they have inspired him to work hard even in the face of true academic terror: statistics.

Despite how important they can be, most of us have not identified our values. Values clarification exercises (like the one in *TRY IT! 3.3*) can help us to realise what we value, and thus increase the likelihood that we will live a life that is meaningful and fulfilling. You can use the following values exercise to help you identify what is important to you. This can then guide you to consider ways of thinking and acting that are aligned with your values.

TRY IT! 3.3

Identifying Your Values

Below is a list of common values that might guide a person in prioritising their goals and time. Consider each word on the list based on what you understand it to mean — don't get hung up on semantics! From the list, select up to 5 values that are important to *you*. This first step should take no longer than about 2 minutes.

You could also briefly think about why each value is important to you (although it might be much more obvious for some values than for others). Then, identify one *valued action* that you can take to live according to that value, including as much detail as possible (e.g., where and when you will undertake that valued action). Rate how important this value is to you on a scale of 0 (low importance) to 10 (high importance). It's okay to have several values scoring the same number. Rate how successfully you have lived this value during the past month on a scale of 0 (not at all successfully) to 10 (very successfully). Finally rank these valued directions in order of the importance you place on working on them right now, with 1 as the highest rank, and 2 the next highest, and so on.

Value	Optional: Why is this value important to me?	Valued action (give as much detail as possible)	Importance	Success	Rank
Integrity	Parents live by this value, and I was raised to do the same	My work is always my own; I will not claim others' work as my own in any assessments or other work.	9	6	1

Abundance	Elegance	Industry	Sensitivity
Acceptance	Encouragement	Integrity	Service
Accomplishment	Enthusiasm	Intimacy	Sincerity
Achievement	Equality	Joy	Skilfulness
Adventure	Excellence	Kindness	Space
Assertiveness	Excitement	Love	Spirituality
Authenticity	Fairness	Loyalty	Success
Beauty	Faith	Mindfulness	Supportiveness
Caring	Family	Openness	Tolerance

Caution	Fitness	Optimism	Tradition
Challenge	Flexibility	Orderliness	Trust
Commitment	Focus	Originality	Truth
Community	Forgiveness	Participation	Understanding
Compassion	Frankness	Patience	Vitality
Compromise	Free Spirit	Peace	Zest
Connection	Freedom	Persistence	Security
Contribution	Friendship	Pleasure	Self-expression
Creativity	Gratitude	Realism	Humour
Curiosity	Growth	Reliability	Independence
Dedication	Harmony	Resilience	Duty
Dependability	Honesty	Respect	Effort
Dignity	Humanity	Responsibility	
Diversity	Humility	Risk Taking	

Chris came to his appointment with Eva armed with knowledge of his top 5 values: integrity, generosity, courage, wisdom, and innovation. Chris was upset, because although he now knew his top values, he was not successfully living them. Eva explained that people often felt confused or even depressed when they were not living by their values, but discovering one's values was just the first step. Over time, Chris would learn to align his decisions and behaviour more closely to those values. It would take some effort, but the more Chris 'lived his values' the better he would feel about his direction in life.

Chris and Eva also discussed why it can be valuable to know the origins of one's values. For example, Chris's value of courage was partly inspired by his grandmother, who had migrated to this country and, through hard work and courage, built a successful business. Chris realised how much he admired his grandmother (even though they didn't always agree).

Know Thy Character Strengths

Chris now felt like he had a better idea of what was important to him, but still wasn't clear about what careers he would be good at, or what aspects of himself he could bring to his studies and his career. To help answer these questions, Eva sent him to the VIA website (see *TRY IT! 3.4*) to discover his character strengths.

Positive psychology argues that it is better to focus on building one's strengths, rather than on correcting weaknesses. Understanding and using our strengths is about focusing on things that we enjoy, and that come easily to us. This doesn't mean that we should ignore our weaknesses (especially those that are critical to our aspirations), but we don't need to excel at everything — sometimes good enough is enough.

Character strengths (as opposed to physical strengths such as running, or other capacities such as cognitive skills) are 24 culturally universal and distinctive characteristics defined by Chris Peterson and Martin Seligman. Each one is unequivocally positive, and contributes to individual fulfilment, satisfaction, and happiness (e.g., bravery and valour, perspective, leadership, love of learning). They are those personal characteristics that allow us to perform well, and that energise us and make us feel at our best. It is claimed that when voluntarily utilising those strengths with which you identify most (signature character strengths), you feel that you are being true to yourself. In that sense, signature character strengths are sometimes conceptualised as 'values in action'.

Although trait-like and stable, signature character strengths can not only be developed, they are also often areas in which we learn fast. There is evidence that purposefully utilising and further developing character strengths (mostly signature, but also lesser strengths), leads to positive outcomes including increased goal progression and wellbeing — thus, it is worthwhile identifying your signature character strengths.

TRY IT! 3.4

Character Strengths Plus

One way of determining your signature strengths is to go to the VIA website (like Chris did) (http://www.viacharacter.org/www/) and complete the **VIA survey.**

Identification of signature and weaker character strengths can facilitate subsequent: (a) building on your signature character strengths, particularly when dealing with novel or challenging situations; (b) building up weaker character strengths, having decided to do so for internal reasons (e.g., you enjoy attempting to be creative, even though you currently do not rate yourself highly on this character strength) or for external reasons (e.g., your current job requires that you be more creative); and (c) shaping your environments strategically so that any weaknesses do not interfere with your aspirations (e.g., ensure there is a creative person on your team).

PLUS: Because the character strengths exercise involves self-rating, and we can sometimes be inaccurate in our knowledge of our character strengths, it is worthwhile asking others who know you (friends, relatives, co-workers) to rate you on a strengths inventory. However, you need to be ready to take on 'discrepant' information in a non-defensive way to get the best outcome (i.e., control your confirmation bias — see Chapter 2). You could ask them which of your behaviours led them to rate you in that way, so you can better understand how your behaviour is perceived by others. On the positive side, of course, you will find that people perceive character strengths you may not realise you have.

The next time they met, Eva and Chris discussed Chris's top five character strengths: creativity; kindness; love of learning; integrity; and bravery. Eva asked him to think about the areas of his life where he is using each of those strengths, and which other areas he could use them more. For creativity, for example, Eva suggested that Chris could find opportunities in his studies to use his creativity to make the learning more interesting. She challenged him to think of at least one thing he could do each day. Chris decided that he would also focus on his strength of bravery, and continue on his path to self-discovery. With Eva's encouragement, he decided to see a psychologist, Dr. Levy, who could conduct a formal personality assessment.

Know Thy Personality

Although you might put money on the fact that at least one of your classmates has no personality, we all actually do have a personality. Our personality can be thought of as stable (and fairly consistent) patterns of thoughts, feelings and behaviours that we express across different contexts. And, although our behaviour in a particular situation is determined not only by our relatively enduring personality traits but also by myriad environmental influences, in the long term, these personality traits *do* predict our general behavioural tendencies. So how can we understand both the stability of these behavioural patterns in ourselves, and our differences from each other?

There are different theoretical approaches to understanding personality and how it is developed. To make things more complex, many factors interact with and contribute to personality, such as genetics, sociocultural environment, and gender. One relatively well accepted model of personality is the **five-factor trait model**. The five-factors are:

1. openness to experience (O)

2. conscientiousness (C)

3. extraversion (E)

4. agreeableness (A)

5. neuroticism (N)

These can be conveniently captured by the acronym 'OCEAN' (particularly useful for those of you high on conscientiousness, who are diligently studying this book!).

A good way of conceptualising personality factors is as **dimensional constructs**, where we differ to varying degrees on *how much* of a particular factor we have, rather than having a factor or lacking it. As an example, let's consider the factor of extraversion. It is commonly and, not surprisingly, misunderstood to mean social confidence (vs. shyness). Instead, it relates more to what energises us. Imagine we all have different reserves of energy (like a battery pack) for getting though our daily lives. Some of us get more charged by external stimulation, such as social events or just being surrounded by others (i.e., more extraverted). Then there are those of us who get more charged through internal stimulation, such as introspection, or even reading a book, and are conversely drained more quickly by external stimulation (i.e., more introverted). Most of us sit somewhere in the middle, enjoying the pleasures of socialisation, yet balancing this with personal time to re-charge. Where we fall on the introversion-extraversion spectrum will influence how we prefer to spend our time and how much we want to interact with others. Having self-knowledge of where we (and those we associate with) fall on each of the OCEAN factors can help us better interact with others and achieve desired outcomes.

Imagine you have recently joined a class and are assigned a group assessment with two people you don't yet know well, Eli and Luca. The assessment requires interviewing to collect data, analysing data, report writing, and a group presentation. There are many things that you might want to know about each other, such as skill set and time-availability, when considering how to allocate roles and tasks. You may also want to know about their personalities. Do they meet deadlines (conscientiousness), are they open to new ideas and change (open to experience), will they challenge ideas or avoid confrontations (agreeableness), do they prefer to work in dynamic social environments or more in isolation (extraversion), and do their emotions fluctuate more often than others (neuroticism)?

As a part of the group-work assignment your tutor asks you to complete a personality assessment, and provides you with the results to share with your group. Focusing again on extraversion, you notice Eli scores quite low — he is less extraverted (more introverted) than 92% of the population. In contrast, Luca's score on extraversion is higher — she is less extraverted (more introverted) than 52% of the population. Luca's score reflects how her battery-pack is a more even split of both extraversion and introversion, whereas Eli's battery-pack is mostly introversion. If we didn't examine personality along a dimension, but rather used a categorical approach, then we would simply conclude that both Luca and Eli are 'introverts' (both less than 50% on extraversion), without recognising the vast differences in their levels of introversion.

All of the OCEAN personality factors, except neuroticism, are positively associated with wellbeing. So what happens if, for example, you are low on extraversion (i.e. high on introversion), just like Eli, which is not unusual, for example, in a university population? You could work on changing aspects of your personality, although that takes much effort and time — perhaps worthwhile if you are high on neuroticism, but not so important or practical for other personality traits. Rather, it may be worthwhile seeing the benefits of different points on the dimensions of each personality factor. For example, being high on introversion has many benefits that can be leveraged — the capacity to be comfortable with solitude can allow for intense learning and creativity. In the group work scenario above, Eli could work productively on certain assignment tasks such as the data analysis and report writing, without draining his battery as much as other group members. At the same time, being aware that he is lower on extraversion than his teammates may lead Eli to engage more effortfully and purposefully in those *compulsory* tasks that require social engagement, such as presenting to the class.

If you want a valid personality assessment (not one in a magazine that tells you which Kardashian you most resemble), how do you proceed? You could find a private career counsellor or psychologist, or if you are a student, there may be a career development office that offers these services. There are also several well-respected online sites that allow you to gain relatively valid and reliable information regarding your personality (see *More Resources*). *TRY IT! 3.5* is a very brief personality inventory.

TRY IT! 3.5

Brief Personality Assessment

Complete the Ten-Item Personality Inventory (TIPI) below:

Here are a number of personality traits that may or may not apply to you. Please write a number next to each statement to indicate the extent to which you agree or disagree with that statement. You should rate the extent to which the pair of traits applies to you, even if one characteristic applies more strongly than the other.

1 = Disagree strongly

2 = Disagree moderately

3 = Disagree a little

4 = Neither agree nor disagree

5 = Agree a little

6 = Agree moderately

7 = Agree strongly

I see myself as:

1. _____ Extraverted, enthusiastic.
2. _____ Critical, quarrelsome.
3. _____ Dependable, self-disciplined.
4. _____ Anxious, easily upset.
5. _____ Open to new experiences, complex.
6. _____ Reserved, quiet.
7. _____ Sympathetic, warm.
8. _____ Disorganised, careless.
9. _____ Calm, emotionally stable.
10. _____ Conventional, uncreative.

Scoring the TIPI

Step 1. Recode the reverse-scored items (i.e., recode a 7 with a 1, a 6 with a 2, a 5 with a 3, etc.). The reverse-scored items are 2, 4, 6, 8, & 10.

Step 2. Take the AVERAGE of the two items (the standard item and the recoded reverse-scored item) that make up each scale. ('R' denotes reverse-scored items):

Extraversion: 1, 6R; Agreeableness: 2R, 7; Conscientiousness; 3, 8R; Emotional Stability (note that this scale uses this subscale as the opposite of Neuroticism): 4R, 9; Openness to Experiences: 5, 10R. You should thus have 5 scores (ranging from 1-7).

Example using the Extraversion scale: A participant has scores of 5 on item 1 (Extraverted, enthusiastic) and 2 on item 6 (Reserved, quiet). First, recode the reverse-scored item (i.e., item 6), replacing the 2 with a 6. Second, take the average of the score for item 1 and the (recoded) score for item 6. So the TIPI Extraversion scale score would be: (5 + 6)/2 = 5.5.

See http://gosling.psy.utexas.edu/scales-weve-developed/ten-item-personality-measure-tipi/ for norms to help you interpret your scores.

Chris showed Eva the results of his personality assessment. Unsurprisingly Chris scored high on conscientiousness, but he had scored at about mid-level for extraversion. Eva told Chris that although you can purposefully work on changing some aspects of your personality, an important potential outcome of a personality assessment is using this information to firstly better understand your past and current behaviour, and secondly better shape your future environments to achieve your goals. The value is in knowing that certain situations, including work situations, may be more suited to your personality than others. For example, Chris would be pushing his natural tendencies if he were in a work situation that required a high level of extraverted behaviour to be successful (e.g., entertainment, sales).

Know Thy Capabilities and Interests

Although motivation and persistence are obviously important factors in success, 'knowing thyself' can also mean knowing what interests you, as well as knowing the potential of your own brain. The most well-known example of the latter is your **IQ**, although there are other aspects of 'capabilities'. Your IQ is not a measure of your worth or capacity in life. Your IQ is a measure of your ability to problem solve, analyse, and adapt to new situations. It provides an indication of your current cognitive strengths and weaknesses (and we all have both), relative to other people your age, or with the same level of education. If you're wondering what your brain is best at, any appropriately qualified psychologist can conduct a valid and reliable cognitive assessment.

In addition to IQ, which measures your general ability or intelligence, you can also find out about your specific cognitive abilities such as abstract reasoning, analytical reasoning, verbal reasoning, or numerical reasoning. You might also want to know about specific aptitudes, such as motor dexterity, artistic ability, creativity, or leadership potential.

These kinds of assessments can help you think about future study and career options, based on your assessed capacities, or they can help you understand where you might need extra help to reach your goals. There are also tools that assess your general and career-related interests (rather than just the specific cognitive strengths you may possess). Thus, it is worth seeking out a career counsellor either in private practice (e.g., an organisational psychologist) or perhaps at your education provider.

Interest inventories, in contrast, help you to identify your areas of interest, to help you find careers that appeal to your specific preferences. When students embark on higher education studies or further training, some will have a clear idea of their career development goals, while others will not. If you fall into the latter category, professional assessment and guidance can be helpful. To get you started on this path, you could undertake an initial analysis of your interests by using one of many career-related surveys, for example, the Career Cluster Interest Survey (http://www.iseek.org/careers/clusterSurvey) This will ask you to identify:

1. activities that you like to do (e.g., be outdoors in all types of weather; play a musical instrument)

2. personal qualities (e.g., adventurous, caring, coordinated, curious, persuasive)

3. school subjects you like.

It will then provide you with the career clusters (e.g., education and training, health science, STEM, law etc) that best match your interests. Complete the survey once quickly to see what career clusters come up. You may or may not find the results helpful. But then, do the survey a second time, more slowly, and in particular, note down those interests that really resonate with you (or copy them into a file and find your top 10 interests). That is, use the exercise to help you to explicitly recognise those activities you really enjoy. Use these to guide your goal formation (see Chapter 7).

The next thing that Eva asked Chris to do was to think about his capabilities and interests. She sent him back to Dr Levy to assess Chris' cognitive capacities and gave him a career interests survey to complete. At their follow-up meeting, Eva and Chris discussed Chris' assessments. In his cognitive assessment, Chris was way above average on verbal reasoning tasks, but just above average on nonverbal reasoning tasks. This was not a surprise to Chris; he was much better with words than he was with diagrams and symbols. The important thing to take away from these results, Eva explained, was that Chris had both strengths and weaknesses. If he chose to, Chris could put some effort into improving his nonverbal reasoning skills, or he could accept that they were not an area of strength for him and keep that in mind when choosing what to study or where to work.

Next, they discussed Chris's interests' survey results which, surprisingly, had come up with Education and Training and Human Services as two of his top career interests. As Eva and Chris dug deeper into the assessment results, a common theme emerged: Chris seemed very interested in helping others to reach their potential. Eva suggested that he seek out opportunities where he could try being a mentor, such as in a local disadvantaged high school.

Then, Eva asked Chris to list the most important things he had learned about himself during their time together. What self-knowledge had Chris gained? Chris said that he had learned about many of his icebergs, that his brain was great with words, that he was not particularly extroverted even though he sometimes pretended he was, that he really valued things like bravery and integrity, and that he was potentially very creative by nature. Eva then asked Chris to quickly list activities he had frequently done over the past couple of weeks. Included on the list were: being in class (where Chris felt the pressure to compete, rather than collaborate, with his fellow students), studying (whereby Chris was tempted to cheat), and drinking with friends. Eva also asked Chris to indicate which of those activities were aligned with his values or interests, and which were not. Chris found this tough, as he noticed that nothing seemed to align with all the things he now knew about himself. He wasn't acting with integrity or bravery, he wasn't putting his great verbal skills to proper use, and he certainly wasn't being particularly creative at the moment. Now that Chris knew himself better, he realised that he wasn't really being himself. It was clear that some things would have to change. Eva then gave Chris one final exercise to complete before their last session. It was called the 'Best Possible Self' exercise, and Eva was confident it would help Chris identify the changes that he needed to make.

TRY IT! 3.6

Your Best Possible Self

First, you need to consider what kind of person you want to be. Not just a nice person or a smart person, but what do you want others to say about you? It is sometimes useful to reframe this question as, 'what kind of person do you want to be remembered as?'.

Picture your 70th birthday party. As people are sharing videos and selfies (and whatever else we're sharing by then) what would the captions read? On your 70th birthday card, **what would you *want* your family or friends to write about you?** Jot down some of these things, focusing on personal characteristics (e.g., 'she has so much integrity'; 'he is so generous'), how you interact with others (e.g., 'she always makes you feel valued', 'he is devoted to his family'), and capabilities (e.g., 'she is an incredible athlete', 'he is really good with money').

The next step is slightly tougher. Now that you have an idea of your 'best possible self', **contrast this ideal with how you see yourself now.** You may already be living some of this stuff (e.g., frequent generosity). However, there are likely other things that you would like people to say, but you might not have given them many reasons to do so just yet (e.g., a person of high integrity). This might be a bit painful if there are important things missing from your current self, but at least you now know where to focus your efforts going forward. List both the things you currently are, or are doing, as well as those you would like to work on, making sure you can differentiate between the two.

Now, think about the **steps that you need to take** to achieve different aspects of that best possible self. Try to think about what you would need to do this year, this month, or this week, to make progress towards the best you. For example, if you want people to say: 'She had such an amazing career', what might you need to do in the short term to realise that ambition? Education is likely. What about networking? What are the potential barriers? Write them down, and then brainstorm some possible solutions.

Finally, decide **what *specifically* you will do today, and this week, to make progress toward your best possible self.** Make sure that what you write down is a clear, achievable task. If you're focusing on your education, what is one thing that you could do today or this week to improve your approach to learning? Write it down; make it your screensaver; tell a friend who you know will hassle you until you do it.

And when things get tough, try visualising that 70th birthday party with everyone celebrating your amazing career. Also, plan to review your progress regularly: once a week, or at least once a month. Chapter 7 will provide you with further strategies to help you lead a meaningful life, and to be your best possible self.

At their next meeting, Eva and Chris discussed Chris's 'best possible self' exercise, and how this reflected Chris's values and interests. Chris really wanted his friends and family to say that he made a positive difference to others, but he just couldn't see many ways in his current life whereby he was working towards this future self. Eva and Chris discussed how he could change his behaviour in class, during study, or with friends, to more closely align with his values. Chris then decided on what he would try first, and Eva helped him to plan it, including anticipating barriers to those changes.

Chris decided that he would start by helping some of the people in class that other students were giving a hard time. Sure, some of his current 'friends' would needle him for doing that, but no one would be able to deny that he was trying to make a difference for his fellow classmates. Eva noted what bravery and integrity Chris was showing by taking this approach. Chris smiled because the pieces of himself that he had discovered now seemed to be fitting together, and for the first time in a while he felt like — well, himself.

Know Thy Identity and Thy Barriers to Self-knowledge

Knowing yourself is partly about self-perception but should also include how others perceive you — which can be different, as we mentioned in the character strengths section. That is, there are barriers to self-knowledge, which are explored further in *Diving Deeper 3.2*. Moreover, knowing yourself is partly about personal identity, which inevitably involves which social groups you are a member of, or perceived to be a member of. Group membership, or the perception of such, can have positive or negative consequences. Some group categorisations (e.g., sex, skin colour) are relatively unchangeable (but there are exceptions to this generalisation), whereas others are more malleable (e.g., religious affiliation). We do not have the scope for a deep examination of social categorisation in this book, but we discuss some aspects of social interaction in Chapter 8, and you may also wish to dive deeper in the next section. Moreover, you can explore how your memory may affect your identity, in *TRY IT! 2.3*.

DIVING DEEPER 3.2

Identity

The concept of identity is a key aspect of self-knowledge. Our memory is the core integrative mechanism underlying our sense of identity. Most of us have a sense of personal identity, a sense of what we feel is unique about ourselves (e.g., capabilities, aspirations, life history). Our social identity is our perception of who we are as part of a larger social group, and what salient attributes we share with group members (e.g., values, meanings). We all have multiple social identities, relating to our multiple social contexts or groupings. For example, you may be a university student (with aspirations such as being academically successful), a partner (with values such as loyalty), and a son (of immigrant parents, which gives meaning to your aspiration to become a lawyer specialising in migration issues). Social identities help define our place in the world, and satisfy our need to be part of a wider group (part of our psychological need for relatedness — see Chapter 7).

Occasionally these social identities conflict (e.g., according to your parents, sex is not allowed until marriage, but to you and your peer group, this is not an issue), and we need to revisit our core values in our attempt to resolve such conflicts. As a subcategory of social identity, ethnic identity is where members of an ethnic group identify with each other using aspects of shared culture, language, and religion (e.g., being a member of the Greek community in Melbourne, speaking Greek and English, and being of Greek Orthodox Christian religion). Other forms of social identity can include national identity, global identity, and social media identities. Particular challenges exist when social identity includes oppressed groups (e.g., LGBTIQ, disabled, 'colonised' Indigenous peoples). For example, as comedian Magda Szubanski commented (seriously) in her award-winning biography:

> ... the crucial difference between [LGBTIQ] people and other minorities is this: in every other minority group the family shares the minority status... but gay people are a minority within the family... we live with the gnawing fear that our parent's love could turn to hatred in an instant. (p. 276)

Perhaps the most important aspect of identity, however, is that it (a) changes somewhat over your lifetime, and (b) you can purposefully work on changing certain aspects of your identity, particularly through realistic goal setting (see Chapter 7). For example, if you have realistic goals and plans regarding academic achievement, and successfully implement those plans, then you are likely to pass your assessments, and form or reinforce your desired identity as a 'successful student'. Then, as you engage in the final year of your degree program, you may focus more on acquiring those career development skills that will help ensure that you become a 'successful graduate' (i.e., a graduate who has obtained a career-relevant employment position).

Thinking about Desired Futures

Thinking about your desired future entails considering a number of *possible* futures and identifying the ones that are most desirable and appealing to you. This can be an important motivator in goal pursuit, especially when comparing it with your current reality. The *TRY IT! 3.7* activity complements the *TRY IT! 3.6* exercise and is designed to help you determine what is really important to you with respect to your imagined future.

 TRY IT! 3.7

Desired Futures Brainstorm

Step A. Here are some initial prompts for thinking about how you would like to be; you don't have to answer all of them — choose those that appeal to you.

1. Write down at least 5 qualities you admire in others.

2. Write down at least 5 things you want to do better.

3. Write about how you would like your career to be in the future (e.g., in 10 years).

4. Write about how you would like your primary relationships to be in the future (e.g., in 10 years).

5. Write down at least 3 things you would like to learn more about, or pursue your interests in.

Step B. Remind yourself of the values you identified in *TRY IT! 3.3*. You may wish to write some of them down.

With some of those ideas in mind, brainstorm at least one **future scenario** for yourself (e.g., in 10–15 years' time), reflecting on the position you want to be in (in your career, personal relationships, and/or other life domains). You might want to return to *TRY IT! 3.6* to help you think about this. Identify what you would be doing, what you would have achieved, and what kind of person you would be at that point in time (i.e., personal characteristics).

Step C. Think about what capabilities you will need to reach that vision. Compare that with the capabilities and personal characteristics you have now (based on your self-knowledge acquired in this chapter) to determine whether you already have these capabilities, or whether there are gaps (and if there are gaps, think about what you need to do to fill those gaps).

Step D. Then think of some goals for this **year**, then for this **month**, then for this **week**, that would move you toward that vision.

Your Journey to Self-Knowledge

When we first met Chris he was pretty despondent, but by getting to know himself he was learning how to live in a way that reflected who he truly wanted to be. Of course, we do not have to wait until we come to a place of despair, like Chris, to trigger self-knowledge-seeking behaviour. Given our imperfect brains and consequent vulnerability for unhelpful thinking about everything including ourselves, we can always benefit from greater self-knowledge. And what we do with that self-knowledge is up to us. Some of us will continue to find ourselves to be perfect, so we don't have to do anything. But the vast majority of us will always benefit from seizing opportunities for self-discovery, especially when we are feeling brave and open to new experiences. Life is always going to throw you curve balls, and the more you know about yourself, the better you will be prepared to make the most of those challenges. And making the most of those challenges goes beyond just self-knowledge; it involves a sense of personal agency and self-efficacy, together with the motivation (and strategies) to make these self-beliefs a reality. That's where Chapter 7 will come in handy.

As mentioned earlier in this book it can be particularly useful to identify your own faulty thinking patterns, so that you can minimise negative impacts on your life. Moreover, you can learn to identify faulty thinking patterns in valued others, gently bring their attention to these, and point them toward solutions. If undertaken sensitively, this has the potential to improve relationships. In general, use psychological science and evidence-based practice to better understand your habits of thinking, feeling, and behaving, so that you can determine what works best for you, what needs improvement, and what can be improved (remembering that some things cannot be changed or improved), and work with that! The bottom line to this chapter is that the more you know about your capabilities, values, and interests, the more likely you can adjust to changing circumstances, and successfully pursue your aspirations.

Summary Points

- It is worthwhile putting in the effort to understand yourself better, because at a minimum, it allows you to make the most of your strengths, and take into account your weaknesses, in striving toward valued goals.

- Self-knowledge is considered a very complex form of knowledge, and there are many barriers to gaining greater self-knowledge.

- Nevertheless, there are a number of different ways in which you can gain greater self-knowledge, for example by undertaking values clarification exercises and cognitive assessments.

- Once you have a better idea of who you are, then you will be better informed about what you want in the short- and long-term.

- Most people want to change some aspects of themselves, but two things are important: having some idea of what you can and cannot change, and knowing effective tools to help you change.

More Resources

- Personality Tests:
  Neo PI-R
  www.personal.psu.edu/j5j/IPIP/

  Big Five personality questionnaire
  www.psychometrictest.org.uk/big-five-personality/

  16 Personality Factors
  http://personality-testing.info/tests/16PF.php

Online Personality Tests
http://personality-testing.info/

- Sample Ability Test:
https://student.unsw.edu.au/ability-tests-sample-questions

CHAPTER 4

The Flexible Mind

Now that you have a sense of who you are and what is important to you, it is time to focus on how to optimise your thinking on a day-to-day basis. Although we have established that your mind is sometimes less than perfect, there are many tools and strategies to help you to get the most out of even the most Imperfect Brain.

To take the idea of a 'rubber brain' further (see Chapter 1), in an ideal world our minds would be like rubber-bands: gleefully elastic, and the perfect weapon against little brothers (well, maybe not that second part). Even when stretched, our minds would bounce back into shape just like rubber, ready for the next challenge. In reality, our minds can seem more like glue: useful when properly applied, but messy once a difficult thought or feeling gets stuck. We can spend so much time trying to get thoughts or feelings unstuck that we miss out on things that are important and meaningful to us (like work, school, or relationships). But we have good news for you: there are evidence-based strategies to help your mind become more flexible like a rubber-band, so that it can bounce back, rather than getting stuck. In the first section of this chapter we'll focus on *understanding* psychological flexibility, and in the second section we'll move on to *using* psychological flexibility in our daily lives.

Understanding Psychological Flexibility

What is Psychological Flexibility?

Broadly speaking, psychological flexibility refers to how an individual acquires and employs mental resources to balance the fluctuating (and sometimes competing) demands of life. In a nutshell, a psychologically flexible or 'rubber' mind can help us change our thinking or our perspective in order to rise to challenges or navigate times of stress. Rubber can easily take any shape forced upon it by external pressures without losing its original constitution. Rubber adapts to the demands of the situation, rather than being broken by them.

Psychological flexibility is at the heart of our SMR model. Being psychologically flexible allows you to identify your unhelpful thinking — your M_{SUB}'s — and really optimise what's going on in your head, leading to more functional responses and healthier outcomes.

To help explain why psychological flexibility might be relevant to you, we'd like to introduce you to Jen. Ninety percent of the time, Jen is an effervescent mélange of scholastic goddess and comic genius. Ninety percent of the time, Jen's flexible mind adapts to the vicissitudes of life like some vicissitude-adapting rubber ninja. However, around exam time, Jen transforms into the academic oracle of doom. Suddenly every lecturer is 'deliberately avoiding' Jen's emails. Jen 'just knows' she's going to fail that ethics exam. All Jen talks about is her impending failure and inevitable career as a rubbish bin. What once was rubber, is now glue.

What happened? Did Jen's brain accidentally erase the 'ethics exam' file, such that nothing was retrievable from her memory when she read the exam questions? Was failure really inescapable? Or did Jen just start to *think* and *feel* that way? It is likely that the upcoming exam stress made Jen start to worry about failure, which triggered some anxious thoughts and feelings about academic performance and self-worth. Jen was yet to acquire the psychological flexibility skills needed to bounce back from her worries, rather than getting stuck in them. So Jen did what we all do sometimes: she turned to unhelpful ways of thinking and acting in order to cope.

If you're honest with yourself, there is probably a part of you that thinks and acts in some unhelpful ways when you're stressed. That's *your* glue. And mental glue tends to spoil things. You get into arguments with people you care about. You get angry or frustrated over minor stuff. You get so stressed that you can't study, so you give up. Soon you start buying into thoughts like, 'I'm never going to be good enough!'. What would life be like if you had enough space to step back, breathe, and choose a way of thinking or acting that was more helpful? How would things have been different for Jen if she could think a bit more flexibly about her grades, her lecturers, and everything else? What if life was a little less glue and a little more rubber?

In this chapter, we will focus on three approaches to psychological flexibility:

- Mindfulness

- Acceptance and Commitment Therapy (ACT)

- Cognitive Behaviour Therapy (CBT).

Despite the fact that ACT and CBT both contain the word 'therapy' in their title, they offer strategies that can be useful outside a therapeutic setting. In fact, the 'T' in ACT and CBT can also stand for 'training'. As you read through, you may notice some similarities between these techniques. For example, ACT borrows components from mindfulness, and CBT and ACT agree on many points — they just approach them from different angles.

Together, Mindfulness, ACT, and CBT provide us with ways of responding to our personal experiences that help us maintain perspective and live the life we want to live. What this means for you is that Mindfulness, ACT, and CBT provide an assortment of tools for developing your psychological flexibility. All three techniques are thoroughly supported by evidence, and ACT and CBT work equally well, so in the interest of providing flexible options (flexible — get it?) we will discuss them all and let you decide which suits you best.

Mindfulness and Contact with the Present Moment

Let's start here, in the present moment. A crucial part of psychological flexibility is an awareness of your own mind. Through this awareness we can create enough mental space to make optimal psychological choices. Using mindfulness, we can observe what's going on in our mind, and choose thoughts and actions that support and nourish us. By staying in the present moment, we can make these choices outside the influence of misgivings about the past, or anxieties about the future.

First, let's clarify what we mean by 'mindfulness'. Mindfulness is not mystical navel-gazing. It is *not* a religious practice. Mindfulness requires no special skills or resources, and it can be done whenever and however you like (you can even do it in public). Mindfulness is simply bringing focus to your momentary experience without judgement. Notice that we said 'simply', not 'easily'.

In terms of the SMR model, Mindfulness can be a great way to create some space between the Situation (S) and the Response (R), to allow you to become aware of your Ms — your thoughts and beliefs — whether they're suboptimal or bursting with optimisation. Being able to be in the present moment also allows you to reflect on the beliefs that emerge in response to a situation. Then you can use the tools in this chapter and throughout the book to take control of those M_{SUB}'s and to create some brand-new M_{OP}'s.

The research on mindfulness is unequivocal. Mindfulness can help manage difficult thoughts and feelings, improve our concentration, help us stay mentally healthy, and even lead to positive changes in our brain. Mindfulness can be very helpful, but like most things that are good for us (such as eating well), it requires some effort in order to reap the greatest benefits.

Contact with the present moment is an ACT technique that intentionally uses mindfulness skills to avoid being swept away by our mind. Once you build up your mindfulness skills, you can use them to anchor yourself when the current of your mind starts to gather pace. Say, for example, you need to make a decision about an important friendship. It can be very easy to get swept away by suboptimal thinking about what terror awaits you in the future, or begin to drown in negative feelings about things that happened in the past. In ACT, these suboptimal thoughts and feelings are called your **conceptualised past** and your **conceptualised future**. They are the past and the future as you *believe them to be*, rather than the past and the future as they *are*, and often our conceptualised past or future is suboptimal to say the least. To make helpful decisions you need space to deal with the facts as they are, not as you conceptualise them to be. You can use mindfulness to connect with the moment you are in right now and remind yourself that you're not stuck in a dramatised past or a catastrophic future. Anchored in the here-and-now, you can make optimised decisions based on facts, not fears.

The Practice of Mindfulness

So, how do you develop your mindfulness skills, and then use them to contact the present moment when things get tough? The first step is developing your mindfulness practice so that those skills are increasing steadily over time. Like any new practice, in the beginning you'll likely need structure and a bit of help. Here is a 4-step plan to building your mindfulness practice:

Step 1. **Set aside time** — designate a time each day (or every few days to begin with) that you will engage in mindfulness exercises. You can put this in your calendar or set a reminder on your phone. There are many mindfulness apps that can gently remind you that it is time to be mindful.

Step 2. **Stick to the point** — the point of mindfulness is not to relax or be at peace. The point is to be aware of whatever is going on at that moment without judgement. If you experience relaxation or peace then that's great, but neither are necessary.

Step 3. **Get creative** — many people repeat the same mindfulness exercises until they decide that mindfulness is boring. Try new exercises when the old ones become stale. Anything that enables non-judgemental awareness of the present moment is all that is required.

Step 4. **Do it!** — sometimes you might feel too tired or sad or angry or hungry to practice. That's fine. You can bring non-judgemental awareness to those feelings during your mindfulness practice!

As you consistently practice mindfulness you will find it creeping into your day-to-day life, which is the ultimate goal. Many people who practice mindfulness for a month or more report feeling less stressed, more connected with what they value, and even better able to manage problems with anxiety and mood. Below we offer various mindfulness exercises that you can incorporate into your regular mindfulness practice (*TRY IT! 4.1*). Remember, the goal of a mindfulness exercise is to spend time bringing awareness to your momentary experiences without judgement. These experiences can be sights, sounds, thoughts, tastes, feelings, smells etc. The more your brain practices focusing on momentary experiences, the more mental room you will have.

Before we move on we want to quickly address one of the biggest misconceptions about mindfulness. Many people who begin a mindfulness practice think that their goal is to maintain absolute focus at all times, and that a wandering mind is a sign that they're doing something wrong. The truth is, every time your mind wanders is a golden opportunity to flex your mindfulness muscles. The process of noticing that your mind has wandered and gently refocusing is one of the core processes of mindfulness. So remember: as you engage in the exercises below, your mind *will* wander! Each time you notice that your mind has wandered and then you gently refocus, *you're doing it right.*

⚑ TRY IT! 4.1

Body Scan

The body scan is one of the most popular mindfulness exercises. First, find a comfortable position, either sitting, standing, or laying down. Take a few deep breaths to centre yourself in the present moment. As you breathe, bring mindful attention to the feeling of air entering and exiting your body. There's no need to label the sensation, just bring your attention to it. After you have centred your attention on your breath, move this non-judgemental attention to the top of your head. What does it feel like? Are there areas of tension or stress? Move your attention down your body in this way, simply noticing what each area feels like without judging the sensations or needing to change them. Some areas might feel soft, tense, tingling, sore etc. Simply notice how each area feels, then move on to the next. If you find your mind wandering, simply notice that your mind has wandered, then bring your attention back to your body.

Suggestion: read aloud (with appropriate pauses) and record these exercises on your phone, so you can play them back at any suitable time (including in the library, lying on the carpet, etc.).

Cognitive Defusion (using ACT)

ACT is grounded in a scientific understanding of what we call **verbal cognition** — the part of your thinking that is expressed in words. The chatter box in your head. Because humans can represent things verbally, we can call to mind people, experiences, feelings etc. using only words; we don't always have to see or experience them. For example, the word 'puppy' is not literally a *puppy*, but using the word you can call to mind what a puppy looks, feels, smells, and acts like. This is an incredible advantage in planning, and also lovely if you want to remember enjoyable moments in your life (such as playing with a puppy).

The wonderful, terrible thing is that these abstract representations (words) come with **associations**. When you think of the word 'puppy', you might get a warm, happy feeling, and even start recalling the day you met that adorable 15-week-old Labrador in the park. The thing that the word refers to doesn't need to be present for you to experience the emotional associations to it. If you think 'puppy', then you feel 'awww'.

But your mind doesn't just talk about puppies. Sometimes it talks about hurtful places, people or events. Try thinking of the word 'failure'. Unfortunately, the same cognitive processes that brought you the puppy fuzzies now bring you hurt, shame, and a lovely story about that time you failed your maths exam and cried in front of everyone. Again, the thing the word refers to doesn't need to be present for you to experience its emotional associations. You don't need to be back in the exam room to 'feel' what it's like to fail. If you repeatedly think, 'I'm a failure', it causes the distress and upset of failure before you've even failed. Soon enough you start to believe you are a failure because you *feel* like one, and your head is filled with examples of when you really did fail. This is what ACT refers to as **cognitive fusion**; binding with thoughts and feelings until their associations feel like reality. Cognitive fusion is suboptimal thinking at its finest!

So, how do we optimise our mind in the face of cognitive fusion? The mind will think what it will, so controlling our thoughts isn't an option (if you don't believe us, see *TRY IT! 4.2* for the Pink Panda experiment). To break this cycle of cognitive fusion, we need to somehow *defuse* the words from the things they refer to. We need to be able to think the word 'failure', but recognise that this thought is just a word, and not a reality. This is what **cognitive defusion** allows us to do. We can look at our verbal cognition without buying into it. We can *have* a thought without *being* the thought.

⊞ TRY IT! 4.2

The Pink Panda Experiment

Some of us believe that we can control our thinking if we just try hard enough, but this is a myth. To bust this myth, we are going to give you one simple task: do *not* think of a pink panda for the next 60 seconds. Ready? Go! ….

How did you do? Many of you will have had a bright pink panda pop into your head the second you began the task. Others might have lasted a few seconds, but soon that furry fuchsia friend popped into your mind.

But what about the few of you who swear that you never once thought of a pink panda? To you we ask: how did you know that you weren't thinking of a pink panda? In order to check for a thought, on some level you need to have a cognitive representation of the thought you are checking for. You can't not think about something because that very process requires you to think of it!

If thoughts can hurt because they bring with them unpleasant images and feelings, and we end up buying into (or 'fusing with') them, what we need are some strategies to help see thoughts as just words. You'll still know what the words *mean*, but you won't feel as though 'hurt' or 'failure' or 'ugliness' are actually present just because you think of them. You will be able to let these thoughts and feelings pass and get on with what is meaningful and important to you.

Let's try an exercise so that you get the idea, then later in this chapter we will try out specific exercises for specific situations. We're going to try and see the difference between *having* a thought and *being* a thought. First, close your eyes (well, read the rest of the exercise, then close your eyes). Say to yourself, 'I'm a loser' ten times in your head. Try it right now! How did it feel? Even if you were having a good day, ten 'I'm a loser's can bring you down a bit! Close your eyes again but this time say 'I'm having the thought that I'm a loser' ten times in your head. How did *that* feel? You might have noticed that you felt a bit of distance from the concept of being a loser. Let's try it one more time, but this time say 'I'm noticing the thought that I'm a loser' ten times. Did you feel even greater distance from the thought? For some people, 'observing' words like 'noticing' or 'seeing' create even more distance between themselves and their thoughts. Rather than buying into the thought, you can observe it come and go.

It is this 'observer perspective' that cognitive defusion is all about. Taking a step back and watching the words come and go. Once you can observe your thoughts, you can really understand the difference between having the thought 'I'm too dumb', and actually being dumb. When you understand this difference, the words lose their power. We feel less like dummies because we can see the phrase 'I'm too dumb' as simply that: a phrase. We become disinterested in the words that our mind throws at us, and turn our attention to the meaningful and important things that we've been missing out on because we had bought into our thoughts. We can go out and *actually study law*, rather than listening to a tape in our head that tells us that we're *too dumb to*.

 TRY IT! 4.3

Cognitive Defusion

Try some of the cognitive defusion exercises with a difficult thought that you have come across recently.

The neon sign

Imagine your thought written like a neon sign. You might see 'I'm a fat loser' written in glossy pink cursive above a doorway. Now make the sign blink. Change its colour. Imagine one of the words shattering. The thought is just words in your mind. Step back and look around at the rest of the scene. Look at the entire street. What else is there in this scene that you might enjoy?

The beach ball

In your mind, write a sticky thought on a beach ball. Now imagine standing in the water at the beach. You try and force the beach ball under the waves but it keeps bobbing up! Let the beach ball float. Take your eyes off the ball and look around the lovely beach. Smell the salt. Feel the sun. Let the ball bob around, bouncing against your legs occasionally.

The comedic commentator

Imagine a celebrity or well-known comedic figure saying your thought at you. For example, imagine Homer Simpson screaming 'You're too dumb to be at uni!'. Imagine his voice getting high pitched and squeaky. Then bring it down low. Keep going until you get a good giggle.

The cognitive interchange

Imagine you are standing on a platform above a large train station, and trains are passing beneath you on many tracks. The trains represent your thoughts. Label each train as it passes. There goes 'judgement'. Here comes the '12 o'clock anxiety express'! That's 'disappointment'. Let the thoughts pass beneath you. Occasionally you'll find yourself swept up in a thought, like you've boarded one of the trains. Gently return to the platform.

The bad news radio

Imagine your thoughts are coming through a tired old radio. Your brain's favourite show is on, 'Disaster Dan Presents All The Ways That You Suck!', and Dan is telling everyone that you're too stupid to get that job you want. You can't always change the tuning dial (and Disaster Dan has a broad syndication deal, so sometimes he's on all the stations at once).

Look over at the volume dial. Try turning it up, so Disaster Dan is screaming. Now try turning it down slowly. Keep going until it's so low that you can hear other things around you. Birds. Friends texting. Your flatmate attempting to bake. Life.

Labelling and Disputing Unhelpful Thoughts and Beliefs (using CBT)

Sometimes we think or believe things based on how we *would like* the world to be, rather than how *we know* the world to be. Because these thoughts or beliefs are unrealistic, they make it hard for ourselves and the world to live up to our expectations. We know from our SMR model that suboptimal beliefs (M_{SUB}'s) lead to suboptimal responding. Take, for example, one pervasive belief that you learned about in Chapter 2: that the world should be a fair and just place. When a person who believes this encounters an unfair situation, they're likely to feel frustrated, betrayed, and even lash out at other people. Talk about suboptimal responding! However, what is really making that person frustrated or angry isn't the unfair event itself, rather it is their iceberg belief (M_{SUB}) that unfair things *shouldn't* happen in a fair world (see Figure 4.1). Think about it for a moment: is the world actually a fair place? Is there written, somewhere, a rule that says the world *should* be fair? Reflecting on your own life, has everything always been fair?

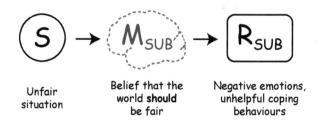

Figure 4.1   Holding the belief that the world should be fair (M_{SUB}) can lead to feeling bad and constantly struggling against reality (R_{SUB}).

Now consider another widely-held belief: if you do something bad then you're a bad person and should be condemned. Have you ever known a 'good' person who did only 'good' deeds, until one day they made a mistake and was forever 'bad' from that point on? Does a single moment of a person's life really define who they are? When we hold tightly to beliefs that don't reflect how things really are, we set ourselves up for heartache. If we continue to use this kind of suboptimal thinking, it becomes impossible for anyone or anything to live up to our expectations (including ourselves).

CBT offers techniques for dealing with these unrealistic thoughts and beliefs: **labelling** and **disputing**. When we label thoughts, we take a step back and evaluate their nature. We know from research that certain cognitive styles lead to suboptimal thoughts and beliefs, so a good place to start can be to step back and label these as they arise. Once we can recognise these thoughts and beliefs for what they are, we can consider more optimal alternatives that are supportive and helpful.

Consider the following list of **unhelpful cognitive styles**. As you go through the list, think about the last time you engaged in this kind of thinking.

Black-and-white thinking

Thinking that things are either one thing or the other, without considering all the options in-between. For example, you decide that if people aren't on your side, then they're against you. This is unhelpful because you fail to consider other more helpful perspectives, such as that people will agree with you on some matters and disagree with you on others.

Catastrophising

Imagining only negative outcomes and predicting disaster, regardless of the evidence. For example, you find this week's revision quiz difficult, so you decide the course is going to be too hard and you'll fail. This is unhelpful because it considers failure the only possible outcome despite very little evidence for this, thus causing undue anxiety.

Blaming

Criticising others for their faults without considering the many factors that lead to someone's behaviour. This is unhelpful because it breeds anger and resentment, and doesn't reflect a person as a whole. For example, you judge someone harshly for excessive drinking without considering the life circumstances they are struggling to cope with.

Overgeneralising

Using narrow evidence to draw broad conclusions about ourselves, others or the world. For example, the first time you met Chi she wasn't very friendly, therefore you hate Chi. This is unhelpful because you have made an absolute judgment based on a single encounter and failed to develop a well-rounded opinion. Chi can have a bad day like anyone, and you might need to spend more time with her before you decide if you like her or not.

Mind-reading

Thinking or acting based on the assumption that we 'just know' what someone else is thinking. For example, not speaking to your friend Judy because she did not say hi to you in the street earlier, and that must mean she's mad at you. This is unhelpful because we assume facts that we cannot possibly know (she may not have noticed you because she was busy thinking about a personal problem), and we use our mistaken knowledge to withdraw from important connections with others.

Categorising

Assigning a person or a thing to a category or label based on isolated events. For example, you decided to ask Greg out but he said 'no', therefore you're an ugly loser, and Greg is a jerk. This is unhelpful because it creates inflexible and often negative perceptions of ourselves, others or the world, resulting in hurt, shame, and anger.

Musterbating

Clinging to the notion of '*musts*' or '*shoulds*' in the world. For example, believing that people must always be polite to you. This is unhelpful because the world doesn't follow a set of absolute rules that you have developed, thus you are often disappointed and frustrated.

How many of those common styles of thinking did you relate to? Most people can relate to at least one or two, and that's fine. That is why they're common! The suboptimal mind can get caught up in these styles of thinking, but the optimised mind is different. The optimised mind can develop an awareness of thoughts and label unhelpful thinking styles as they arise. For example, the next time you meet someone and think, 'I can tell by the way she's talking that she thinks she's better than me', try taking a step back, notice that you're mind-reading, and re-engage with the conversation. If you're willing to be more psychologically flexible in this way, you may find that you have something in common with this person, or that they have recently received some upsetting news and aren't really themselves today.

At this stage some of you might be thinking (or screaming), 'but some people really are jerks!', or 'sometimes the worst possible scenario really does happen!'. True, but until you know for certain that someone is a jerk, or a disaster is imminent, you're likely wasting a lot of time and energy making yourself anxious about it. It can also be tempting to dismiss this all as just positive thinking, but optimised thinking is very different from positive thinking. Optimised thinking involves being aware of a thought and deciding if it is useful or not. If someone is standing in front of you with a knife, disaster probably *is* imminent (and they're probably a jerk, too) so the optimal thing to do would be to run! But these situations are rare. In most cases, all we are doing is clinging to unhelpful thinking that gets in the way of things that are meaningful and important to us.

Once we have the psychological flexibility to label suboptimal thinking (M_{SUB}), the next step is to try out an alternative. One evidence-based way of trying alternatives is called **logical disputing**. Relax, this doesn't mean talking to that annoying guy from Philosophy 101 who wants to argue every point (even we don't want to talk to him). Disputation, by definition, requires offering an alternative point of view. Therefore, logical disputing means challenging overly rigid or unrealistic thoughts and beliefs with a more balanced, optimised take on things.

Think back to the belief that the world is and should be fair. You already know that this doesn't reflect the real world, and unrealistic beliefs lead to upset, so why not try an alternative belief? What if you would like the world to be fair, but you accept that sometimes there is injustice? Take a moment to try on this belief. How does it fit? Does it better reflect the world as you *know it to be*, rather than how you *would like it to be*? See Figure 4.2 for how this fits with our SMR model.

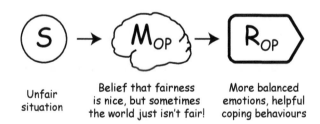

S	M_{OP}	R_{OP}
Unfair situation	Belief that fairness is nice, but sometimes the world just isn't fair!	More balanced emotions, helpful coping behaviours

Figure 4.2   A more flexible and realistic belief about fairness (M_{OP}) can help us balance our emotions and give us the mental space we need to come up with more helpful ways to cope (R_{OP}).

Consider some common thoughts and beliefs below and an example of a balanced, optimised perspective that you could use to dispute each.

Thought/Belief	Optimised Alternative
My way of doing things is the right way, and everyone must do things this way.	I like my way of doing things, but other people have different approaches. There is no law stating that everyone must do things the same way I do them.
I must be approved of by everyone or I will be unlikable.	It's nice when people approve of me, but not everyone will. The opinions of a few people don't make me unlikeable; they don't actually change anything about me!
If other people can do something, then so can I.	Other people have skills and abilities that are different from my own. Others have achieved what they have by playing to their strengths. I can do the same, however it won't necessarily lead me to precisely the same achievements as others.
When I fail at one thing, it makes me a failure at everything.	Experiencing failure is different from being a failure. Everyone makes mistakes! I have had both successes and failures, and none of these define me as a person.
Other people should have the same beliefs as me, and share the same values.	Other people, including my friends and family, often express opinions that conflict with what I believe. People are entitled to their own beliefs and values, just as I am (as long as they don't lead to behaviour that is against the law). Differing beliefs needn't prevent me from enjoying someone's company or showing them courtesy.

By disputing rigid or illogical thoughts and beliefs we can change how we feel, and consequently how we act. If you truly believe that others should share your values, you will likely get angry and argue with your friend Paul if he expresses any opinion that differs from your own. Pretty soon, Paul will simply stop discussing things with you. Alternatively, if you believe that other people are entitled to their own values, you might let Paul keep talking, and move the conversation on. You might even find Paul's point of view intriguing and begin wondering if your old ideas could do with an update. By being more psychologically flexible in this way, you have avoided an argument, allowed Paul to be heard, and maybe even learned something.

Experimental Reasoning and Behavioural Experiments (using CBT)

Experimental reasoning sounds like utter nerdery, but it's actually a very useful tool that just happens to resemble nerdery. As you learned in Chapter 2, the experimental method in science requires that unanswered questions be framed as predictions or hunches — called **hypotheses** — for which we must collect evidence, before we place too much stock in them. Using experimental reasoning, we treat our thoughts and beliefs as hypotheses. Each thought or belief represents our best guess, then we go out into the world and collect data that will test our hypothesis. 'Collecting data' sounds like nerdery too, but collecting data is actually just doing stuff and watching what happens.

When we reason experimentally, instead of buying into our thoughts and beliefs, we turn them into a *maybe*, and then seek out information that tells us whether or not we should be paying them much attention. For example, imagine that you think you're not smart enough to study physics. You could buy into that thought, or you could treat it as a prediction, then go and try studying some physics and see if you're smart enough or not. *Maybe* you're not smart enough; *maybe* you are. The world can start to feel lighter when our harshest thoughts become *maybes*, rather than *musts*.

Now that we have our hypothesis (our *maybe*), we need to work out how to test it. Scientists call these tests **experiments**; they're basically a script that tells us what we're going to do, and what we're going to be looking for while we do it (*see Diving Deeper 2.2*). In CBT, we use this same approach to test our *maybes*, using **behavioural experiments**. Research tells us that behavioural experiments are a powerful tool for challenging unhelpful thoughts and beliefs, such as the belief that you're not smart enough to study physics. When we actually do something that we thought we couldn't do, the new information is incompatible with our old way of thinking, so our brain updates and thus optimises our perspective on things. It's a bit like the final scene of most 80's teen movies: the geek shows up at the prom looking amazing, everyone's perception of them changes, and they drive off in a shiny Corvette to the honeyed tones of Kenny Loggins (disclaimer: that last part may not happen in your behavioural experiments).

As the name suggests, behavioural experiments require us to actually *do* stuff, rather than just thinking about it. Doing stuff is one of the most effective ways of challenging our thoughts and beliefs. In a behavioural experiment, we set out clear guidelines about the stuff we will do, when and how we will do it, and what information we will be looking out for. For example, if we were going to test the hypothesis that we aren't smart enough to study physics, we would need to be clear and specific about a few things:

- First, we define what we *mean* by 'study physics'. Reading a chapter from a textbook? If so, which text book? Which chapter? You get the idea. Get as specific as possible, and include dates, times, places, resources etc. You might decide that tomorrow, at 2pm, you will sit quietly in your bedroom and read the first chapter of *Introductory Cat Physics, by Dr. Schrodinger.*

- Next, we need to define how we are going to *measure* 'smart enough'. Answering 50% of a quiz correctly? Being able to explain a concept to a friend?

- Finally, we need to write down our hypotheses, or predictions about what will happen. For example, you might predict that you will try and explain a concept to your friend, fail, and they will laugh at you while you cry.

So now you know exactly which book you will read, how much of it you will read, when and where you will read it, and how you will measure if you're 'smart enough'. Once you have read the first chapter of Dr. Schrodinger's book, you call a friend and explain one concept to him or her. Suddenly, the belief that you're not smart enough to study physics is on shaky ground. You *can* study physics, because you just *did*.

Now you're probably wondering, but what if I do the experiment and I really am not smart enough and everything I believe about how stupid I am comes true and I die of embarrassment? The good news is that when we do these experiments we get lots of new information, not just information about our hypothesis (for example you'll quickly notice that embarrassment isn't fatal). You may notice that physics isn't as interesting as you thought. You may notice that you find some parts of physics quite difficult, but other parts come easily to you. You may try the experiment again with a different chapter and do better. You may even conclude that in life there are bits that we find easy, and bits that we find hard, and it is persistence that makes the difference (whoa, that was meta). That's the great thing about behavioural experiments: new information often comes along that challenges more than just our target beliefs. In *TRY IT!* 4.5 you can try your own behavioural experiment using an adaptation of a form from www.psychologytools.com.

TRY IT! 4.4

Design a Behavioural Experiment

Think of a situation in which a belief that you have about yourself is holding you back from doing something you really want to do.

Prediction

What do you expect will happen?

How would you know if it came true?

Rate how strongly you believe this will happen (0–100%).

Experiment

What experiment could test this prediction? (when and where)

How would you know if your prediction came true?

Outcome

What happened?

Was your prediction accurate?

Learning

What did you learn?

How likely is it that your prediction will happen in the future?

Rate how strongly you agree with your original prediction now (0–100%).

DIVING DEEPER 4.1

The Birth of the Cognitive Model and Cognitive Behaviour Therapies

In the 1960's, psychiatrist Aaron T. Beck began a rigorous empirical enquiry into the then gold-standard psychiatric treatment for depression: psycho-analysis. As this enquiry went on, Beck found little support for psychoanal-ysis, forcing him to consider alternative hypotheses for why people become depressed, and how they could be treated effectively. Beck noticed that his depressed patients shared particular ways of thinking that seemed to explain their lethargy, apathy, and sorrow. In particular, Beck found that depressed patients held negative beliefs about not only themselves, but also about other people and the world at large (in our SMR model, M_{SUB}). Beck theorised that, because of these beliefs, as depressed individuals went through their lives they would 'automatically' think that everyone and everything was inescapably awful. As these thoughts stuck, the depressed individual would feel increasingly hopeless and withdraw — both physi-cally and mentally — from the things that had once held so much meaning for them.

From this theory, the cognitive model of mental illness was born. The cog-nitive model posits that as we interact with the world, our deeply held beliefs (M) influence our 'automatic' thinking in a given situation (S). This thinking leads us to feel a certain way, which in turn, leads to how we behave (R). When our thoughts are supportive and accurate (M_{OP}), we feel good and generally act in ways that keep us well (R_{OP}). When our thoughts are unsupportive or inaccurate (M_{SUB}), we feel sad, angry, afraid, or any number of unpleasant emotions, and these often drive us to either attack or avoid (R_{SUB}). The cognitive model and cognitive behaviour therapy have been validated in studies too numerous to mention, but Butler and col-leagues provide an excellent overview (see Bibliography).

Since the development of the cognitive model, many therapeutic approaches have been developed that seek to help people understand and/or modify their thoughts and feelings, so that they can live a life worth living. These approaches are all considered 'cognitive behaviour therapies', and they include not only traditional CBT, but also some 'third wave' ther-apies such as ACT, which are also discussed in this chapter. Taken together, these cognitive behaviour therapies represent a tectonic shift not only in treating mental illness, but also in how we understand and bring about psy-chological *wellness*. Decades of research now tell us that the old adage is true: to change our mind is to truly change our lives.

Using Psychological Flexibility

In the previous section you developed your psychological flexibility toolkit using strategies taken from Mindfulness, Acceptance and Commitment Therapy (ACT), and Cognitive Behaviour Therapy (CBT). In this section you will start using your psychological flexibility tools to manage some of life's challenges. As you'll shortly discover, even some tough problems — such as failing a university course — can be navigated using the tools you learned in the previous section. Below we will present some common problems that people experience in work, study, and life in general. We'll pit each problem against your new psychological flexibility toolkit to give you ideas on how to use your tools to manage everyday problems.

Managing Self-defeating Thoughts and Beliefs

Sometimes we have thoughts about ourselves that are so suboptimal that they're a bit mean. We might think we're not smart enough, not thin enough, or not *something* enough in order to succeed in life. When we start seeing the world through these thoughts, they become part of what we *believe* to be true. When our beliefs are self-defeating, we start avoiding or withdrawing from things that are important and meaningful to us because we believe that we are 'not X enough' to have them.

For more optimised minds, self-defeating thoughts are short-lived and easily dismissed (sometimes with the help of a loud but well-meaning friend). For the less optimised minds amongst us, self-defeating thoughts start to stick and become what we believe to be true. While self-defeating thoughts are dis-heartening in and of themselves, when they become how we see ourselves and the world, things can get a bit tough.

Let's think back to Jen. Jen got a lower mark than she was expecting on her biology paper, so she started thinking, 'I'm just not smart enough to be a biol-ogist.' The more this thought stuck, the more Jen recalled other times that she hadn't gotten the mark she expected. Soon there was enough evidence for Jen to support the belief that she truly wasn't smart enough. If she truly isn't smart enough, then why bother trying? Jen is deep into self-defeating belief territory.

Once self-defeating thoughts have become entrenched in our belief system, they start to affect how we see the world and what we expect from it. If you have the belief that you're not strong enough, you're probably not going to try Crossfit. That's fine, unless fitness and strength are meaningful and important to you, and you've always wanted to try Crossfit! It's not that you *can't* do

Crossfit; rather because you believe you aren't strong enough you expect to fail at it, so why try? It's not hard to see that this type of thinking can get in the way of us thriving. Fortunately, the negative influence of these suboptimal self-defeating thoughts and beliefs can be reduced, by optimising your thinking.

Self-defeating Thoughts vs. Mindfulness

You can use your mindfulness skills to gain some distance from self-defeating thoughts. As we learned earlier, the point is not to relax or feel better, you are simply noticing your self-defeating thoughts without judging them. Sit quietly and try focusing on an anchor to the present, either your breath, sounds, or sensations. If self-defeating thoughts arise, let them come and go as much as they like. Because self-defeating thoughts are usually accompanied by emotions and images, try switching between noticing what's happening in your mind and what's happening in your body. How does it feel to have this thought? What does your heart feel like? Your stomach? Your shoulders?

You might find yourself getting lost in the self-defeating narrative, for example your mind might wander off to a time when you really did do something poorly, or someone made you feel like you weren't good enough. Thank your mind for the story, return to your anchor, and gently resume noticing thoughts come and go. Remember, these moments of distraction are the small successes of mindfulness. Noticing the distraction and returning means you're doing it right.

Self-defeating Thoughts vs. Behavioural Experiments

CBT offers us a powerful way of undermining these suboptimal beliefs and, at the same time, building new beliefs that better support the life we want to live. You might remember that rather than treating our beliefs as truths, we can treat them as hypotheses to be tested. Self-defeating thoughts like to tell us all the things we cannot do. Consider the previous example: you value fitness but believe that you'd never be strong enough to do Crossfit. Why accept the belief that you're not strong enough if it is just a prediction? After all, did you try Crossfit for a month and fail at every turn? No! You have little evidence to support the hypothesis that you're not strong enough. Why are you so attached to it?

If you forget how to design a behavioural experiment, flick back to *TRY IT! 4.5*. Bring to mind a self-defeating thought or belief that is getting in the way of you doing something you really want to do. Sometimes it can be helpful to first think about things that you are avoiding doing, then ask yourself what you believe about yourself, others, or the world that keeps you from doing these things. Write your target thought or belief down, then design an experiment to test your prediction. In the Crossfit example, this will mean *actually doing* Crossfit. Remember, you'll need to be specific about what you will do and when, you will need to define what 'doing Crossfit' is, and you'll need to make clear predictions about what you think will happen.

At the end, review the evidence. How did your hypotheses turn out? Perhaps you're not as strong as you'd like to be, but you have new skills to develop your strength. Maybe you're not strong enough for advanced Crossfit, but there's actually a program designed specifically for people at your level of strength. Either way, what will likely happen is that you will learn new information about your self-defeating thought or belief, and this will change the influence it has on you.

Self-defeating Thoughts vs. Cognitive Defusion

Often, our self-defeating thoughts are linked to what is most important to us. Say, for example, you desperately want to be a lawyer. You're working hard but you're finding your Contract Law course really tough. You might start thinking, 'I'm not smart enough to be a lawyer!'. Remember, that's just a thought. They're just words that have unpleasant associations. Buying into the thought 'I'm not smart enough to be a lawyer!' might leave you anxious, avoiding your studies, or even considering changing degrees. What if instead of *living* that thought, you were simply *having* that thought? Rather than buying into the idea that you're not smart enough to be a lawyer, notice the thought as it comes and goes. Let the thought be there, for now. Even thank your brain for the lovely story, the way you might thank your 3-year-old nephew for the 'lovely' picture he drew of a ten-headed cat vomiting rainbows. Once you gain some distance from your suboptimal thinking you are better able to come up with a more optimal response (in this case, finding a good contract law tutor!). See Figure 4.3 for how this applies in our SMR model.

Try using one of the cognitive defusion techniques from the previous section with a self-defeating thought. You might imagine the thought 'I'm not smart enough to be a lawyer' up in lights. Change the colour of the lights. Make them blink. Change the font. You'll soon notice that the thought really is just words! Having the thought does not change anything about your actual abilities, and there's certainly no reason to let it stop you from working hard to achieve the career you really want. Thank your brain and get back to living the life you want to live.

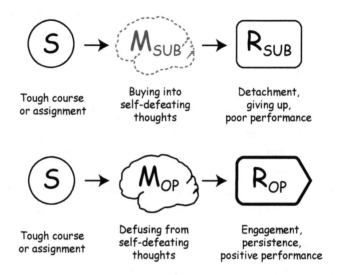

Figure 4.3   Buying into self-defeating thoughts (M_{SUB}) can make us feel like giving-up (R_{SUB}), and we can end up disconnecting from things we value. By using defusion techniques we can take a step back from self-defeating thoughts and see them as nothing more than an unhelpful story our brain is telling us (M_{OP}). The more we defuse from suboptimal thinking, the freer we are to engage with the things that are meaningful and important to us (R_{OP}), and the healthier we become.

Managing Overwhelming Emotions

Most of the time our emotions are manageable, but for some of us, some of the time, emotions can get out of hand. We might feel extremely sad about not achieving a particular grade, or exceptionally angry about something someone said to us. When emotion overwhelms us, we can act in some pretty suboptimal ways, such as lashing out at people or avoiding them all together.

Unless you live in a Shakespearean play, the consequences of overreacting to overwhelming emotions can be worse than the emotions themselves. If you lash out at a classmate because of something they said, you might find yourself in trouble with your university. If you avoid class altogether you might find yourself failing the course after putting in a lot of hard work. It's OK to have overwhelming emotions, but it is important to manage them in a way that makes things better, not worse.

Strong Emotions vs. Mindfulness

If you have begun building mindfulness practice into your week you will have spent a great deal of time noticing the thoughts and sensations that arise in your momentary experience. One way to short-circuit strong emotions is to apply these skills to the experience of the emotion itself. Find a comfortable position, close your eyes, and begin by focusing your attention on your breath. Don't worry if this is especially hard right now, that's to be expected if you're experiencing strong emotions. Be kind to yourself as you engage in this exercise.

Now, turn your attention to how this emotion presents in your body. Without judging or labelling any feelings, notice where in your body you can feel this emotion strongest. Is it in your stomach? Your chest? Your face? As you focus on how this emotion is presenting itself to you, ask yourself what colour it is? What shape? What texture? As you breathe and focus on these sensations, imagine the breath coming in and connecting with these areas of sensations. Let the breath contact the emotion. As you observe how this emotion presents in your body, you might notice that you feel a bit of space from it. Anger that at first felt very strong might seem less powerful. Sadness that weighed you down might seem a bit lighter. If nothing else, you will likely have gained enough mental space to consider other options, rather than simply reacting to the emotion. Those options might be calling a friend, speaking to a counsellor, removing yourself from the situation, or shifting your perspective.

Managing Emotional Reasoning

Emotional reasoning doesn't mean breaking into histrionics while completing your philosophy essay (although many of us have done that). Emotional reasoning refers to using how you are feeling at the time to draw conclusions or make decisions. If we are honest with ourselves, we use emotional reasoning a great deal when deciding if and when we will do things. For example, we have all put off an assignment because we 'just don't feel like it', or we 'aren't in the right head space', or we 'just aren't feeling creative today'. By that reasoning because you don't *feel* like doing it you either *can't* do it, or you *shouldn't* do it. Ask yourself this: of all the assignments that you have completed, did you *feel like* doing all of them? It's likely that many assignments got done, regardless of how you were feeling, but usually at the last minute (sometimes literally at 11:59pm on the due date).

Emotional reasoning is suboptimal because how we feel often doesn't reflect the way the world really is. If you have ever been in a bad mood at a party, you will know this. Everyone is having a good time, meanwhile you think it's the worst party ever thrown. Think about it for a moment: if it really were the worst party ever thrown, then no one would be enjoying themselves! The facts don't match your mood, which makes your feelings a poor vantage point from which to draw conclusions or make decisions.

Think back to that assignment that you didn't 'feel' like doing. Did you decide not to do it because you had read several peer-reviewed articles that listed 'feeling like it' as a crucial factor in academic success? Did you decide not to do it because, in the past, you had attempted assignments before you 'felt like it' and your fingers physically couldn't connect with the keyboard? What reason do you have for basing this decision on your feelings? And how do you *know* that you can't because you don't feel like it? Emotional reasoning doesn't work because our feelings don't always reflect the real world, and we have no basis for using them in our decision-making. Therefore, we end up making decisions that don't actually lead to our desired outcome, and that often stop us from doing things that are meaningful and important.

Emotional Reasoning vs. CBT

CBT provides us with an antidote to emotional reasoning. As you may remember, using experimental reasoning our thoughts become hypotheses to test. In the case of that assignment, you can test the hypothesis that you can't do it because you don't feel like it.

Rate your 'feeling like it' before you start, and rate how much work has been done (likely 0%). Set yourself a reasonable writing goal, say 30 minutes. Write for that time, then revisit your ratings of 'feeling like it' and note how much of the task you completed. You might find that your 'feeling like it' rating increases over that 30 minutes. Even if it doesn't, your completion rate certainly will! But did your 'feeling like it' rating have to increase before you began? No! You just began, regardless of how you felt, and the second you hit the first key on that keyboard (or drew the first line on that page), you were on your way.

Now that you know about emotional reasoning you will start to see it everywhere. You're not going to go to the gym because you're not feeling very energetic. You're going to skip today's lecture because you're just not quite up to it. You're going to cancel on your friend again because you're just not in the mood to socialise. Luckily, you can use experimental reasoning to counter it every time.

Managing Perfectionism

Imagine that you are ready to buy a new computer. You walk in to the store and you see the model you have been lusting after for months. It's beautiful, sleek, and powerful. As you're about to hand over all your hard-earned cash, the salesperson tells you that they have another one just like your dream machine, only it has a scratch on the back that no one will ever see and doesn't affect the machine in any way. They are willing to sell it to you at 10% off the original price. Which do you choose?

For some people, they'll take the discount happily, but for others the scratched machine will never do. They know it 'works just as well' as any other computer, but it's not *perfect*. In this case, the cost of perfection is an additional 10%. When we insist on perfection in other areas of life we often end up paying dearly for our 10%. It's easy to think that perfection is the optimal outcome in any situation, but not if it comes at a cost, and the true cost of perfection can be late nights, arguments, stress, and illness. Instead of handing over our wallets we end up handing over our well-being.

Think back to a time when you stayed up all night to be the perfect student, exhausted yourself to be the perfect friend, or made yourself sick being the perfect employee. Was it worth the cost? Did anyone even notice your extra effort? Are you willing to keep paying? What happens when you can't afford it anymore?

You might have heard of perfectionism as a good thing, but sometimes people can get confused between *perfection* and *success*. Consider Eileen and Alexi, who both attribute their 'success' to being a 'perfectionist'. Eileen pays due attention to detail, and as a result, completes tasks to a high standard. Alexi labours over every detail in the never-ending pursuit of flawlessness, often missing deadlines in order to turn in work that he feels is perfect. Eileen achieves success while Alexi is still rapaciously obsessing over his use of adverbs (Alexi has also failed to realise that adverbs like 'rapaciously' are verbose and redundant. Or maybe we are being too perfectionistic?).

The difference between success and perfection is often the difference between *high* standards and *impossible* standards. High standards are achievable, and provide acknowledgment of both our strengths and our weaknesses. When we hold ourselves to high standards we strive to achieve the very best we can. When we hold ourselves to impossible standards, by definition we set ourselves up for failure. We strive for levels that cannot be reached. We agonise over details that don't matter. We ignore our strengths and weaknesses and continue to insist on perfection at the cost of our productivity, our success, and in some cases, our health.

One aspect of perfectionism that commonly rears its head at work and study is what's sometimes called **analysis paralysis**. This refers to a tendency to dissect a task so painstakingly that we never actually get started, or we become so fearful that something might be overlooked that we avoid the task all together. For some students, this means meticulously analysing every essay question, agonising over what the lecturer 'really wants', or labouring over every word, often to the point that the essay is either late or only partially completed. If you can relate to that scenario you're not alone. When you notice that perfectionism is making you less productive and more anxious, try using some of your psychological flexibility tools to set standards that are high, but not impossible.

Perfectionism vs. Logical Disputing

If you struggle with perfectionism, take a moment to consider your need for things to be perfect, or 'just so'. Imagine you are writing a very important assignment or email. What are some of the specific thoughts that come up for you? As the thoughts come up, write them down and then try and come up with a more balanced and realistic version, just like we did earlier. Here are a few common perfectionistic thoughts and some optimised alternatives:

Thought/Belief	Optimised Alternative
I have a reputation for doing well and I must uphold this reputation.	I enjoy being a person who is known for success, but not everyone succeeds at everything, all the time. I am more than just my successes.
I must get a minimum mark for every assignment. Any mark below this is the equivalent of failing.	High marks are nice, but they aren't always achievable. Decide what the best possible outcome is (an A), worse possible outcome is (an F) and most likely outcome is (a B or C), given my resources and abilities at that time.

If I can't do something perfectly then I shouldn't bother doing it at all.	There is a difference between perfect and satisfactory. I might not be able to complete everything perfectly, but that needn't stop me completing tasks satisfactorily.
If I don't do things perfectly then other people will suffer.	I will do my best, but I am not solely responsible for others' happiness or health. Others have their role to play and it's OK for me to expect effort from them.
If I don't achieve a given milestone it will be a disaster, or my future goals will be ruined.	I will do everything I can to achieve a given milestone but it may not be realistic for me just now. I can spend time acquiring additional skills to help me achieve the milestone in the future, or I can explore other options for achieving my goals.

Perfectionism vs. Behavioural Experiments

Perfectionism is partly driven by the belief that everything can be and should be perfect. If you didn't believe this on some level, you wouldn't care! An effective way of challenging this belief is purposely falling short of 'perfection' and observing the consequences (if you struggle with perfectionism, this idea may have caused a lump in your throat!). The goal of this approach is to collect data on what the standards of success *really* are (versus what you *think* they are), and to reflect on whether or not your strivings for perfection are worth the associated cost.

As you now know, behavioural experiments involve us doing something and observing the outcome. Using our behavioural experiment guidelines from earlier, design an experiment where you do something less than perfectly and observe what happens. Decide what specifically you will do. Make sure you define 'perfect' so you will know if you have fallen short of it, and be clear about your hypotheses. If you are perfectionistic about your writing, then you likely re-read each email several times before sending it. As an experiment you might like to send an email without checking it, perhaps with something deliberately left out, or even a with a typo (gasp). What do you predict will happen? Will someone criticise you? Will you feel bad? How bad will that feeling be? How long will it last?

As you evaluate the evidence at the end of this experiment, we will get you to reflect on one more thing. What was it like not putting in 100%? Did you get something else done? Did you feel less stressed? What might life be like if you accepted some criticism or discomfort in return for less stress and more time to do other things?

Managing Setbacks

Sometimes life doesn't go according to plan (excuse us while we accept the award for the greatest understatement ever written). When we experience setbacks life can seem painful, uncaring, or even hopeless. When things don't work out, remaining psychologically flexible can help us navigate the situation and get ourselves back on track. You can use your psychological flexibility toolkit to manage difficult thoughts, make helpful decisions, and cope with the emotional rollercoaster of disappointment.

Setbacks vs. Cognitive Defusion and Disputing Unhelpful Thoughts

Setbacks are the perfect breeding ground for some of the suboptimal cognitive styles you learned about in the previous sections. When we experience setbacks we can fall into the trap of catastrophising, over-generalising, blaming, and engaging in black-and-white thinking. This exam result is a disaster. If James were smarter, then our group wouldn't have failed. If I can't succeed at this, then I can't succeed at anything. Sound familiar? When you experience a setback, you can combine cognitive defusion with disputing unhelpful thoughts to manage the mental fallout.

First, defuse from your mind by taking an inventory of all your thoughts. You might like to use the list of 'unhelpful cognitive styles' from the previous section as a field guide. Sit comfortably for 10 minutes and watch what goes through your mind as you think about the setback. Let the thoughts come in whatever form they do. When you spot a particular cognitive style, simply label this, and then let the thought go. You might notice blaming. Then over-generalising. Oh, look, there's catastrophising.

If thoughts are particularly persistent, write them down, along with the cognitive style they represent. Try using one of the cognitive defusion techniques from the previous section to remind yourself that those thoughts are just words. You may find that this process alone provides enough space from your thoughts to make the setback feel more manageable.

Next, try disputing the most persistent thoughts just like we did in the previous section. Offer an alternative point of view, and try it on for size. Say you notice the thought, 'If I can't succeed at this, I'll never succeed at anything'. What is an alternative point of view? How about, 'I didn't succeed this time, but I will try again. Even if I still don't succeed, there are other options, and I have succeeded at many other things'. How does that feel? Softer? Lighter? Does the setback seem quite as awful?

Bringing it all Together

So now you not only *understand* psychological flexibility, you have practical tools to *use* psychological flexibility to optimise your mind. You have learned about unhelpful stuff that can keep your mind stuck in a gluey mess, like emotional reasoning and self-defeating thoughts. You have also learned research-based tools to help your mind flex like rubber to avoid getting stuck; tools like behavioural experiments and cognitive defusion.

Some of you might even be starting to see how many of these techniques work perfectly with our SMR model. Jen certainly can. At the beginning of the chapter, exam time made Jen's mind sticky with suboptimal thoughts of impending failure, leaving her anxious and more than a little tough to get along with. Now, Jen has decided to use some psychological flexibility tools to optimise her thinking so that she can feel better (and be nicer to be around, too). When self-defeating thoughts start to stick, Jen might identify the unhelpful thinking styles and dispute them. Or Jen might put her new mindfulness skills to good use as she defuses from her thoughts and focuses on something far more important, like her friendship with you.

As Jen heads back out into the world with her psychological flexibility tools she will notice many situations in which being psychologically flexible can help her succeed and thrive. Over time, as Jen replaces her suboptimal thoughts with more optimal alternatives, Jen's mind will come to automatically use psychological flexibility tools, and her old, sticky ways of thinking will fade. Occasionally when Jen gets tired or stressed those sticky thoughts may sneak back in, but by then Jen will have some well-practiced tools to deal with them.

Summary Points

- Psychological flexibility refers to how an individual acquires and employs mental resources to balance the fluctuating (and sometimes competing) demands of life.

- Being psychologically flexible allows you to identify your unhelpful thinking — your M_{SUB}'s — and really optimise what's going on in your head, leading to more functional responses and healthier outcomes.

- The psychological flexibility toolkit includes mindfulness, ACT, and CBT.

- Using mindfulness, we can observe what's going on in our mind, and choose thoughts and actions that support and nourish us.

- One of the most useful ACT tools is cognitive defusion, which help us to deal with fusion, which is the binding with thoughts and feelings until their associations feel like reality.

- Two useful CBT tools are labelling and disputing unhelpful thoughts and beliefs, and, experimental reasoning and behavioural experiments.

- The toolkit is applied to managing: self-defeating thoughts and beliefs, overwhelming emotions, emotional reasoning, perfectionism, and setbacks.

More Resources

- CBT approaches to increasing psychological flexibility:
  See Sarah Edelman's book *Change your thinking*.

- ACT approaches to increasing psychological flexibility:
  See Steven Hayes' book *Get out of your mind and into your life*, and Russ Harris' book *The Happiness Trap*.

CHAPTER 5

Stress

Imagine that you're walking into class and your teacher reminds you that she is giving you a test that you need to pass in order to continue in the class. And somehow, between the assignment due last week and the group presentation this Friday, you had forgotten all about it! It might not be your favourite subject, but you have made some really good friends in this class and it's a compulsory unit in your degree program, which is really important to you. So, passing this test is pretty crucial, BUT all the stuff you have learned this semester feels like a distant memory. You can recall the teacher's name, and you definitely remember the name of the really cute student who sits behind you, but you are pretty sure that neither of those answers will help you on the test! You know that you would have studied for it if you had remembered to, but without studying, there is no way that you are going to pass. How do you feel?

Regardless of the cause — whether it is the situation described above, going on a date with that cute student who sits behind you, or taking a driving test — the symptoms of **stress** are usually the same: your heart races, your breathing quickens, you feel butterflies in your stomach, you start to sweat profusely, your throat dries up, you blanch as your blood moves away from your skin to fuel your muscles and brain, and you might feel like you are about to throw up. All of these symptoms reflect the activation of the sympathetic nervous system together with the release of stress hormones, such as adrenaline and cortisol. This is your body's well-tuned way of responding to a stressful situation, which we refer to as a **stressor**. Even in its extreme form, stress is a very adaptive response. This extreme form is known as the **fight or flight** response — your body's way of protecting you from a perceived threat, and allowing you to stay alert and energised to deal with that looming threat. It's kind of like a super-power, which your body can call on when things get tough. All of these changes prime you to be alert and ready to act. You are Wolverine!

The purpose of stress, then, is to help you rise to a challenge. When we think of challenges we often think in terms of threat, and so stress too is usually framed as something bad and to be avoided. However, stress can also be positive — such as when you are walking along (probably daydreaming about that cute student from your class) and suddenly you notice a $100 note floating in the breeze, and so you chase after it!

In this chapter, when we talk about stress we will often refer to stress in the face of threats, such as unexpected tests, looming deadlines, mean bosses, and other scary beasts. It is true that beyond a certain point stress can start interfering with your optimal functioning and can be both physically and psychologically harmful. However, a certain amount of stress can actually be a positive tool to help your body and brain best meet the challenges that you face. Seeing stress as *unequivocally** problematic is a great example of the suboptimal thinking (M_{SUB}) we introduced in Chapter 1.

This chapter will help you to shine a light on your thinking around stress and to learn that stress does not *necessarily* lead to negative outcomes; stress can actually bring out the superhero in you, motivating you to try harder and to achieve more. We'll start the chapter by defining stress and how it can become problematic if left unchecked. Then we'll move to some more helpful ways of thinking about stress, and finally we'll consider ways of keeping stress under control.

---

* It should be noted that some events *are* unequivocally negatively stressful, such as rape or physical assault. We are certainly not asserting that your negative reactions to such events are 'all in your head', with the responsibility being yours to change. Dealing with such experiences are beyond the scope of this book, and we strongly advise you to seek appropriate professional help.

Understanding Stressors, Stress, and the Stress Response

In everyday language, the word 'stress' usually refers to the negative feelings we experience when we are under pressure. As you now know, stress is a process that helps us rise to the challenges of life, so it's not really helpful to think of stress as always negative. To start optimising our thinking around stress we need to understand the 'stress response system', which involves a stimulus — the stressor — and the response to that stimulus — the **stress response**. Stressors can be either positive (that rogue $100 note) or negative (that forgotten test) events or situations that represent a *disruption of the equilibrium between you and your environment.* Simply put, this means that when stressors come along they disrupt your tidy little corner of the world and *require you to adjust.*

The stress response helps us rise to the challenges of a stressor. It can be thought of as the internal processes that arise when a stressor comes along, which can be emotional (including the feeling of negative stress under pressure), cognitive, physiological, or behavioural (actually, usually all of these). For example, when you experience stress your liver releases sugar and fat into your bloodstream to provide fuel. Your breathing speeds up to increase the oxygen in your blood. Your heart rate increases to deliver the sugar and oxygen to the muscles and brain where they are needed most, and stress hormones ensure that these fuels are utilised efficiently. Adrenaline also ramps up your senses, dilating your pupils to see better and sensitising you to hear better. Your brain processes information more quickly and concentrates attention on the problem at hand. See, it really is like a super-power!

DIVING DEEPER 5.1

The Stress Response

Regardless of the cause of the stress response, Hans Selye, the noted Hungarian-Canadian endocrinologist (1956; see Figure 5.1) outlined 3 phases of the typical threat stress response:

1. *Alarm Reaction* — you are alerted to the threat, prompting the 'fight or flight' response. Your autonomic nervous and endocrine systems prepare for action, with adrenaline, noradrenaline, and cortisol released by the adrenal gland, and oxytocin from the pituitary gland. These have numerous effects, including increasing your heart rate, blood pressure,

muscle tension, blood sugar, respiration, and perspiration. They also reduce blood flow to your skin and reduce your digestive activity.

2. *Resistance* — you continue to mobilise resources in an attempt to adapt to the ongoing stressor, for example, through elevated stress hormones. Your temperature, blood pressure, and respiration remain high. Your body works hard to adapt to the enduring stressor; and

3) *Exhaustion* — when the stressor is enduring, your resources become depleted and you become exhausted, rendering you susceptible to illness, and even collapse.

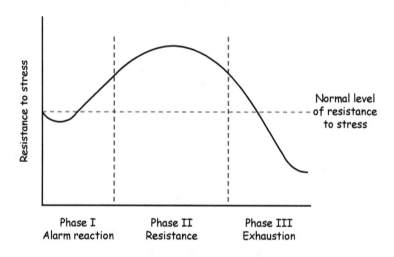

Figure 5.1   Selye's (1956) model of resistance to stress.

So, What's So Bad About Stress?

While the stress response is highly adaptive in the short-term, severe or prolonged stress that leads to extended activation of our nervous and endocrine systems can have a seriously negative impact on our health. There is extensive research linking chronic stressors to poor health, including a reduction in bodily processes that protect us from myriad ills, including infections, tumours, psychological problems, and sleep disorders. Stress can also involve inflammation, which delays wound healing and makes us vulnerable to infection, heart disease, and arthritis. Prolonged elevation of cortisol and adrenaline is associated with increased blood pressure and cholesterol, weight gain, heart disease, reduced bone density, and impaired learning and memory. Moreover, elevated cortisol levels have been associated with decreased psychological resilience and increased mental illness. To take a metaphor even further than is really necessary, a prolonged stress response can be like Kryptonite to our superhero.

In addition to these physical aspects of the prolonged stress response taking their toll on your body, there are also psychological responses to stress, which may be emotional, cognitive and/or behavioural. Emotional responses include feelings of anxiety, anger, frustration, fear, and sadness (which can themselves induce physical sensations such as dizziness, heart palpitations, headaches, or stomach aches). You may become withdrawn, tearful, irritable, or tense. You may find yourself unable to concentrate, remember things, or make a decision. You may have trouble sleeping, lose your appetite, or you may find yourself turning to alcohol, drugs, or food for 'stress relief'. All of these reactions can form part of the stress response, but the stressor itself and individual differences in body and mind will determine which reactions you experience. Redundant summary alert: being overly stressed is not good for your health or your wellbeing!

What Does Suboptimal Thinking Have to Do With the Stress Response?

There is an important role for our mind — including how we think about a stressor — in determining if we experience a stressor as threatening. While you can feel stressed by a situation itself, you can also be stressed by *the way you think* about that situation. Think of how you would feel if you were about to have a job interview. Some events, like interviews, are objectively stressful, as they would cause a stress response in anyone who experiences them (even Wolverine). However, people differ in the amount of stress they feel in the face of the same stressor, because part of our stress response is guided by how we think about the stressor. An interview can become even more stressful if you think 'if I don't get this job, then I'm a loser, and I'll never be employable'.

Your cognitive appraisal — that is, your assessment of a situation and how it could affect you — influences how you respond. In our SMR model, where S is the stressor, M is your cognitive appraisal of it. Whether that is optimal or suboptimal influences whether you will have a negative response to that stressor, or a more positive one.

107

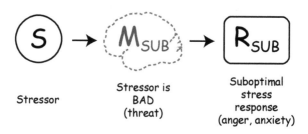

Figure 5.2   Having a suboptimal mindset (M_{SUB}) that a stressor is negative, can lead to suboptimal responding (R_{SUB}).

Daniel and Dylan both work at a local café on weekends. One Sunday, their boss calls them in to tell them that they are being let go. Even though this wouldn't be a fun experience for anyone, their cognitive appraisal of the situation influences their emotional response to it. Daniel's cognitive appraisal is that this is not related to his performance but is more about the company needing more full-time staff and fewer casuals. He still feels disappointed but is not stressed about finding another position. In contrast, Dylan's cognitive appraisal is that he is being fired because he's useless at everything. Dylan feels ashamed, and very stressed at the thought of applying for other jobs. Immediately you can see how suboptimal thinking has increased Dylan's stress levels.

According to psychological scientist Richard Lazarus, there are two steps to the cognitive appraisal that determines your response to a stressor. The first step, or **primary appraisal**, is the evaluation of how the stressor will impact you and your wellbeing — is it potentially threatening or harmful, or is it harmless (either benignly positive or irrelevant)? If you determine that it is harmless, you simply move on. For example, imagine you have just walked into class, and been given a group presentation assignment to work on over the next month. If you are a confident and competent presenter, you know the topic, you like your team members, and the assignment is not heavily weighted, then your primary appraisal is likely that this it is not a threatening situation, and your thoughts will probably flitter calmly between the job at hand and what you might eat for lunch (mmm, meatball sub).

If, on the other hand, your primary appraisal is that this event is potentially harmful or threatening, a **secondary appraisal** of the situation occurs. At this stage, you think about what coping strategies and resources you have, and whether they can be successfully recruited to manage the perceived stressor. In the example of the group assignment, you may be uncomfortable with public speaking, or know that one of your team members never does any work. However, if you remember that you have plenty of time to complete the task, *and* the other students in your group have proven themselves to be highly capable, *and* your teacher has provided significant amounts of material to help you, *and* your sister has agreed that for the next month she will be doing all of your cooking and laundry, then your secondary appraisal will likely be that you have adequate resources to manage the stressor; thus, you will not experience a negative stress response. If, on the other hand, you realise that you have *all* your assessments due that same week, *and* your team-members haven't even shown up for this class, *and* you were out all weekend and didn't get enough sleep, *and* you feel like you are coming down with the flu, then it is highly likely that your secondary appraisal will be that you most certainly do not have adequate resources to manage the stressor, and you will experience a negative stress response.

We may have rambled on a bit in the previous example, but it was strategic rambling to illustrate that there are numerous factors that interact in determining whether a situation results in a negative stress response, many of which are controllable to varying degrees, and determined by whether you have an optimal or suboptimal mindset towards the stressor. This means that you have some control over how much a given situation evokes your stress response. Controllable factors that can optimise your thinking include being optimistic rather than pessimistic (see Chapter 6); your self-efficacy; and your values, beliefs, and goals that determine the importance of the event, and thus its potential to impact your wellbeing. Other controllable factors include your lifestyle (e.g., whether you are getting enough sleep and exercise), and your level of social support. However, one of the most important controllable factors that can optimise your response to a potentially stressful situation is your appraisal of whether a difficult situation is judged to be challenging (M_{OP}) or threatening (M_{SUB}). With the right skills, you can optimise your thinking about stressful situations (and even about stress itself) to change how you respond in the face of stress.

The Positive Side of Stress

Stress is a Performance Enhancer

For over 100 years we have known that stress, up to a point, can actually enhance performance, thus the amount of stress we experience actually predicts how we respond to a given situation. According to the Yerkes Dodson curve (see Figure 5.3), stress produces arousal, which leads to action. As arousal increases, performance increases up to a point, however if arousal continues to rise beyond this point, performance actually begins to decrease. The Yerkes Dodson curve suggests that there is an 'ideal' level of stress that yields optimal performance (like you might see in a *Gatorade* commercial). Imagine a basketballer with his team 1 point down, 5 seconds to go, surrounded by the noise of the crowd yelling their support; he is able to run a little faster, and shoot with a little more accuracy to nail the 3-pointer that wins the game. That basketballer is surfing the peak of the Yerkes Dodson curve (and earning his *Gatorade* sponsorship deal). Put simply, when you feel sufficiently stressed, you are sufficiently motivated, and how you channel that motivation is up to you. You might put extra effort into studying for an upcoming exam or do some extra prep for a job interview. Either way, you are pumped and ready to perform.

At other times, you might find yourself at either end of the Yerkes Dodson curve. Too little stress and you are not sufficiently aroused or challenged to perform optimally. Think of this as the 'meh' zone, where you would rather be in front of Netflix or Snapchat (or both) than the textbook for that exam. Too

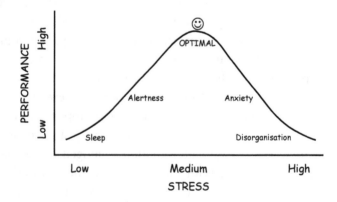

Figure 5.3   The Yerkes Dodson arousal-performance U-curve illustrates the connection between stress and performance.

much stress, however, and your performance declines. You become overwhelmed and don't know where to begin. Or you feel burnt out and unable to take on another task. The amount of optimal stress or arousal is closely linked to the task itself, and there is no 'correct' level of stress. The key point is that experiencing *no* stress is just as detrimental to performance as experiencing *too much* stress, and that a certain amount of stress can actually enhance your performance. Now that we know this, we can begin to consider stress as our friend, rather than our enemy.

 TRY IT! 5.1

The Positive Side of Stress

Think about a time where being stressed 'enough' energised and helped you to achieve what you needed to.

Stress Can Be Your Friend (If You Let It)

In one of the 25 most-watched TED talks of all time, health psychologist Kelly McGonigal makes the surprising claim that when you change your mind about stress, you change your body's response to stress (see *More Resources*). This is our SMR model in a nutshell: by turning your M_{SUB}'s into M_{OP}'s you end up with a more positive response. As you recall, the stress response evolved to help us adjust to the shifting demands of life. Those symptoms that we have learned to identify with the experience of stress — pounding heart, rapid breathing, sweaty palms — are actually age-old signs that our body is preparing to rise to a challenge. In her TED talk, McGonigal describes how when she put people in a stressful situation but told them that their stress response was helpful — for example, that their pounding heart and rapid breathing were getting more oxygen to the brain and body — they were less stressed and more confident. However, McGonigal notes that the most incredible finding was that with this mindset, although participants' heart rate increased, their blood vessels remained relaxed (rather than constricting, as is typical of the negative stress response). This cardiovascular profile is more like that of joy than distress, and does not have the negative effects on health that we discussed earlier in this chapter. McGonigal's take-home message is that even in a pressured situation, if we acknowledge our physiological stress response as being helpful, then we can benefit from the experience.

McGonigal also found that although high levels of experienced stress increase the likelihood of dying prematurely, this is truer for people who believe that 'stress' is harmful to their heath. Across her studies, McGonigal noticed that people who experienced stress but did not consider it to be harmful were least likely to die prematurely. This suggests that it is not stress, per se, that negatively affects our health; rather it appears to be the combination of the experience of a stressor combined with the belief that it is harmful. Indeed, other research tells us that people with a positive view of stressors are more satisfied with their life, less depressed, more productive and energised, and are happier and healthier.

Optimising Thinking About Stress and Stressful Situations

Cultivating A Positive Stress Mindset

McGonigal suggests that those with a **negative stress mindset** are more likely to try to avoid or escape the stressor. In contrast, those with a **positive stress mindset** are more likely to cope with the stressor more proactively, by facing challenges head on, and building resources for dealing with the stressor. So, what are the benefits of stress that we could acknowledge to help us cultivate a positive stress mindset? First, the stress response helps you meet the challenge of the stressor. The physiological and cognitive components of the stress response mobilise your energy, increase your motivation, sharpen your senses, and focus your attention. Second, the stress response connects you with others through the release of oxytocin. Stress activates your social instincts, enhances social cognition and connection, and increases courage, described as the **tend and befriend** response. Finally, the stress recovery process helps you learn and grow, as stress hormones increase activity in brain areas responsible for learning and memory. Ultimately, the stress response system prepares you for current challenges and future encounters with similar stressors, so appreciate it for the super power that it is!

We can also optimise thinking about stress by seeing it as a challenge to be risen to (see Figure 5.4). When we begin to think that a stressor is a challenge, we become energised and motivated to solve problems and achieve goals. Successful athletes, leaders, performers, and even teachers and students can thrive in the face of challenge. Part of optimising your thinking about stress is

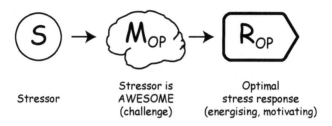

Figure 5.4   Having an optimal mindset (M$_{OP}$) that a stressor is positive, can lead to optimal responding (R$_{OP}$).

learning to view each stressor as a challenge. Viewing stress in this way increases self-confidence, motivates us to act, and helps us learn from experience. This is closely related to the research on growth mindset (see Chapter 6) in which a difficult problem is reappraised as an opportunity to grow. If we think back to the group presentation example given in the previous section, the student could have reappraised the situation as a challenge to learn more about the given topic, work well with teammates, become better at oral presentations, and/or utilise resources (internal and external) more effectively.

TRY IT! 5.2

The Positive Mindset

Try cultivating a 'positive stress' mindset by reflecting on your past stress responses, including those that were helpful. There are 3 steps to this process:

1. **Notice the experience of stress** — allow yourself to acknowledge the stressor and your physiological, emotional, and behavioural responses to it. Research suggests that this can positively impact the stress response by shifting neural activity from lower brain areas to more conscious, higher order areas.

2. **Welcome the experience of stress** — connect with the value of what is at stake and thus causing you to feel stressed. Meeting stressors head on with a proactive mentality reduces anxiety, improves your sense of control, and energises you.

3. Use the stress — channel the energy of the stress response to focus on actions that reduce negative aspects of the stressor.

Cultivating Coping Resources and Strategies

Lazarus's model suggests that when an event is perceived as negatively stressful, the presence or absence of coping resources determines the impact of that stressor on our health and wellbeing. Resources include time, money, knowledge, skills, and social support, as well as psychological coping strategies to deal with the stressor at hand. Such strategies can be divided into **problem-focused strategies** — those that focus on removing or resolving the source of stress — and **emotion-focused strategies** — those that aim to regulate the emotional consequences of the stressor. Moreover, emotion-focused strategies may actually enhance problem-focused ones, as they manage emotions that might otherwise interfere with problem-solving ability. Emotion-focused strategies can also be useful in reducing distress when a problem can't be solved in the short-term (see Chapter 4 for examples).

It is important to note that not all coping strategies necessarily lead to helpful outcomes. Coping strategies tend to either be approach-oriented or avoidance-oriented. Approach strategies address the stressor and associated emotions (e.g., problem-solving), while avoidance strategies sidestep the stressor (e.g., denial, substance abuse). Approach strategies tend to be associated with better outcomes than avoidance strategies. Occasionally, however, avoiding a situation is the best course of action, such as when your stressor is a person with a knife. Even superheroes run away sometimes (which is why it is called the 'fight or flight' response, not the 'fight to the death' response!)

Following are some activities that will help you manage your experience of stress.

Helpful Problem-Focused Strategies

Cognitive Reappraisal. We learned in this chapter that our stress response is based on our perceived ability to cope, so another part of optimising thinking during times of stress is reappraising the skills and resources we have in order to cope with a given stressor. For example, next time you find yourself in a traffic jam on your way to work, and your stress levels rise as you realise you will be late, ask yourself '*what do I believe about my ability to cope with this situation?*' You might be thinking: 'If my boss yells at me I will go to pieces' or 'there's nothing I can do!'. Your boss may be mad, but if being late was unavoidable (e.g., due to a 12-car pile-up) then you can explain that to her. While stopped in the traffic you can even send her a message warning her you will be late (but make sure you are stopped — no texting and driving!). If being late was avoidable (e.g., you hit the snooze button too many times) then maybe you need to take her anger on the chin and learn from the experience (e.g., put two alarms on — one on the other side of the room). You could also offer to your boss to make the time up at the end of your shift. In the face of a stressor, reminding yourself of what you can do may help you to reduce maladaptive aspects of your stress response, and to engage in solution-focused strategies (see Chapter 4 for more information on managing unhelpful thoughts).

Putting things in Perspective. Ask yourself whether this is really important in the long run, and whether it is worth the amount of energy you are devoting to it. Put it in context, and perhaps adjust your expectations of yourself and the situation. For example, having an extreme anger or anxiety response in the 'caught in traffic and will be late for work' situation described above, could be put into perspective by imagining events that truly do deserve such responses (e.g., having your car stolen, or being physically attacked by a road-rager).

Time-management. Utilising some of the time-management strategies from Chapter 7 should help you to channel your time more effectively and thus reduce the impact of the stressor.

Social Support. As 'they' say, a problem shared is a problem halved. By seeking advice from friends and family, or from experts (a teacher, manager, or psychologist), you are more likely to arrive at a range of possible strategies or tools to deal with the stressor, and indeed, any one of these people may be physically helpful as well (e.g., your sister agreeing to do your chores at particularly demanding times — as long as you pay her back when she is in a similar situation, of course!).

Helpful Emotion-Focused Strategies

Sometimes a problem can't be solved in the short-term, or you're just not thinking clearly enough to address the problem as it stands. In this case there are always things you can do to get some emotional distance from the problem.

Physical Activity. Get moving! Surprise, surprise, regular exercise has been shown to facilitate adaptive responding to negative stressors as well as to protect you from the effects of such stressors. You could create the fight (e.g., boxing) or flight (e.g., a spin class) experience in a positive way. Or, just get out the door and go for a brisk walk (no equipment needed). Any form of physical exercise that gets you sweating releases endorphins that enhance your mood and relieve tension and anger. This includes riding a bike, putting on music and dancing, exercising with a friend, or power-walking home from school or work. Aim for at least 20 minutes, 3 times a week.

Mindfulness. As outlined in Chapter 4, mindfulness is a moment-to-moment awareness of your experience, without judgement. It encompasses attention to your bodily sensations and thoughts, intention to focus on being in the moment, and an attitude of acceptance. Any activity can be done mindfully — cleaning your room, exercising, walking, or even eating. For example, through-out the day, stop and become aware of where you are, what you are doing, and how you are feeling. You might choose a given action to remind you to do this, for example, each time you walk through a doorway, or each time you sit down. Another example is mindful breathing, where you stop and take a few deep breaths, which also activates the vagus nerve, signalling your parasympathetic nervous system to reduce your heart rate, blood pressure, and cortisol levels. You can do this any time or place, for even a few minutes.

Mindfulness Meditation. Mindfulness meditation has become a very popular strategy for reducing your feelings of negative stress. There is much research to support its effectiveness in reducing the negative aspects of the stress response and in activating the parts of the brain responsible for emotional control. There are numerous apps, YouTube clips and websites to introduce you to mindfulness and other types of meditation (see *More Resources*, and Chapter 4). The principle is to mindfully focus on your breath or your body, returning your attention each time you become distracted. You can practice by sitting in a chair with your feet on the ground and your back straight. 'Take a few deep breaths, and allow your body and mind to become relaxed, while remaining alert to the present moment. Notice the areas of your body that are relaxed, and those that are tense, those that are in contact with the chair or the floor, and those that are not. Notice your breath, and where it enters and fills your body. Notice sounds and the space between sounds. Simply feel the sensations, and let any thoughts and images come and go, like clouds floating past. If you notice that you are engaging with your thoughts, just bring your attention back to your breath — over and over.' [You could read the above words out loud, while recording it on your phone, and then play it back any time!] Another type of meditation is loving-kindness meditation, in which you meditate while generating feelings of kindness and love towards yourself, and others. For further information on mindfulness meditation, see *More Resources*, and Chapters 4 and 7.

Connectedness. Social contact is one of the most efficient strategies to reduce negative stress experiences. McGonigal suggests that the neurochemical oxytocin (the 'love hormone' that affects our social functioning), which is released as part of the stress response, facilitates stress reduction. Just like the release of adrenaline primes your body to respond to the stressor, the release of oxytocin has been suggested to motivate you to seek support, and to surround yourself with those who may be able to help you. This not only has an impact on finding solutions (as above), but also has an impact on satisfying your need for relatedness, thus leading to positive feelings (see Chapter 8). The vagus nerve, which is connected to your face, heart, and stomach, also responds to human face-to-face contact and connection, thus activating your restorative parasympathetic nervous system. If physical connectedness isn't possible, calling or emailing a friend can also have a positive impact on reducing your stress.

Positive Experiences. Having positive experiences, laughing, and enjoying yourself all lead to a reduction in cortisol and adrenaline levels. There are numerous effects of regular, hearty laughter, including lowered blood pressure, enhanced immunity, muscle relaxation, pain reduction, and even reduced risk of heart disease. Laughter has even been equated to 'internal jogging', with suggestions that a minute of laughter is as positive as ten minutes of exercise, including providing cardiac and abdominal muscle conditioning. Humour also connects us to others, providing an additional benefit. Try to do something you enjoy every day, particularly during times of stress. See Chapter 6 for examples of how to enhance the positivity in your life.

Music. Listening to your favourite music has been shown to reduce levels of cortisol and improve mood.

Look After Yourself. Have a good night's sleep, or a massage, or a healthy meal. Give yourself time to relax each day, and aim to do something calm and soothing before you go to bed.

Research suggests that both problem-focused and emotion-focused coping can be used in almost every type of stressful situation, and you might use both types of strategies to deal with a given situation. However, there is also evidence that optimists are more likely to use problem-focused coping strategies that directly address the stressor, whereas pessimists are more likely to use unhelpful strategies like denial and avoidance. Gender differences in coping styles also exist, with males more likely to get angry, avoid stressors, or both, whereas females are more likely to invoke their social support networks.

The key message is that, rather than seeing stress as the big bad wolf to be avoided at all costs, we can optimise our thinking about stress and acknowledge that the stress response can be seen as an adaptive and even positive thing, potentially leading to growth and success. So, the next time you find yourself in a stressful situation, with your sympathetic nervous system activated, and stress hormones coursing through your veins, be grateful that they turned up to help you channel your inner Wolverine, and deal with whatever life throws your way!

Summary Points

- Stressors are stimuli or situations that disrupt our equilibrium in some way.

- Some stressors are undeniably negative; for most stressors it is how we think about them that determines how we respond to them — in an optimal, or suboptimal way.

- The models of and orientations toward stress help us understand how to optimise our responding to stressors.

- There are many problem-focused and emotion-focused approaches for dealing with negative stressors; both can be helpful, but certain emotion-focussed approaches can be suboptimal in some situations.

More Resources

- Kelly McGonigal's TED talk:
  https:ww.ted.coks/kelly_mcgonigal_how_to_make_stress_your_friend

  See also McGonigal, K. (2015). *The Upside of Stress: Why Stress Is Good for You, and How to Get Good at It.* Avery.

- Mindfulness mediation:
  http://www.positivityresonance.com/meditations.html

CHAPTER 6

Positivity

'There's nothing good or bad but thinking makes it so.'
— William Shakespeare

Some people (usually parents) like to ramble on about the importance of 'being positive' or having a 'positive mindset'. While this sounds like hippie nonsense, research tells us that our mindset and our capacity for positivity really do play an important role in our wellbeing. To illustrate just how important positivity and mindset can be, we'd like to introduce you to two very similar (yet very different) people: Padma and Nelly.

First, let's meet Padma. Padma has recently started university and moved in with three friends as her parents live too far away for Padma to commute. Although she misses her mum's cooking, Padma enjoys her new independence and has set herself the challenge of preparing new and interesting meals each week. Padma lives close enough to university that she can walk there every day if she gets up 30 minutes earlier than she normally would. Padma is sometimes tired, but she reminds herself that this gives her the opportunity for some free exercise each day. She has a part-time job that helps her to pay the rent, and there is even a little left over to treat herself, or to give a few dollars to the homeless man she passes on the street every now and then. She is grateful for her family, especially for her aunt who has her over for dinner twice a week. There is nothing like a home-cooked meal, and Padma secretly enjoys having her laundry done by her aunt. Her aunt often comments on the clothes Padma brings, which makes Padma feel like her aunt is genuinely interested in her. One of Padma's tutors suggested that the students who do best in her degree program are those who engage with community service, so she goes to a preschool for disadvantaged children once a fortnight to help with the breakfast session, which she really enjoys. All in all, Padma is very happy with life.

Next, let's meet Nelly. Nelly has recently started university and has also had to move in with three friends because her parents live so far away, which she is quite annoyed about. She finds it particularly inconvenient to have to shop for groceries and cook her own meals. The bus stop is half way between Nelly's house and the university, so she has to walk there every day, which she hates because she has to get up 30 minutes earlier than she would like. She has had to get a part-time job to pay the rent and has barely enough left over for herself, so it really annoys her when the homeless man that she passes everyday asks her for a handout. Nelly feels obligated to go to her aunt's house for dinner twice a week, but at least it's better than cooking herself, and she has a deal with her aunt that she will only go to dinner as long as her aunt also does her laundry while she is there. Nelly is sure her aunt is judging her because she always makes some comment about the clothes Nelly brings. One of Nelly's tutors said that the students who do best in her degree are those who engage with community service, so now Nelly feels guilted into doing community service. Nelly drags herself to a preschool for disadvantaged children once a fortnight to hand out breakfast for the bratty kids who never even thank her for her time. All in all, Nelly is not all that happy with her life.

Our Naturally Negative Mindset

If you are like most people, you are more likely to think about what is wrong with your life, your relationships, your study, your career etc., rather than what is right with these things. Before you start feeling bad about yourself, we should tell you that human beings are actually hardwired to focus on the negative events in life, rather than on the positive. So when you focus on the negative, that doesn't make you a bad person or even a Negative Nelly. Your brain was built that way to help you survive.

Imagine yourself as a caveperson traipsing through the prehistoric forest. How much more important is it to notice and remember the location of the big hairy beast's lair, rather than the field of pretty flowers? Very important! You remember where the hairy beast lived because your brain evolved to focus on negative or fear-eliciting stimuli, and that saved you from becoming a big hairy breakfast. So, it is not necessarily a bad thing to be aware of the negatives in life, however constantly seeing the world through a negative filter can be detrimental to your physical and mental health (and besides, you might find some nice food in that field of pretty flowers). Fortunately, there is increasing evidence coming out of the field of **positive psychology** (PP) that being *consciously and intentionally* aware of the good in our lives can have significant and wide-reaching benefits!

Now that you know that our mind is naturally attuned to the negative parts of our world, if you think back to our SMR model (see Figure 6.1) you can begin to understand how this default mode of negativity can often lead to suboptimal responses. These responses may be destructive emotions, such as anger, contempt, or sadness. These responses usually lead to poor health outcomes such as raised blood pressure, or to unhelpful behaviour, such as yelling, blaming, or even turning to drugs or alcohol. All in all, our naturally negative mind is one big reason why sometimes we default to suboptimal thinking. One way of optimising our thinking is shifting our mindset to notice the good, rather than just the bad. We need to 'hunt the good stuff' in life and reflect on the positive things that happen (and they do happen!). As we do this, we start to add positive stuff to our mental playlist, rather than constantly listening to your brain's favourite album, 'Life Sucks and So Do You'.

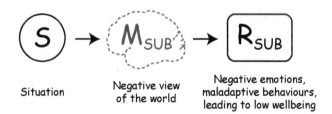

Situation   Negative view   Negative emotions,
             of the world   maladaptive behaviours,
                              leading to low wellbeing

Figure 6.1   Having a negative world view (M_{SUB}) can lead to suboptimal responding (R_{SUB}), leading to poor physical and mental health.

TRY IT! 6.1

Three Things

Think of 3 things that you are happy with or satisfied with in your life. Write down these 3 things — things that you are already good enough at or have enough of. Do you have enough friends? Are you good enough at cooking? Are you funny enough? Instead of listing things that you want or need, or pondering what is missing or wrong with your life, try thinking about what is good about it, what you have, and what you are grateful for.

Before we begin let's get one thing clear: positivity is *not* about being happy all the time. It is not about forcing a Marsha Brady trill every time you open your mouth, or constantly squishing your face into a Cheshire grin (both would be extremely creepy). In fact, that kind of 'always happy' mentality leads to unrealistic expectations that can actually undermine your wellbeing. Instead, the goal of positivity is to help you to be mentally healthy and filled with emotional vitality. So positivity is not about 'being happy'; positivity is about shifting away from our natural negativity by actively using positive experiences to help us grow and flourish.

 DIVING DEEPER 6.1

Positive Psychology (PP) and Flourishing

Most of the time we think of psychology as 'helping cure psychological illness', but that is just one branch of a very broad science. PP is the branch of psychology that studies psychological *wellness* (as opposed to *illness*), such as positive emotions, and human strengths and virtues. For example, when you have a cold, it is obviously important to treat the illness so that you can recover. But surely there is more to wellness that simply 'not being sick'? Beyond simply recovering, many of us seek to be as healthy as we can possibly be. PP, therefore, is about helping people to climb beyond the mere absence of mental illness. PP is about helping people to *flourish*. Flourishing is positively correlated with academic achievement, not to mention self-control and perseverance.

PP research has uncovered many factors that explain why or how some people flourish. Happiness is one factor. Happy people are more successful at work, have more satisfying relationships and better health. Happy teenagers earn significantly more income later in life than less happy teens. Authenticity is important: females who have genuine smiles in photos at age 18 experience less divorce and greater marital satisfaction later in life than those displaying fake smiles. In developed countries, money has only a small effect on happiness. Optimism also helps people flourish. Optimistic people are less likely to die of heart attacks than pessimists, even when we take into account physical risk factors.

Martin Seligman, who is universally acknowledged as the father of positive psychology, suggests that wellbeing has 5 components: Positive Emotion, Engagement, Relationships, Meaning, and Accomplishment, referred to as **PERMA**.

PERMA

Positive Emotions

There are many positive emotions — joy, gratitude, serenity, interest, hope, pride, amusement, inspiration, awe, and love. All of these emotions are associated with greater life satisfaction, decreased vulnerability to depression, and enhanced learning, especially creative learning. Moreover, positive emotions motivate people to take action in order to make the most of potentially rewarding opportunities.

Engagement

Basically, we thrive when we engage with our life and our work. This idea is closely linked to Mihaly Csikszentmihalyi's concept of **flow**, which entails doing a task for its own sake and being fully immersed in the present moment such that time seems to stand still. Flow can be experienced when doing a challenging task that requires skill and concentration, such as sport, dancing, studying, reading, or working. When people are in 'flow', they concentrate more, and feel happier, stronger, more active and creative, and ultimately feel more satisfied.

Relationships

Wellbeing is enhanced by surrounding ourselves with people — family, friends, colleagues, neighbours — with whom we can share our positive experiences. For example, teenage participants feel more happy, motivated, and strong when they are with their friends, than when they are alone (see also Chapters 7 and 8).

Meaning

As outlined by Viktor Frankl in his inspirational *Man's Search for Meaning*, our deepest desire and greatest task is to search for meaning and purpose in life — in work, in love, and in courage during difficult times (something that Frankl knew better than most, based on his experience in concentration camps in the Holocaust). Meaning is closely related to personal growth and the pursuit of valued goals, as well as to belonging to and providing service to something bigger than oneself, such as family, community, society, justice, religion, or spirituality.

Accomplishment/Achievement

Accomplishment or achievement is about setting goals and working towards achieving them. Successful achievement of meaningful goals leads to increased feelings of wellbeing and self-efficacy, which enable the formulation and successful pursuit of further achievable goals (see Chapter 7).

Positivity Can Be Cultivated

You might be a bit sceptical at this point. Is positivity *really* changeable? Aren't some people just happier and more positive than others, like Positive Padma and Negative Nelly? Absolutely! We can all think of a miserable, grumpy neighbour, colleague, or relative who could win the lottery, get a promotion, marry their dream partner, read this book cover to cover and *still* be a miserable grump. In fact, there is a lot of evidence to indicate that each person has a characteristic and stable level of happiness — like a baseline level (and much of this research comes from studying twins, so if you are a twin and you are reading this book, the scientific community thanks you). This 'baseline' is so stable, in fact, that research into lottery winners showed that although their happiness level increased after their win, it soon returned to their initial baseline (and this had nothing to do with whether or not they had spent their money). A similar effect was observed when researchers spoke to accident victims. Understandably, their happiness levels took a turn for the worse initially, but over time they too returned to their original happiness baseline.

But this doesn't mean that the Negative Nellies should just pack up and go home and leave the world for the Positive Padmas! Baseline happiness isn't the *only* contributing factor to our overall happiness and wellbeing. Only about half of your level of happiness is stable. That means that the other half is *changeable*. So even if you are a bit of a Negative Nelly (or a Grumpy George, or a Miserable Mika) there is hope for you. Of course, *some* of your happiness is determined by your circumstances — such as whether you have money, a good job, are healthy etc. These things contribute to your overall level of happiness, although not as much as you might think that they do. The rest of your happiness, however, is something you can change, and there are several ways you can build happiness and start to flourish.

Learning to Flourish

So, is there a Holy Grail of happiness? A Light Sabre of optimism? A Phaser of positivity? Just how can we go about learning to flourish? Whether you're flourishing or floundering is influenced by how you think and what you choose to do. You may be preparing an eye-roll for our answer, but it's a simple fact: you can learn to flourish by optimising your thinking. One road to flourishing is moving away from our natural negativity and cultivating a mindset that seeks out and celebrates positive experiences. In this next section, we will show you how to learn to flourish. We will focus on 3 main approaches for optimising thinking by shifting away from our tendency to focus on the negative:

1. Growth Mindset

2. Realistic Optimism

3. Positive Activity Interventions

You can apply each of these approaches to our SMR model to help you optimise thinking (see Figure 6.2). Each of these approaches involves changing your mind to have a more positive outlook (M_{OP}), which, in turn, can help you to optimise your responses (R_{OP}). As your responses become more optimal over time, you will begin to see how a more positive mindset can have a meaningful and sustained impact on your happiness and wellbeing.

 DIVING DEEPER 6.2

Broaden and Build

Another key figure in the area of positive psychology is Barbara Frederickson. Frederickson and her colleagues have proposed the **Broaden and Build** theory of positive emotion, which suggests that experiencing

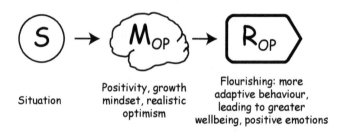

Figure 6.2 Having a positive outlook (M$_{OP}$) can lead to optimal responding (R$_{OP}$).

positive emotions encourages us to engage with our surroundings, *broadening* our world-view and cognitions. This results in a widening of our attention, unusual patterns of thought, creative thinking, and more holistic thinking. Conversely (as you might expect), negative emotions narrow our thinking and consequent actions, usually resulting in action tendencies such as fight or flight responses.

In addition to broadening our perspective, positive emotions also *build* personal resources, such as cognitive, physical, social, and psychological resources, which can have long lasting benefits. For example, Fredrickson and her team have shown that positive emotions not only improve cardiovascular health, but also undo the cardiovascular effects of negativity such as increased heart rate and blood pressure. Positive emotions can serve as a buffer against the effects of negative emotions, and as such, seem to have a protective role against the negative stress response and anxiety. Experiencing positive emotions can also increase our sense of connectedness to others, enable us to recognise their perspectives, and enhance our compassion towards them. Interestingly, this extends to those from other cultural backgrounds, with evidence that positive mood improves memory for faces of people from different races, as well as promoting greater compassion for them.

Finally, Fredrickson speculates that there exists an **upward spiral** effect, whereby the broaden-and-build effect of experiencing positive emotions leads to more positive emotion, which continues to build one's resources.

Growth Mindset

Have you ever been told that you are really smart, or good at sport? Or have you ever overhead your mother tell someone that 'he just doesn't have a head for maths' or that 'she's my artistic one'? How did hearing those things make you behave? Did it motivate you to become better at the thing you were told you were good (or bad) at? Or, did it make you feel like giving up? Research tells us that how you respond to being told that you are good (or no good) at something depends on your mindset (sounds like our SMR model, doesn't it?).

Psychological scientist, Carol Dweck, has identified two different types of mindsets: **Fixed** mindset and **Growth** mindset. Each of these mindsets leads to different responses to both success and failure. People with a Fixed mindset believe that basic qualities, like intelligence or talent, are fixed, unchangeable traits, and that these traits are more important than effort in determining success. They see success in terms of winning (i.e., performance), rather than in terms of personal development (i.e., learning). Conversely, people with a Growth mindset believe that (within reason) abilities can be developed through effort and hard work. These people are more likely to be learning-oriented, and to focus on mastery and competence. That is, their goal is to get better at something. People with a Growth mindset believe that although we all differ in our initial talents, abilities, or interests, anyone can change and grow through effort and experience.

TRY IT! 6.2

Do you Have a Growth or Fixed Mindset?

Growth Mindset Scale: To what extent do you agree with these statements. Be honest; there are no right or wrong answers:

Strongly Disagree	Disagree	Neutral	Agree	Strongly Agree
1	2	3	4	5

☐ 1. You can learn new things, but you can't really change how intelligent you are.

☐ 2. You can always change basic things about the kind of person that you are.

☐ 3. No matter how much intelligence you have, you can always change it quite a bit.

☐ 4. You can do things differently, but the important parts of who you are can't really be changed.

☐ 5. You are a certain kind of person, and there is not much that can really be done to change that.

☐ 6. Your intelligence is something very basic about you that can't change very much.

☐ 7. No matter what kind of person you are, you can always change substantially.

☐ 8. You can always substantially change how intelligent you are.

Scoring

Reverse score items 1, 4, 5, 6 (i.e., 1 = 5, 2 = 4, 4 = 2, 5 = 1). Add up your scores across the 8 items. If you scored 8–15, you are very high on Fixed mindset; if 16–23, you are relatively high on Fixed mindset; if 24–31, you are relatively high on Growth mindset; if 32–40, you are very high on Growth Mindset. What does this mean, and what can you do to change your mindset? Read on.

Importantly, the type of mindset you have helps determine how you respond to setbacks. When faced with a difficult situation, people with a Fixed mindset tend to fear failure, which can cause anxiety and loss of self-esteem, and often results in disengagement and feeling defeated. In contrast, in terms of our SMR model, having a Growth mindset is a great example of optimised thinking — people with a Growth mindset see difficulties as opportunities to learn, and challenge themselves to try new things. They see effort as integral to success and respond to setbacks by trying harder (see Figure 6.3). For people with a Growth mindset, challenging and stretching themselves is how they flourish.

Thomas Edison became the ultimate poster-boy for Growth mindset when he stated, '*I have not failed, I've just found 10,000 ways that won't work*'. More recently, Michael Jordan (arguably the most successful basketball player in recent times) was quoted as saying, '*I have missed more than 9,000 shots in my career. I have lost almost 300 games. On 26 occasions I have been entrusted to take the game-winning shot... and missed. And I have failed over and over and over again in my life. And that is why I succeed*'. Until the end of his career, despite how capable a player he was, Jordan was renowned for being the first to arrive at the gym and the last to leave.

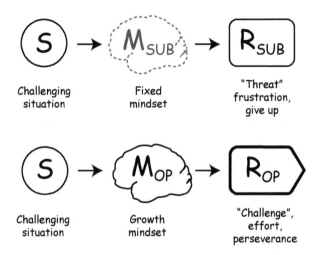

Figure 6.3 A Fixed mindset — a suboptimal belief that talent rather than effort creates success (M_{SUB}) — leads to a sense of threat or avoidance in the face of a challenge, frustration and ultimately giving up (R_{SUB}). Adopting a Growth mindset (M_{OP}) in the same challenging situation is an optimal way of thinking, leading you to embrace challenges, see effort as the path to success, and persist in the face of setbacks (R_{OP}).

But few of us are an Edison or a Jordan, so let's consider some new people who are slightly more relatable. Meet Fabio. Fabio has a Fixed mindset — he thinks of himself as 'not really a stats person' but 'very talented at basketball' (OK, so Fabio's a tiny bit of a Jordan). When faced with a stats assignment, Fabio becomes anxious, and is sure that he will fail. He convinces himself that there is no point even spending time on it, so he avoids even starting the assignment until it is too late to give it the time that it needs. Not surprisingly, Fabio fails the assignment, which he sees as evidence for his belief. 'See I was right! I'm just not a stats person,' says the voice in his head, patting himself on the back in an act of metaphysical contortionism, while at the same time whispering 'loser' under its cerebral breath (which, Fabio notes, could be fresher). When it comes to basketball, clearly Fabio doesn't need to practice as hard as everyone else (given what he describes as his 'Jordan-esque' talent). When his team loses the semi-finals he is really angry and is quite sure it is because the rest of the team isn't quite as good as he is! He storms off the court and considers quitting basketball for good (or at least finding a team that can handle his swagger).

Now let's consider Gavin. Gavin has a Growth mindset. He wears a t-shirt declaring 'It's not how good you are, it's how good you want to be'. He has a poster on his wall declaring 'FAIL = First Attempt In Learning'. His favourite word is 'yet', as in 'I'm not good at stats... yet'. Gavin might sound like a walking museum of lameness, but when presented with the same stats assignment as Fabio, Gavin realises that because he finds stats challenging, he will need to devote extra time to it. Gavin knows that although stats assignments can suck, this assignment is a learning opportunity that will benefit him in the long run, and that he might even learn to love stats (a big call, we know, but Gavin is open to the possibility). Gavin is also on Fabio's basketball team. Although he knows he is not the best player on the team, Gavin still spends hours practicing his 3-pointers, as he knows that practice is the route to improvement. Sadly, his team loses, but Gavin is content that he had given the game his best effort, and that he will try again next season. He knows that he is slowly but surely improving, and he truly loves playing basketball. After the game, Gavin stays on the basketball court and does what his hero Michael Jordan was rumoured to have done after each game — he re-shoots every basket that he had missed during the game.

Interestingly, people don't always have just one type of mindset. Many people may have a Fixed mindset for some things, and a Growth mindset for others. For example, Dweck suggests that you can have Fixed or Growth mindset for Love. People with a Growth mindset prefer a partner who encourages them to learn and helps them to become a better person and partner. Conversely, those with a Fixed mindset tend to want their ideal mate to put them on a pedestal and make them feel perfect and worshipped like a god! But the key message is that mindsets are just a system of beliefs, and just as you can change your mind, you can change your mindset in 3 'simple' steps:

1. **Identify your mindset.** When facing a challenge, what is the voice in your head saying to you? Is it telling you 'I can't do this' or 'I'll be a failure if I get it wrong, and everyone will laugh at me'. When you do end up failing (because we all do), does that voice throw a pity party and say, 'I knew I would fail because I'm just terrible at everything' or a blaming BBQ of 'that failure was X's fault, not mine!'. If some (or all) of this sounds familiar, you might be temporarily stuck in a Fixed mindset.

2. **Choose a Growth Mindset**. Remember, how you interpret challenges, setbacks, and feedback (even harsh criticism) is up to you. You can interpret setbacks with a Fixed mindset: as a sign that you are a failure and there's nothing you can do; or with a Growth mindset: as a sign that although you aren't there yet, you can increase your effort and improve yourself. Try to remind yourself that all successful people have experienced failure on the way to success, and that you can reframe failure as learning (if you're willing to). Try to have patience for your weaknesses, learn to view challenges as opportunities, and see if you can value the journey at least as much as the destination. These might seem like things your mum would say, but they are all about changing your mindset and that accompanying voice in your head that pops up when things don't go the way you had hoped.

3. **Don't stop trying**. When you do fail — and you will — instead of seeing it as an endpoint in the journey, think about what you can learn from that experience and the steps you need to take to improve. In basketball speak, go out and re-shoot those missed hoops! Of course, sometimes there is no amount of trying that can help you overcome an obstacle. Instead, you may have to adjust your goals. For example, your goal may have been to become the next Michael Jordan. First of all, you may not be tall enough to make it to the major leagues. Second, even if you are tall enough, despite all your effort you may simply not make the grade. Thus, you will need to adjust your goal to being good enough to make it to the minor leagues, and be willing to consider all the positives that might come from that achievement (because it would still be quite an achievement!).

Realistic Optimism

You might think that optimism is best captured by the Monty Python song, *Always Look on the Bright Side of Life* (Google 'songs that old people love'). Optimists have future expectations that are generally positive, whereas pessimists expect things to be generally negative. Optimists more easily see the positive in the world. But blind optimism can be unhelpful because it can lead to unrealistic expectations. Apart from making most people want to hurl, those sing-song Pollyanna-types who just know that everything is going to be fine (gosh darn it!) can find themselves struggling when a challenge arises that they can't sing their way out of, and they often ignore important warning signs that things might not be fine after all. In this section, we are going to focus on

realistic optimism, which is that brand of optimism that remains positive, but also acknowledges that 'everybody hurts', sometimes (Google 'songs that Generation X loves').

TRY IT! 6.3

How Optimistic are you?

Please answer the following questions about yourself by indicating the extent of your agreement using the following scale:

Strongly Disagreee	Disagree	Neutral	Agree	Strongly Agree
0	1	2	3	4

Be as honest as you can throughout and try not to let your responses to one question influence your response to other questions. There are no right or wrong answers.

☐ 1. In uncertain times, I usually expect the best

☐ 2. It's easy for me to relax

☐ 3. If something can go wrong for me, it will

☐ 4. I'm always optimistic about my future

☐ 5. I enjoy my friends a lot

☐ 6. It's important for me to keep busy

☐ 7. I hardly ever expect things to go my way

☐ 8. I don't get upset too easily

☐ 9. I rarely count on good things happening to me

☐ 10. Overall, I expect more good things to happen to me than bad

Scoring
Reverse code items 3, 7, & 9 (0 = 4, 1 = 3, 3 = 1, 4 = 0)
Sum items 1, 3, 4, 7, 9, 10

If you scored 19 or above you are highly optimistic, 14–18 reflects moderate optimism, and a score of 13 or below represents a low level of optimism. What does this mean and how can you change your level of optimism? Read on.

Some people think of optimism as a personality variable, very much like the happiness baseline that we described earlier. From that point of view, optimism might seem like a fixed thing: either you have it, or you don't. However, as you will find out shortly, optimism is something that can be learned. Optimism also goes much further than just being a 'glass half full' kind of person. It also influences how you explain to yourself (and to others) the causes of successes and failures, and how this influences your expectations for the future. There are a number of different stories we tend to tell ourselves to explain events. When something happens (be it good or bad) we can think of it as being due to internal factors (i.e., something we did) or external factors (i.e., something someone else did). We can think of the causes of this event as enduring (i.e., will always be there) or temporary (e.g., changeable), and we can think of them as global (i.e., relating to all the things) or localised (i.e., relating to only this thing). Whether you are an optimist or a pessimist will influence which of these stories you tell yourself when things go wrong, or when things go right (see Figure 6.4).

Imagine that you had a class test that you and your mates, Pierre and Ollie, failed abysmally. Pierre tells you that he failed because he is not very smart, then suggests that he is going to fail the subject because he won't be able to pass *any* assessments, and he is probably going to have to drop out of university because he is going to fail all his subjects, then his degree, then life itself (i.e., Pierre isn't great with failure). Ollie, on the other hand, tells you that the test was very hard, and he wasn't feeling his best today. He is confident that this was just a one-off, and that if he studies harder and more effectively for the rest of the semester, he will be fine.

Pierre is being a pessimist (in case you were unclear about that). Pierre leaps to attributing his failure to internal causes (he is not smart), permanent causes (he will fail all assessments in this subject), and global causes (he will fail everything that cometh hereafter) related to his learning. Ollie, on the other hand, is an optimist, attributing the same outcomes to external (hard test) and temporary (felt unwell) causes, with more local attributions (if I study harder and more effectively, I will still do well overall). In this way, Ollie reacts to setbacks

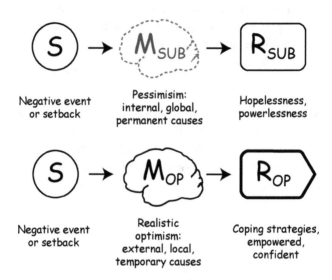

Figure 6.4 A suboptimal Pessimistic outlook, incorporating an attribution for a negative event to a cause that is internal, global, and permanent (M_{SUB}), results in a sense of powerlessness and lack of control over future events (R_{SUB}). A more optimal and optimistic belief in causes as local, temporary, and external (M_{OP}) fosters a sense of control over the situation, promotes the use of coping strategies, and ensures a more confident and empowered response to adversity (R_{OP}).

from a position of empowerment, in a manner that fosters his self-confidence, encourages him to persist, and contributes to greater wellbeing. If you were in the same situation as Pierre and Ollie, what would you attribute your failure to?

TRY IT! 6.4

Optimistic Mindset

Think of an event that happened that had a less-than-desired-for outcome. Write down your explanation for it.

Looking at your explanation, identify if it was:

- due to factors of an internal *or* external nature,
- temporary *or* permanent,
- isolated to a particular situation *or* global.

If your explanation included internal, permanent, and/or pervasive causes, try to reframe it to incorporate more external, temporary and/or specific causes.

Let's think back to that test that Pierre and Ollie failed. After the test, twins Opal and Pearl ask Ollie and Pierre to accompany them to the campus party the following weekend. Opal and Pearl are straight-up hotties, and Pierre and Ollie have been crushing on them all semester. How do optimists and pessimists deal with positive events such as this? In exactly the reverse way! Ollie fist-pumps the air, telling himself that Opal asked him out as he is a nice guy (and a fabulous dancer), reminds himself that every time he has spoken to Opal they seem to get on well, and thinks that, in general, people tend to like him. Pierre also accepts Pearl's invitation, but he is convinced that she only asked him because she feels sorry for him, that this will be a one-off date, and that he is generally a complete dating disaster!

Learning (Realistic) Optimism

The good news for Pierre (and you) is that how you explain events is a learnable skill, rather than an unchangeable personality trait. Again, these pessimistic beliefs about the cause of failure are simply an example of suboptimal thinking — M_{SUB}'s that can be changed.

But we need to take care that we are learning a realistic form of optimism. As we have already mentioned, unrealistic optimism, or wishful thinking, can have negative effects on an individual's wellbeing. For example, if Ollie didn't study at all for the test but still attributed his failure to the (unusual) difficulty of the test, he runs the risk of approaching other tests this way and may continue to explain away his failures rather than learning how to prepare for exams more effectively. Unrealistic optimism leads us to underestimate risks. As a result, we are more likely to get ourselves into risky situations. Sadly, one of the biggest groups of unrealistic optimists is adolescents and young adults, who often consider themselves to be bullet-proof! Unrealistic optimists tend to believe that bad things won't happen to them, which can have seriously negative consequences. So, as we learn optimism, it is important that we keep it realistic.

DIVING DEEPER 6.3

Optimism

Although average levels of optimism are roughly the same for men and women, research reveals some interesting gender differences regarding the things we are optimistic or pessimistic about. Men tend to be optimistic about work, attributing failure to external, temporary, and localised causes — however they seem to be pessimistic about interpersonal failures, often invoking permanent, pervasive and personal causes. In contrast, women are often more optimistic about social setbacks but less optimistic in their interpretations of failures in the workplace.

There are many benefits of a realistically optimistic outlook. Optimists experience less distress than pessimists when dealing with difficulties in life. Optimists are more likely to adopt approach strategies (rather than avoidance strategies) to deal with stress (e.g., help-seeking), and are less likely to suffer from depression and anxiety. Optimists tend to be more productive in the workplace and perform better at individual and team sports. Interestingly, in one study in the USA, optimism predicted academic performance more accurately than SATs.

Positive Activity Interventions

Positive activity interventions are simply activities that increase positive emotions, thoughts, and behaviours, leading to an increase in pleasure, engagement, meaning, and overall wellbeing. There are many, many different activities that have been shown to have this effect, including counting blessings, gratitude letters, doing good things, and using strengths. All of them have the same effect of optimising our thinking by making it more positive, as shown in Figure 6.5.

Each of the following positive activities is short and can be done daily, but not every strategy will work equally well for everyone, so part of the process is trying a few activities, and noticing whether they are enhancing your positive mood. Once you have identified those activities that lift your mood, you may like to mix them up and do a variety of different activities, rather than feeling like you must do the same one every day.

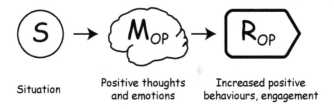

Figure 6.5 Positive interventions, which increase positive thoughts and emotions (M_{OP}), result in flourishing, in the form of increased engagement and positive behaviours (R_{OP}).

Three Blessings

Remember how your brain is hardwired to notice the negative in life, rather than the positive? One way of countering this natural negativity is to intentionally pay attention to the good stuff around you. There are many different ways of describing this task, but it all comes down to the same thing — regularly writing down things that went well for you, or that you are grateful for. People who do this on a regular basis describe feeling better about their lives in general, more optimistic about the coming week, and more connected with others. They also report being in a more positive mood, sleeping better, and feeling calmer. At first, you might find that you have to hunt quite hard in a *Where's Wally* kind of way for good things that have happened each day. However, as you continue do this, you might catch yourself increasingly noticing good things as they happen, so that you can capture them on your list at the end of the day.

One of the benefits of this task is that thinking about the good things that happened strengthens their memory trace and makes you more likely to remember them in the future — otherwise, they might just be forgotten. Another benefit is that you are savouring positive memories, which leads to positive emotion when you recall how you felt at that time.

⚑ TRY IT! 6.5

Using Three Blessings to Hunt the Good Stuff

Write down three good things that happened to you during the past day. They are likely to be relatively small like 'I had my favourite lunch today' but occasionally they will be big like 'I was offered a job today that I really wanted in the area I have chosen to study'.

1._____

2._____

3._____

Once you have recorded your three entries, rate your day on a scale of 1–10 where 1 is a bad day and 10 is the best day you could have had. This is a global rating of your entire day not just the three events you have recorded. Notice how this changes over time and reflect on what caused these changes.

Attempt to count your blessings at least 3 times each week.

The Gratitude Letter

In addition to the three blessings task, which is a private way to capture the goodness in your life, you can think about someone who has touched your life or done something to change your life for the better, and thank them for it. The three blessings activity encourages you to think about *what* you are grateful for; this activity focuses more on *why* this positive thing happened, and more specifically *who* helped it to happen. Saying thank you is nice, but fleeting. Writing down what you are grateful for not only affirms the positive aspects of your life but reminds you that there are people who care enough about you to make positive things happen. Although writing a gratitude letter has been shown to have a positive impact on the writer, the icing on the cake is hand-delivering the gratitude letter to the recipient (if you don't believe us, search 'Gratitude Letter' on YouTube, and get a box of tissues ready).

TRY IT! 6.6

Writing a Gratitude Letter

Focus on the times in your life when someone was particularly helpful, supported you, or made a positive difference in your life. Think of the people that fall into this category that are still alive — parents, grandparents, friends, partners, mentors, teachers, colleagues — who may not have heard you express your gratitude.

Write a letter of gratitude to the person you have chosen. The letter should be specific. You should describe why you are grateful to this person, what they did for you and precisely how it affected your life. You should also include how you remember their efforts and what you are doing now because of their efforts.

It is up to you whether you send the letter, or not. However, there is often much joy as a consequence of delivering that letter.

Do Good Things

The Dalai Lama says 'Be kind whenever possible. It is always possible'. This strategy involves doing exactly that — performing acts of kindness that benefit others, or make them happy. Kindness can be as simple as a smile, a thank you, or a kind word. It usually involves connection with another person, but not always. Kindness doesn't have to cost anything, but it might. At its heart, kindness embodies genuine thoughtfulness and caring for another person.

There are unlimited possible acts of kindness; we just need to look for opportunities to help those around us. You might make someone laugh, take time to listen, give (correct!) directions, donate your clothes to charity, or even just press the 'Door Open' button in a lift when you see someone approaching (as opposed to smashing the 'Door Close' button as hard as possible). People who regularly do things to help others have been shown to be happier, healthier, and feel a greater sense of connection and belonging. And the more good things you do, the happier you become!

🏳 TRY IT! 6.7

Doing Good Things

Each day, consciously carry out one or more acts of kindness.

Whether you do it individually, or as part of a volunteer group (that you may already be a part of) doesn't matter; the key is that the act is voluntary with the aim of helping someone.

Your act of kindness can be as small as washing a roommate's dishes, or helping a friend with an assignment, or can be something that requires more of your time like tutoring a student or volunteering at a local community centre. It doesn't matter what you do, as long as you are helping. Everything counts.

Try to vary the kinds of acts that you perform each day.

Cultivating Signature Character Strengths

What is best about you as a human being? What comes naturally to you and what do you enjoy doing? Are you the type of person who likes to watch the sunrise over the ocean? Are you the one most likely to make people laugh in an uncomfortable situation? Or are you the type of person who is constantly learning something new? Character strengths are the qualities that show you at your best. However, character strengths are different from your talents or capabilities, which are skills you are good at.

Think about what you consider to be your key character strengths from the following list:

Appreciation of beauty

Bravery

Citizenship

Creativity

Curiosity

Fairness

Forgiveness and mercy

Gratitude

Hope

Humor

Integrity

Judgment
Kindness
Leadership
Love
Love of learning
Modesty and humility
Persistence
Perspective
Prudence
Self–regulation
Social intelligence
Spirituality
Zest

Knowing our personal character strengths is powerful as it enables us to nurture what we are good at. Our strengths can affect everything that we do, and intentionally harnessing our strengths has a positive effect on wellbeing. People who use their strengths tend to be happier, more confident, more resilient, have more energy, feel less stressed, and are more likely to achieve their goals.

Having identifed your signature character strengths you might like to pick one strength to work on. The goal is to use this strength in a new way at home, school, work, etc. It should be an activity that you are not already doing. Remember that the emphasis is to work on a strength, not a weakness.

Some ideas for using your key character strengths are listed below.

Open-mindedness:

- Play devil's advocate on an issue that you have strong opinions about.

- Identify reasons for three actions that you are not happy with (e.g., not following through with a goal) and brainstorm better ideas for the future.

Perspective:

- Find purpose in the last five of your significant actions/decisions.

- Find someone wise (alive or someone who has passed on); read or watch a film on their life and identify how their life can guide your decisions and actions.

Persistence:

- Select an activity that you find engaging and meaningful and give 100% to it.

- Set 2–5 small goals weekly. Break them into practical steps, strive to accomplish them on time (or near to time), and monitor your progress from week to week (see Chapter 7).

Integrity:

- Refrain from telling small, white lies to friends and family (including insincere compliments), unless you know that at that time, they are too fragile to hear the truth. If you do (unnecessarily) tell a lie, admit it and apologise.

- Monitor every time you tell a lie, even if it is a small one. Try to make your list shorter every day.

Social Intelligence:

- Listen to your friends and family members empathically, without preparing rebuttals.

- Note and appreciate others in the light of their positive attributes.

Forgiveness and Mercy:

- Make a list of individuals against whom you hold a grudge, then either meet them personally to discuss it and forgive them, or visualise letting bygones be bygones.

- Evaluate your emotions before and after forgiving someone.

Humility/Modesty:

- Resist showing off if you notice that you are better than someone else.

- Notice if you speak more than others in a group situation and try to encourage others who have not spoken to do so.

Gratitude:

- Express your gratitude to someone who hasn't fully heard your gratitude before, through a personal visit or a letter.

- Every day, select one small yet important thing that you take for granted. Work on being mindful of this thing in the future.

Hope:

- Visualise where and what you want to be after one, five, and ten years. Sketch a pathway that you can follow to get there.

- Read about someone who succeeded despite difficulties and setbacks.

Spirituality:

- Spend some time every day in at least one activity that connects you with a higher power or reminds you about where you fit in the larger scheme of things.

- Spend ten minutes daily in breathing deeply, relaxing, meditating, and accepting your thoughts/emotions for what they are (see Chapter 4).

Note that a recent study reported that those who focused on improving their mid- or even low-level character strengths showed as much increase in wellbeing as did those who focused on signature strengths. This is congruent with the Growth mindset approach, that is, if we set our mind to it, including using effective learning strategies, we can 'grow' our capacities. Nevertheless, in a resource-limited world, it may make sense to focus on strengths first, unless there is a compelling reason to do otherwise (like that stats assignment!).

Savouring

Imagine you have been taken to one of the best restaurants in town and ordered the most incredible dessert. You have never seen or tasted anything like it in your life. What do you do? You probably take a photo, post it on the hippest social media site, and then start eating it slowly, taking small mouthfuls and letting them melt on your tongue so that you not only make the most of the experience, but also have a rich memory of the experience that you can revisit. Savouring is about being consciously aware of the experience of pleasure, both at the time of the event, as well as afterwards. At the time, you can sharpen your awareness of the event through taking photos, focussing intensely on different elements of the event, and thinking about what you have done to bring about the event. Afterwards, savouring includes conjuring up recollections of the event, reminiscing with others who were present, or bragging about it to those who weren't.

There is evidence for the effectiveness of savouring strategies in increasing positive emotions. Some examples include **Being Present**, that is, deliberately directing attention to the pleasant experience (see also the Mindfulness exercises in Chapter 4); **Positive Mental Time Travel**, where you vividly recall a positive event; and **Capitalising**, that is, communicating and celebrating positive events with others (See Chapter 8). Each of these is associated with an increase in positive mood.

Bringing It All Together

Choosing to do one or more of these strategies to enhance your positivity, adopting an optimistic explanatory style for when things go wrong, and fostering a Growth Mindset are all ways to optimise your thinking in order to help you to flourish in life. At the beginning of the chapter we met Padma and Nelly, who had very similar life circumstances but very different levels of life satisfaction. One morning Nelly missed her bus and grudgingly walked to uni. On the way, she passed Padma. Recognising Nelly from one of her classes, Padma struck up a conversation. The two girls shared stories from their week and soon realised how similar their lives were. At first Nelly was irritated by how positive Padma seemed about everything, but eventually she asked Padma why she seemed to flourish while Nelly was floundering.

At Padma's suggestion, Nelly started writing her 3 blessings at the end of her day and she soon realised how lucky she was to be living with friends, and to be seeing her aunt so regularly (yet sometimes she struggles to come up with a 3rd blessing!). Nelly even wrote her aunt a letter to express her gratitude for all that she has done for her. Every now and then when she passes the homeless man, Nelly gives him some change, or even just a smile. Nelly has concluded that although she is finding university challenging and doesn't always do as well as she hopes, she is trying her hardest and it is all a learning experience for her. And Gavin, a boy from her stats class who she asked for help, suggested that they go out for a drink, and they had a really nice time. Not-So-Negative Nelly suddenly can't keep the smile from her face and is looking forward to sharing her good news with her friends, Opal and Pearl.

Summary

- Although our mind is naturally attuned to the negative parts of our world (in order to survive), we also need to be able to switch to a more positive mindset when appropriate (in order to thrive).

- Seligman's PERMA is one approach to using tools to increase positivity and wellbeing.

- People with a Growth mindset believe that (within reason) abilities can be developed through planning, effort, and experience. Thus, they are more learning-oriented, focusing on mastery and competence.

- Realistic optimism is about focussing on the causes of events in a way that enables you to better control your future, by attributing bad events to local, external, and temporary factors (aligned with reality, rather than wishful thinking).

- Positive activity interventions are simply activities that increase positive emotions, thoughts, and behaviours, leading to an increase in a sense of meaning, and overall wellbeing.

More Resources

- What is positive psychology?
  https://www.youtube.com/watch?v=1qJvS8v0TTI

- Gratitude:
  https://www.youtube.com/watch?v=oHv6vTKD6lg

- Smiling Mind:
  https://smilingmind.com.au/

CHAPTER 7

Getting Motivated and Getting Things Done

It's a bright, sunny Sunday morning, and you have all day ahead of you free to work on that huge assignment that is due way sooner than you would like it to be. As you lie in bed contemplating your toenails, and checking all the overnight happenings on social media, you think to yourself 'All I need is a bit of motivation so I can get out of bed and get started'. Ah, motivation! That mythical magic bullet, that elusive beast you imbue with the power to solve all life's problems — our best friend, and worst enemy. But how do you get... and stay... motivated?

Motivation seems simple, but there are many aspects to it. We often think of motivation as the drive to take action to achieve a particular outcome or goal. This motivational drive can take us in different directions and can vary in how intensely we experience it. We can be motivated to move *toward* something (e.g., an adorable tiger cub), or to move *away* from something (e.g., the tiger cub's protective mother). The intensity of your motivational drive to move toward or away from the tiger cub can range from very mild (if you're not fussed by baby animals) to very strong (if the cub's mother is in an especially bad mood). Although there are different types of motivation, this chapter will focus on one specific type: intentionally moving toward your desired goals.

Our goal in this chapter is to provide you with an overall understanding of what motivation is, and give you tools for working out what your goals are and how you can achieve them. The idea is that if you use these tools to help you achieve a few small or simple goals, this will increase your confidence to take on new goals, and so on, leading to an 'upward spiral' of goal attainment, and a boost to your wellbeing.

But what is motivation really? One thing is for sure, it is not simple. It is tempting to think that motivation is just 'drive', but we can bust that myth by thinking about motivation as if it were a shiny new Tesla. True, the first thing a Tesla needs is power. Without power, you just sit there and don't go anywhere! But you don't buy a Tesla just to charge it; you buy it to go places in. So, motivation is about (a) the charge you need to get moving, and (b) the place you want to end up. In terms of motivation, that could be a destination (i.e., goal). How important your destination is to you will determine the 'charge' you start with, and thus how far and how fast you can go. You'll also need to map out the best *route* to get to your destination so that you do not waste time or get lost. Along the way you'll pass **milestones** (e.g., *sub-goals*), which can act like charging stations, topping up your energy to keep pursuing your ultimate goal. But despite your best planning efforts you might hit some road blocks on your journey, so you may need a few *back-up plans* and *alternative routes*. You may even decide to change your destination or goal, or you might be forced to take a detour. So, while fully charging your Tesla is a good start, it is only one part of the motivation story.

The main messages from this analogy are (a) choose a goal that is important to you (so that you start with a full charge), (b) develop tools to most effectively move toward that goal, and (c) think about back-up plans. Clearly motivation is not simply charging your Tesla. There are some more myths about motivation that need busting, so put your critical thinking caps on for the next section.

Motivation Myth-Busting

Some of the most common motivation myths come from the pseudoscience industry. Ordinary people (like you and me) often pay large amounts of money for 'the book', 'the program', or 'the motivational speaker' that will transform their lives. The false premise underlying most of these is that there are quick and easy ways to get motivated and stay motivated. Below are some myths needing to be busted before we move on to the reality of effectively defining and pursing our goals.

- **'Just think it, and it will come true.'** (To the tune of Walt Disney's 'When you wish upon a star'.) Yes, a positive attitude can make goal attainment easier, but just wishing for something won't make it happen. Neither will buying a book that claims this is true (for the science on busting this myth, see Gabrielle Oettingen's book, *Rethinking Positive Thinking).*

- **'I can do anything if I put my mind to it.'** People with little experience of life are often prone to this particular motivation myth. Only a very few people get to do 'anything' if they put their mind to it. Even then, although their effort and skill may have played a significant role in their goal achievement, luck would also have been a major player. For every Steve Jobs or Beyoncé there are thousands who put in enormous effort (and who were perhaps more skilled), but who unfortunately experienced the dark side of chance and so did not become tech billionaires or superstars. Because you may not wish to become a billionaire or a superstar, here is a more realistic example: many young people wish to become a lawyer. However, entry to law programs is highly competitive, usually involving special entrance examinations. Despite their best efforts (and despite the fact that they may have made great lawyers), many will fail to achieve a high-enough grade (even with many attempts) to gain an offer in a training program. Thus, at some point it will be realistic to revise career goals. This is not to say that one should not try more than once, because *some* people are successful on the second or third attempt. Just not *all* people, which may include you. Thankfully, humans are relatively resilient, and usually recover from the disappointment of not achieving something they really want, and they move onto a new, more achievable goal. So be prepared with a back-up plan.

- **'If at first you don't succeed, try, try, try again.'** If you fail at a task or at trying to achieve a goal, don't try again before you ask yourself the following questions: (1) did I fail because I had bad luck?; (2) did I fail because I do not *yet* have the relevant knowledge and skills, but I can acquire them?; or (c) did I fail because I don't 'have what it takes', and so I should give up this goal and try another? Let's say Aiden tried out for his local football team, hoping to become a professional football player, but he was not chosen. Perhaps he had bad luck — one of the two selectors was his sporting nemesis. Aiden might then contact the other selector to ask him how to improve his game before the next selection round. If Aiden has what it takes, the selector's advice, and lots of practice, will help him improve. But if the selector says that although Aiden is skilled, he can never make up for his lack of football-required-bulk, then Aiden knows that it is unlikely that he will make it as a professional football player, and he needs to give up that goal and just enjoy the local club competition. Instead Aiden may aim to become a sports physio, so he can make reasonable money while hanging out with the football superstars.

- **'Crash or crash through'** or **'All or nothing!'** This means that you throw everything you have at achieving a particular goal, and if you don't achieve it, then you will have failed and you should give up on this kind of goal forever. Perhaps some goals *are* a bit like that. For example, if Shynae wants to be the *first* to pilot one of Elon Musk's rockets to Mars, by definition she only has one chance, and so she should probably focus all of her resources on trying to achieve that goal. However, if she does not achieve that goal, she does not have to give up her rocket-pilot career, but rather change her goal (e.g., focus on achieving a long, successful, and enjoyable career in interplanetary piloting).

- **'Once I feel the motivation, everything will come together'** or **'I'm just not motivated, so there's no use trying'.** What you're doing here (and as in the opening paragraph) is reasoning with your emotions, which (as mentioned in Chapter 4) is unhelpful. Motivational drive doesn't just suddenly appear when you drink a can of Red Bull (despite what the ads say). Getting valued things done requires hard work on your part, which sometimes means *creating* the energy to initiate and maintain goal pursuit behaviour. The good news is that once you start on a particular task that you initially had low 'motivation' to undertake and manage to complete the first couple of sub-tasks, you should find yourself energised enough to continue. This is partly because of the automatic reward you get from accomplishment. Sometimes putting in the work to progress towards a goal is what is needed to help you to find a source of motivation, rather than the other way around.

- **'If I am not doing something just for my own sake, then how can I be motivated to do it?'** Although having an interesting and personally valued goal can make you more energised and increase the likelihood of achievement, we need to recognise that complete autonomy in goal choice is not always possible. If you do believe that you need to be completely captivated by something before you can pursue it, you may have been raised to value autonomy (being able to do whatever you want to do) above other psychological needs, such as relatedness (feeling that others care for you, and vice-versa; see *Self-Determination Theory* later in this chapter). Thus, we need to broaden our perspective on what is important in our lives, beyond our individualistic personal wishes. For example, Brody's parents want him to become a doctor or lawyer, but Brody is more interested in the economics and IT underlying crypto-currency. Because Brody values his relationship with his parents, and understands their need to provide him with opportunities for a secure future, Brody decides to study law, with economics and IT as minors. The minors will keep him interested enough to tolerate his law subjects, and who knows, he may end up enjoying law, even though this goal was not initially autonomously motivated. Moreover, Brody already knows there are significant legal challenges in the crypto-economics world, so studying law won't be a total waste of time. And if he finds that it is really *not* relevant to what he wants to do, he can always change the focus of his study after a year.

Preparing and Planning for Positive Change

Motivation is really about change. If your current state is not the state that you want to be in, then you feel a need to change from one state to another. For example, when you feel hungry you have an urge to consume food and lessen that feeling of hunger. So, you do what is necessary to acquire some food. Or, you decide that there is a particular job that you would find enjoyable and fulfilling, so you plan and work toward acquiring that kind of position. Basically, your psychological equilibrium or balance has been disrupted for whatever reason, and you feel a need to restore that sense of equilibrium. In terms of how this relates to our SMR model, see Figure 7.1.

Striving toward desired goals means that a change is needed. You want something that you currently do not have (you are in a state of wanting), and you need to make a change in order to obtain that desired outcome (a state of having). However, sometimes you may not be ready to even consider change, and this is particularly relevant in the health domain, where the impact of healthy or unhealthy behaviour is long-term rather than short-term. Psychologist James Prochaska and colleagues have identified the stages people go through in behavioural change, which we consider next.

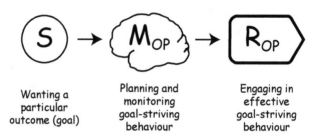

Wanting a
particular
outcome (goal)

Planning and
monitoring
goal-striving
behaviour

Engaging in
effective
goal-striving
behaviour

Figure 7.1 The situation (S) is a state of 'wanting' a particular goal or outcome, which will lead to thoughts relevant to planning and monitoring goal-striving behaviour (M$_{OP}$), which will lead to effective goal-striving behaviour (R$_{OP}$).

The Stages of Readiness for Behavioural Change Model

In some situations our behaviour is well practiced and has become habitual; for example most of us can cook, flirt, and pick up a textbook (often all at the same time) when needed. In other situations, however, this behaviour requires intentional improvement, for example cooking healthy food, negotiating safer sex, or boosting our study skills. A key to managing the difficulty you might experience in changing your behaviour is to better understand how *ready* to change you actually are, and this is where the **Stages of Readiness for Behavioural Change Model** is useful (see Figure 7.2). The model may help you understand where you are in this process. Note that this approach comes from health psychology, whereby behavioural change is usually directed toward changing from a state of un-healthiness (e.g., lack of exercise; smoking) to a state of healthiness.

A key part of change is identifying that change is needed. People in the **pre-contemplation** stage (Stage 1) often aren't ready to acknowledge that their target behaviour — be it nail-biting, procrastination, or poor eating habits — is problematic. This is a stage that many of us can get stuck in. For example, you may be a smoker in the pre-contemplation stage, where you are not ready to admit that you have a health problem. Once you acknowledge that there may be a better way of doing things, and intend on making some changes (Stage 2), the next step is to set about making concrete plans for change (Stage 3). For example, you might sign up for a stop-smoking program and ask your friends and workmates to support you while you are trying to quit. Taking **action** (Stage 4) to implement the plan and maintaining change (Stage 5)

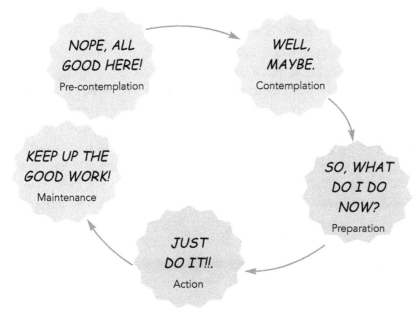

Figure 7.2   Prochaska et al.'s (1992) Stages of Readiness for Behavioural Change Model.

despite occasional lapses, are critical steps to sustained behavioural change. This last stage requires that you learn new strategies to prevent or recover from relapse to old behavioural patterns. In reality, this journey is usually a bumpy one, and most people move back and forth between stages (e.g., 2 & 3) and experience some gains and some losses along the road to more permanent behavioural change. This stage model may seem a little simplistic, but it allows us to work out where we are in the process of significant behavioural change, which in turn guides us in determining how to progress through the stages. It is important to note that while we often have intentions to change (Stage 2), sometimes implementing these changes (Stage 4 and 5) doesn't quite happen. This is called the **intention-behaviour gap**. Many of the tools in this book should help to bridge that gap.

In terms of our SMR model, you might be able to see how optimising our thinking can help us at each stage in this model of change. For example, believing that there is no problem at Stage 1 likely leads to suboptimal responses

(R_{SUB}'s). More optimal beliefs that there is a problem and that change is possible, even though it will be difficult and there may be lapses, can lead to more optimal behaviours (R_{OP}'s) and outcomes.

Let's consider a more detailed example of how motivational issues and the need to change relate to our SMR model. Ruby has just started at university and is living by herself in a tiny apartment. She is struggling on all fronts and is finding it increasingly difficult to get out of bed each morning. When Ruby was in high school she knew what she wanted: to move away from home to this great university, get a good degree, and then catapult herself into a wonderful career. Yes, it was pretty exciting packing up and moving into her own place, but the reality of life at uni is a new situation (S) for Ruby, one for which she was under-prepared. The demands of university study are very different from those at high school, with little structure and support. She did not have the psychological strategies (M) necessary to optimally manage herself and her academic workload (R), which left her struggling. Due to her belief that she needed to 'do it alone' (M_{SUB}), she was not seeking help (R_{SUB}). On weeknights, Ruby would be up late trying to study (with many interruptions from WhatsApp), and on weekends she was working late at a local bar. During the weekdays, Ruby would roll out of bed 15 minutes before class started, throw some clothes on, and arrive just in time, having had a nourishing break-fast of M&Ms. Ruby was barely scraping by in a highly competitive degree and couldn't afford any academic slip-ups. Ruby sometimes wondered why she was even going to uni, and whether she was cut out for it.

By chance Ruby came across Olivia, a psychology student who encouraged Ruby to: (a) learn more about herself and about being ready for change (M_{OP}), and (b) learn self-management and academic skills (M_{OP}) that she could apply to redefine her goals and engage in effective goal-pursuit behaviour (R_{OP}). For example, Olivia told her about the Stages of Change model, and Ruby decided to apply this to her goals of getting to bed earlier and having some breakfast. A week after Ruby had made her initial intentions, she reflected on her progress thus far. She had managed to turn off her screens at 10pm once, and to get out of bed in time for breakfast on one or two occasions. Ruby realised that she had fooled herself into thinking that she was in the action stage, when actually she was stuck in the contemplation phase. She hadn't successfully put her plans into action because she wasn't fully committed. She decided then and there to review her preparation and have a better go at taking action.

🏳 TRY IT! 7.1

Are You Ready to Change *Your* Behaviour?

This exercise will give you a taste both for applying the Stages of Change model, and for some of the strategies that we will focus on in many of the exercises to come in this chapter.

Step 1. Choose a behaviour that you have been thinking about changing, such as getting more exercise, or improving how you communicate with your partner.

Step 2. How important is changing that behaviour to you? Put a number to it (0 = not at all important; 5 = moderately important; 10 = extremely important).

Step 3. If it is at least moderately important, consider why it is that you have not yet changed that behaviour (i.e., the barriers). Are you not yet fully committed (Stage 2)? Have you not yet put in the necessary preparation (Stage 3)? Have you made a change, but then slipped back to your old way of doing things (Stage 5)? What would increase the chances of you making positive progress through each of these stages?

Step 4. Now, write down a plan for changing the behaviour you want to change. What will you do? When? Where? Try to be specific.

Step 5. Next, list all of the resources (e.g., equipment, people with particular skills) you will need to help you implement the change (Stage 3).

Step 6. Make a plan for how/when/where you will obtain those resources.

Step 7. Next, brainstorm possible barriers or setbacks (Stages 3/4/5), write them down, then brainstorm how you will handle those setbacks, proactively (preventing them from happening) and reactively (when/if they do happen).

Step 8. Finally, *publicly* commit to taking the first step (preferably today or at least this week), for example by telling your friends on social media. In short — do it!

It is useful to consider whether the goals we set simply help us survive, or if they also help us thrive. Also, we take things for granted, like having enough good food, adequate sleep, and loved-ones who care for us. A useful framework for considering if we're surviving or thriving is Maslow's Hierarchy of Needs Model, which we consider next.

Maslow's Hierarchy of Needs Model

Maslow identified a pyramid of needs, whereby the most basic needs include a need for food, water, and shelter, followed by the need for safety and security, love and belonging, and acceptance and esteem. At the top of the pyramid is self-actualisation — the realisation of one's full potential (see Figure 7.3).

Figure 7.3 Maslow's hierarchy of needs.

A major tenet of Maslow's model is that the basic needs at the lowest level (e.g., food) must be satisfied before you can begin to satisfy higher needs (e.g., esteem or self-actualisation). Imagine you turned up at your favourite restaurant for a meal with a friend but had to wait for 45 minutes to get a table. By the time the food arrived you may have noticed yourself becoming hangry. You were in no fit state to discuss your friend's relationship woes until you had some food in you, after which you were all ears and compassion. This reflects Maslow's hierarchy, where your lower level physiological need for food must be satisfied before attending to higher order needs like love and belonging. It should be noted that there are exceptions to this 'rule', but nevertheless the model remains a useful taxonomy for people to understand their own needs and behaviours, and to acknowledge possible *conflicts* between different needs. The model also reminds us to set goals not just to survive, but also to thrive (see Chapter 6).

In addition to the needs outlined by Maslow, it is also useful to consider whether or not our goals cover the three basic **Psychological Needs** identified as essential to our wellbeing by Ryan and Deci's Self-Determination Theory (SDT).

Self-Determination Theory (SDT) and Psychological Needs

SDT encompasses three psychological needs (somewhat similar to the needs in Maslow's model): *Competence, Autonomy,* and *Relatedness.* **Competence** refers to your sense that you can do things well and are able to improve your abilities. **Autonomy** is feeling a sense of choice and control in what you do in your life. Finally, **Relatedness** is the feeling that you are connected to and cared about by others (see Chapter 8).

It is important to note that a high sense of wellbeing is achieved only if all three needs are satisfied. Take the example of Mahreen. She is very good at her job (i.e., high level of competence) and has satisfying relationships with family and friends (i.e., high level of relatedness), but she does not like the work she does, and feels a lack of control over non-work domains of her life (i.e., low level of autonomy). As such, she does not feel a high sense of wellbeing.

Research suggests that individuals can benefit from (a) assessing the extent to which each of their psychological needs is being met, and then (b) changing or creating at least one aspect of their life to help fulfil each need. For example, Mahreen may not be able to immediately change her employment situation, but she may choose to commit extra time to a meaningful hobby, thus increasing her sense of autonomy. Additionally, once her family is no longer dependent on her income, she may even retrain in an area that she always wanted to pursue. Thus, despite the reality that one cannot always pursue intrinsically motivating activities, there may be a number of options for realigning activities to achieve adequate satisfaction of all three basic psychological needs.

When considering your goals, for example in the next section, work out whether achievement will satisfy your basic psychological needs. Are all needs equally represented? If not, why not? Are you taking some things for granted (e.g., that your girlfriend will 'always be there' to satisfy relatedness — and other needs). If so, perhaps you should be creating a goal to help ensure that the 'taken for granted' is maintained (i.e., focussing on spending time and effort on your relationships).

Remember Ruby? Ruby realised that sometimes she felt a bit lost and lonely, living alone and so far from her family. She also realised that although she really *did* want to be doing her degree, she did not know how to manage the academic workload. She took some workshops that helped build her study, communication, and organisation skills, and while she was doing that, she made some new friends who ended up helping each other study better by hosting group study sessions. Although Ruby's need for Autonomy was already being met, as she was doing a program that she really wanted to do, her need for Competence and Relatedness were met by building up her skills and making new connections. Although there were still some challenges, including disappointing grades, uncompromising professors, and lazy group-work class-mates, enough of Ruby's needs were being met that these challenges did not get her down too much.

Tools to Help You Make Change Happen

So, are you ready to consider how you can best change your behaviour to meet your goals? As we said at the beginning of the chapter, we'd like to start with some small goals you already have in mind, using simple tools, and build from there. We hope that achieving some initial small goals will give you the confidence boost you need to tackle more challenging goals. For this reason, we've split the upcoming motivation tools into two categories: Simple Tools and Super Tools. The Simple Tools are designed to quickly get you on track toward achieving your existing goals. We give you just an introduction to the more complex Super Tools, which are designed to help you really flesh out how you will achieve larger goals that require a bit more thought and planning. Our advice is to read through both sections and decide whether your goal needs a little Simple, or a lot of Super. You can either take a very considered approach with Super Tools, *or* if you have a goal or two ready to go, try the Simple Tools in the next section (note: you might want to refer back to *TRY IT! 3.6* and *3.7* in Chapter 3, where you identified some goals).

Simple Tools

These Simple Tools are primarily about Prochaska and colleague's Stage 3: Preparation.

The GROW Model

The GROW model asks you to consider how important your goal is, and the reality and obstacles relevant to that goal. Then you'll need to decide on some concrete behavioural plans to pursue your goal. This model has been used extensively within the coaching domain where an individual endeavours to identify and maximise their potential.

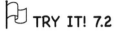 TRY IT! 7.2

The GROW Model

The GROW model has four steps. Write down your response to each.

G = Goals

Identify your Goals and write them in a list, rating the importance of each goal out of 10 (10 = most important).

Then, for the most important goals, list all *measurable* sub-goals (i.e. essential steps along the path toward achieving your goal).

R = Reality

Consider the Reality of your current situation, other demands, any conflicting goals, and potential barriers to achieving your goal.

O = Options

Brainstorm the full range of options/strategies for achieving your most important goals. For each option, use the headings below to help you consider the pros and cons, as well as any challenges and possible solutions. Then, decide which option/strategy to try.

Option/Strategy:

Pros:

Cons:

Challenge/Obstacle:

Solution:

W = Way forward

Having identified your preferred behavioural strategy, likely challenges, and their possible solutions, write down your plan of action. Make steps specific and specify time frames. Also, determine how you will measure your progress toward your goal.

SMART GOALS

SMART stands for: **Specific, Measurable, Attainable, Relevant, Time-bound.** This is a popular approach in the business world, with some evidence to support its effectiveness. For example, when students applied the SMART goal method to the formulation of their goals, they were more likely to attain their goal, and to report increased satisfaction of their basic psychological needs and increased sense of meaningfulness in their lives.

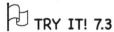 TRY IT! 7.3

SMART Goals*

Write down your goal (i.e., 'I intend to ...'). Now answer the following questions to make sure your goal is truly SMART.

S = Specific

A specific goal has a much greater chance of being accomplished than a general goal. For example, a general goal would be: 'Get in shape.' But a specific goal would say: 'Join the gym and workout 3 days a week, for the next three weeks.' To help you set a specific goal, consider answering these 'W' questions:

Where: Identify a location.

When: Establish a time frame.

What: What *exactly* do I want to accomplish?

Who: Who is involved? Consider who can help you achieve the goal (e.g., if you are studying for a test, ask a fellow student to study with you or test you on the material beforehand).

Why: Specific reasons, purpose, or benefits of accomplishing the goal. Consider which Maslow/SDT needs this goal would satisfy.

M = Measurable

Establish concrete criteria for measuring progress towards the attainment of each goal you set. This may be in terms of sub-goals that you can check off. When you measure your progress, you are more likely to stay on track, reach your targets, and experience the exhilaration of achievement that spurs you on to continue making effort towards reaching your goal. Ask questions such as: 'How much? How many? How will I know when it is accomplished?'

A = Attainable

You can attain most goals you set when you *plan your steps* wisely and establish a *time frame* that allows you to carry out those steps. Goals that may have seemed far away and out of reach eventually move closer and become attainable, not because your goals shrink, but because you grow and expand to match them. Write down the steps required on your way to attaining your goal, what resources you will need, and how you will acquire those resources.

This will help you to determine whether your goal is attainable, or unattainable (SMURT!).

R = Realistic

A goal must represent an objective toward which you are both *willing* and *able* to work. A goal can be both high-level (e.g., an A on an assignment) and realistic; you are the only one who can decide how high you aim when setting your goals. A realistic high goal is often more achievable than a low one because a high goal (if you are really committed) results in high motivational energisation. Ways to know if your goal is realistic:

- Have you accomplished anything similar in the past?
- What conditions would have to exist to accomplish this goal? Do they exist?
- Do you have the necessary resources?
- Would others you respect see this goal as realistic (ask them!)?

Know thyself, and set realistic goals!

T = Time-bound

With no time frame tied to a goal, there's no sense of urgency. If you want to lose 5 kilos, when do you want to lose it by? 'Someday' won't work. But if you anchor it within a timeframe, 'by May 1st', then you've set your unconscious mind into motion to begin working on the goal.

What is your time frame? Why?

* adapted from Bahrami & Cranney (2018)

Super Tools

Now that you have a few Simple Tools to get you started, it's time to introduce you to some more in-depth Super Tools. This approach focuses primarily on

Prochaska and colleagues' Stages 3 (preparation), 4 (taking action), and 5 (maintaining change). In this section, we're going to assume you have undertaken some of the initial work regarding your 'desired future', including working out what your values, interests, and capabilities are (see Chapter 3). We're also going to assume that you have some long-term, medium-term, or short-term goals in mind. The model we present here takes the best aspects of several efficacious approaches to achieving goals. Take a look at the full model in Figure 7.4. You'll notice there are 8 steps, roughly divided into three phases (we don't call it Super Tools for nothing!).

Getting prepared (goal-planning behaviour):

1. Write down **4–5 goals** that will help you to achieve your desired future.

2. **Elaborate your goals** to fully flesh out potential benefits to yourself and others.

3. **Evaluate and prioritise your goals**, and revise if necessary.

4. Determine preparation and implementation of **sub-goals** and **behavioural strategies**, including **milestones**, and revise if necessary.

5. **Identify specific obstacles** to achieving your goals and identify **strategies for dealing with those obstacles** (and have **back-up plans**), and revise if necessary.

Getting it done (goal-pursuit behaviour):

6. Start getting going by taking action to attain the **first implementation sub-goal**.

7. Keeping it going by continuing with the **goal pursuit plan**, including **monitoring and reviewing** progress, and **revising** sub-goals and behavioural strategies when necessary.

Getting goal wise (goal-review behaviour):

8. Reflect on whether the goal is attained or not. A final step is to **review** your goal-related behaviour and determine **what you can learn** from the process to inform future 'getting valued things done' behaviour.

Before you get started, we should probably clarify what **goal planning** and **goal pursuit** is, with the help of our friends Simon and Michael. Simon is in the last year of his history and politics degree program. When he chose his majors in

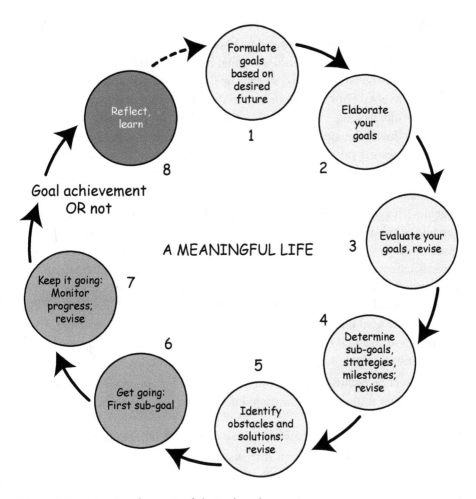

Figure 7.4 Intentional pursuit of desired goals.

first year, he was very interested in the subjects, and he expected he'd get some kind of graduate job when he finished his studies, but he has not done any serious research on job prospects. Although he's been fairly distracted with extracurricular activities, he is keeping his grades up to at least a B.

Michael is also in the last year of his history and politics degree program. When he chose his majors in first year, he was very interested in the subjects, and knew he wanted his first graduate job to be in a government department, although at that time he did not know exactly which one. During his early years at university, Michael took whatever opportunity he could to explore possible career paths. For example, he organised volunteer work in a different department in each vacation period. Also, with the help of the university's career centre, he is setting up informational interviews with people in positions that he thinks he would enjoy, so that he'll have a better idea of what those positions involve. Thus, although he still does not know exactly where he will focus his job-seeking efforts in the second half of the year, Michael has narrowed down the options, has a plan for further investigation, and has chosen interesting subjects and extracurricular activities that will also give him further knowledge and skills that government employers value.

In these scenarios, Michael has set a relatively specific goal and created a plan to achieve it (goal planning), which he is in the process of implementing (goal pursuit). On the other hand, Simon only has a vague wish about gaining graduate employment (not really goal planning) and has not taken any real steps towards achieving this wish (not even close to goal pursuit). Research tells us that people who set explicit goals are more likely to attain those goals, and tend to be more successful, happy, and healthy. But goal-setting is not enough. You also need effective goal planning and goal pursuit tools to help you get there. There is strong evidence that improved goal planning and analysis skills increase your goal attainment (including increased grades) and wellbeing.

In the section below, we set out our simplified 8-step approach for goal setting. See the Rubber Brain website for more information (www.therubberbrain.com).

STEP 1: Formulate Goals to Help Move Toward Your Desired Future

You might be surprised to learn that just writing down your goal appears to increase the probability of obtaining that goal. But you can go further. Having identified a goal, you can make it more achievable by undertaking some planning and analysis activities.

STEP 2: Elaborate the Positive Outcomes/Consequences of your Goals

Thinking about the consequences of your goals both for yourself and others can help energise you to take action. This step should help you to gain a better understanding of how important the goal is for you, as well as the consequences of achieving this goal. For example, Robert may feel some pressure to achieve at least B grades for all his subjects, even the ones he does not particularly like or finds tough. For Robert to become energised to put in the required work, it may help if he spends some time thinking about the positive consequences of obtaining at least a B in each course, even the very boring challenging ones. For example, those grades may help him to get a job at a top global company, which will provide him with exciting work alongside talented colleagues (not to mention the opportunity to travel).

STEP 3: Evaluate and Prioritise your Goals

Now that you have chosen your specific goals to help you achieve your desired future, you need to step back and analyse your goals to check that they are realistically attainable. Moreover, a key challenge in the early stages of getting things done is prioritising your goals and associated tasks. Often we prioritise things that are easiest, or most enjoyable, or that seem to be urgent. Stephen Covey suggests that, although urgency is a critical dimension of prioritisation, the other key dimension is importance (see Figure 7.5).

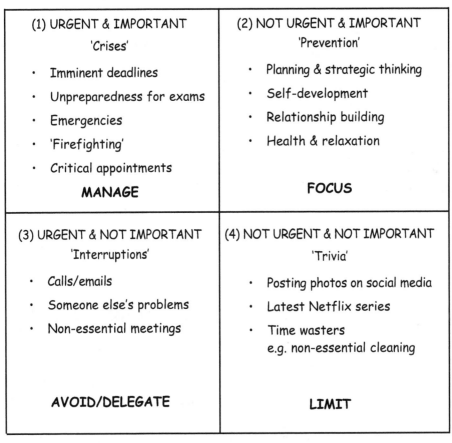

(1) URGENT & IMPORTANT 'Crises' • Imminent deadlines • Unpreparedness for exams • Emergencies • 'Firefighting' • Critical appointments **MANAGE**	(2) NOT URGENT & IMPORTANT 'Prevention' • Planning & strategic thinking • Self-development • Relationship building • Health & relaxation **FOCUS**
(3) URGENT & NOT IMPORTANT 'Interruptions' • Calls/emails • Someone else's problems • Non-essential meetings **AVOID/DELEGATE**	(4) NOT URGENT & NOT IMPORTANT 'Trivia' • Posting photos on social media • Latest Netflix series • Time wasters e.g. non-essential cleaning **LIMIT**

Figure 7.5 Covey's (2004) Important x Urgent Matrix for goal prioritisation. Adapted from http://alumni.sae.edu/2015/03/17/get-things-done-creatively-coveys-time-management-grid/

We can categorise our list of tasks or goals according to whether they are urgent and important (Quadrant 1), important but not yet urgent (Quadrant 2), unimportant and urgent (Quadrant 3), or neither important, nor urgent (Quadrant 4). Clearly you need to prioritise those things that are both important and urgent ('do it!'). But once you have identified those things that are important but not yet urgent (Quadrant 2 items), you should try to proactively 'devote time' to dealing with them before they become urgent, and try to stick to that commitment. Quadrant 2 activities require proactivity, and produce increased effectiveness, less distress, and less need to engage in Quadrant 1 'fire-fighting' activities. Less time, if any, should be spent on Quadrants 3 ('delegate it') and 4 ('dump it') because you have already identified that they are not important, so don't let them hijack you from getting important things done! As urgency (and even importance) changes over time, it is important to undertake this exercise of reviewing quadrants on a regular basis (i.e. daily or weekly).

STEP 4: Determine Sub-goals, Behavioural Strategies, and Milestones

At this point you should have a list of goals that you really value. Now to the nitty-gritty: what do people actually *do* to reach their valued goals? Step 4 is the beginning of the process of making specific plans for goal pursuit. When you have a complex goal, you must first determine the general approach or route toward your goal. There may be several. For example, if you wanted to lose 5 cm from your waistline, you could try dieting, exercising, or both! Then, you need to form the necessary sub-goals or tasks for both the *preparation* and *implementation* and work out your specific behavioural strategies for pursuing those sub-goals (e.g., *preparation*: buying gym shoes; *implementation*: going to the gym Tuesday, Thursday, and Saturday at 6am). Sub-goals provide a way to measure your progress toward your goal.

Sometimes our good intentions to achieve a goal do not translate into action, perhaps unsurprisingly! This is what is called the 'intention–behaviour gap', and it often leaves us feeling disappointed in ourselves. Fortunately, a technique called **implementation intentions** can help you close the intention–behaviour gap by helping you to implement what you will do and how you will manage the obstacles that inevitably arise. Implementation intentions have been shown to be particularly effective when they take the form of **If-then** statements. For example, a goal such as 'attend 3 gym sessions per week' may include the following If-then statement: '*If* it is near bed-time on Monday, Wednesday, and Friday, *then* I will set my alarm for 5:30am, get all my gym gear ready, and ask my partner to positively encourage me to go to the gym once the alarm goes off'. Make sure you have your if-then statements in an accessible place, so that you can read them when necessary, and re-memorise them when you have a few spare minutes. Making your implementation intentions 'automatic' by rehearsing them is more likely to result in successful attainment of goals.

There are often specific resources and skills that you need in order to achieve a specific goal. For example, if your goal involved attending a gym for fitness, you would need concrete items like running shoes and a gym membership. However, if you are writing an essay, you will need to know the essay requirements (e.g., the assessment description, a marking rubric), have access to the research materials, and know about how to construct an essay. In addition, for most types of goals you will need some general resources, such as time-management skills. If you do not have these resources and skills, it is best if you acquire them before you begin, or at least during the process, so factor in the time to do this in your overall plan. And to help you out in terms of studying for an exam, this chapter comes with some evidence-based principles to make the most of your study time (unfortunately we cannot offer you free gym membership).

Setting concrete milestones for each goal helps you to monitor your progress, as well as to increase the perceived attainability of your goal, which increases your motivation. There are two ways to approach this, depending on the kind of goal. If the goal relates to a quantifiable characteristic or activity that you can make continuous progress toward, then you can identify progress milestones. For example, Tom wishes to increase his upper body strength by being able to bench press 60kg within 4 months. He can now bench press 40kg, so he knows that he needs to gain a minimum of an additional 2.5kg each fortnight. Setting fortnightly milestones serves as a valuable way to track your sub-goals and give a clear sense of the incremental achievement of your goal.

The other kind of goal involves qualitatively different sub-goals that may or may not happen in sequence, that can also be thought of as milestones. In the earlier example of Michael gaining a graduate position in a government department, there were qualitatively different tasks he had planned to undertake, which he could 'tick off' along the way. Each 'tick' would energise him to put in the effort to accomplish the next task.

Regardless of the type of goal, an essential task is to set up a customised 'tracking system' of your milestones that will enable you to see when your behaviour is moving you towards your goal. This might be in terms of a qualitative 'to-do' list of tasks, or a more quantifiable set of milestones that can be measured. There are apps that can assist you to do this, or you can go old-school with pen and paper.

Time-management is also relevant to Step 4 in terms of determining the timeframe of your goals and sub-goals, and whether your timeframes are feasible, particularly given your many goals that 'compete' for your limited time. See the 'Additional Tools' section later in this chapter.

STEP 5: Identify Specific Obstacles, and Strategies for Dealing with those Obstacles

Step 5 asks you to identify potential obstacles to the achievement of each goal/sub-goal, and to devise plans for dealing with or preventing those obstacles. In the example above, you might have the following **If-then** statements to deal with obstacles: 'If it is raining when the alarm goes off, *then* I will drive my car to the gym instead of running there; If I am feeling very tired or demotivated when the alarm goes off, *then* I'll have already asked my partner to be especially supportive of me making the extra effort'. Sometimes there are different routes to achieving a particular goal or sub-goal. Thus, if you encounter insurmountable obstacles in a particular route, you may be able to try a different approach. Other times there is only one route, or all routes are blocked. You may then have to accept that you will need to change your goal. Thus, you not only need back-up plans for your approach to achieving your goal, but also a back-up goal in case those back-up plans do not work.

STEP 6: Getting Going (Implement Sub-goal 1 Strategy)

Once you have completed your preparation checklist, your tracking system and obstacle-busting if-then approach, you are ready to take action! Taking the first step (e.g., going to gym on Saturday) means that you have entered the goal pursuit stage (nice one!). Taking this first step can be the most difficult for some people. If things don't go exactly according to plan, remember that everyone makes mistakes occasionally (but you're unlikely to, given all your preparation). The only way you can see if your goal is achievable and that your plan works is to just *do it!* Beware procrastination (see 'Additional Tools' section) — perhaps set yourself a non-negotiable starting date (and stick to it).

STEP 7+: Keeping it Going (Work Through Sub-goal Pursuit Plan)

Once you have taken the first step you'll likely be feeling more energised, and now you need to continue with the goal-pursuit plan, with a particular emphasis on remembering and following your if-then intentions. Step 7 also includes monitoring and reviewing your progress (using the milestones you identified in Step 4), and revising sub-goals and strategies when necessary. In particular, you will need to monitor the timeliness of your sub-goal completion and consider what is happening with competing goals/tasks/demands in your life (revisit Steps 1 and 3; also, see the Time Management Tools in 'Additional Tools' section). You might find that despite adhering to your strategies, achieving your sub-goals takes longer than you had anticipated, so you might need to tweak your strategies and sub-goals. By reflecting on your progress as you go, you may even find that you need to modify or even let go of the goal if it no longer seems feasible or important.

STEP 8: Goal Review

Whether the goal is attained or not, a final step is to *review* how you set, planned, and pursued your goal, and determine *what you can learn* from the process. Ask yourself a series of questions to help you decide what worked well, and what to do differently next time.

For example:

- Did you enjoy the goal pursuit process, such that you'd want to do something similar again, or not? Why?

- Was your goal pursuit behaviour in line with your values and interests?

- Did you have the required knowledge and skills, and if not, do you need to work on that more before you pursue a similar goal?

- What do you think were the strengths and weaknesses in your goal setting, planning, and pursuit behaviour? How can you improve for next time?

- Did you find out who is able to support you in your goal pursuit, and who is not?

This new knowledge will inform what goals and strategies you choose next.

Let's check in with Ruby. Ruby had tried goal setting for her essay but was disappointed with her result. Ruby reminded herself that she was new at this university game, and that she could still gain something positive from the experience. She realised that she could learn from 'not quite achieving' a goal, so that she is more likely to achieve her goal next time. For Ruby, this might mean approaching the marker for more feedback, and getting more instruction in essay writing.

In general, this chapter is mostly about ways to satisfy your psychological need for competence, primarily through your choice of effective goal-related behaviours. We all begin new roles without much knowledge or experience, so it makes sense that we might have to purposefully learn new information and skills to succeed in those roles. When you fail at achieving a goal in any new role, instead of criticising yourself, try critically analysing where things may have gone wrong, using the previous steps as a guide. When you successfully achieve a goal, you will acquire greater confidence to take on new tasks, creating an 'upward spiral' of success, self-efficacy, and continued motivation and engagement. By achieving goals within the different domains of who you are — for example, partner, entrepreneur, student — you consolidate your sense of identity within that domain — that is, you are a successful partner, entrepreneur, student.

Additional Tools for Getting Things Done

In this section we provide you with some general tools for getting things done in many areas of your life (e.g., time-management, problem-solving), as well as some specific tools, such as study strategies. Even with the general strategies, we often use examples relevant to university students, partly because tales of all-night studying, last minute essays, and homework-devouring dogs abound in the university setting. In this section we attempt to understand what can be done about these issues (well, not so much the dogs) and provide a variety of tools for getting things done. Most of the tools, however, *are* applicable to domains beyond study.

Time Management

Liang suddenly found himself with two assignments and one exam due in the next week, and he had not started work on any of them. How was he going to submit two passable assignments and study enough for the exam within the next 6 days? Liang has no idea how he got into this situation, which indicates that he undertook little (if any) planning and time-management. Effective time management involves prioritising (see Covey's Quadrants, Figure 7.5) so that you use your time and energy on the projects and tasks that matter most. Importantly, your ability to plan and organise is associated with both current and future academic success.

In order to improve your time-management, it is often a good idea to first **monitor** how you are spending your time now. A simple timetable including all 168 hours of the week is a good way to start, so that you can fill in exactly how you spend your time each day. Use this to keep track of what you are doing, and when, throughout your day (e.g., sleeping, exercising, socialising, studying/working on assessments). As you monitor your activities, try to identify whether you are spending enough time on important tasks (see Covey's Quadrants, Figure 7.5), on basic essentials such as sleeping and eating healthily (see Maslow's Hierarchy, Figure 7.3), and on fulfilling psychological needs such as relatedness. Also identify those activities that are either time-wasting or unnecessarily prolonged. Once you have identified how you have been spending your time, you can start scheduling your time. Note that there are many apps and services available that can help you to schedule your time. For example, many people use Google Calendar, Pomodoro apps, or project coordination platforms.

Scheduling Time

Every day we think about things we *want* to achieve, but how many of them do we *actually* achieve? The first step to good time management is to plan ahead for the upcoming days (short-term), or months (medium-term). Planning your time in this way allows you to spread your work tasks over an extended time period, avoid work piling up, and thus cope with stress.

As an example, let's look at how you might deal with time scheduling as a student.

Planning the Semester/Term Ahead. At the beginning of semester or term, try creating a planner to help you to *plan your work* and *remind you about deadlines and upcoming commitments*. Use a large single-page calendar wall chart, or a calendar app.

- Write in the dates that assignments are due, and exams are scheduled. If you're using an app, set reminders.

- Work out how long you will need to complete each task. Allow yourself plenty of time.

- Remember to allow for extra workload. If you have several assignments due at the same time, you will need to begin each task even earlier than usual.

- Write start dates for each task on your planner.

Planning the Week Ahead. Use an electronic or paper calendar that shows the time across the week (168 hrs). Fill in all the main demands on your time, for example:

- Paid employment.

- Classes.

- Travel time.

- Meal times and regular family and/or household commitments.

- Sleep time.

- Physical exercise.

- Any regular leisure or community commitments.

When you have written in the main demands on your time, look at the blank time slots that are left. This will help you work out how many hours a week you actually have for uni-related work. Fill in times that could be used as study periods and/or for working on assignments, including short-, medium- and long- duration slots.

Remember:

1. Short time-slots (e.g., on the bus) can be used productively, for example, to review lecture notes or do short readings.

2. You can dedicate regular weekly study time-slots to particular subjects or determine at the beginning of the week what study tasks have priority and attempt to work through those tasks one at a time as effectively as possible (see the Study Strategies section).

3. Take breaks during the longer time-slots (unless, of course, you are in the zone).

Identifying Time-wasters

Even when time is scheduled, you may not make productive use of your time because of 'time wasters', including putting things off, which is a hallmark of **procrastination** — see below. Learn to recognise your most common time-wasters so you can deal with them *before* too much time is lost.

Creating busy-ness. You can't possibly start studying yet because you are so 'busy' with other things (like trawling Facebook pages searching for increasingly obscure and ironic memes about studying, to send to your struggling, time-poor classmates).

Possible solutions include: Make a To Do list, then using Covey's matrix, classify all your tasks. Anything in Quadrants 3 and 4 can be ignored! Then, get started on the first priority task!

Competing Distractions. We are surrounded by a multitude of distractions competing for our attention. You must resist, as surrendering to their temptation can derail your productivity and stop you from getting things done.

Possible solutions include:

- Identify what distracts you, then block it! For example, if the Snapchat alerts on your phone are drawing your attention, leave your phone in another room, or turn it off.

- Reward yourself for finishing a task by giving yourself 5 minutes of unadulterated Snapchat bliss (but only if you have remained focused and completed the task).

- Hang a 'do not disturb' sign on the door (but don't waste an hour making yourself one!).

Daydreaming. Often it is hard to sustain a focus on your work because you find yourself 'drifting off' and thinking of far more exciting things than the essay you are supposed to be finishing — like your upcoming holiday ... ah, beaches, cocktails, dancing...oops, where were we?

Possible solutions include:

- Ensure that you are getting enough sleep and are well-fed and hydrated (remember Maslow's hierarchy).

- Take a short break every hour or so. Get active — go for a walk or a run.

Studying Effectively

When Nick received his mark for his mid-semester exam, he was very disappointed. He had spent hours and hours studying in the library, scouring textbook chapters and lecture notes, and highlighting every possible point. Nick could not understand why his efforts had not paid off. He wondered whether he was just not smart enough to succeed at university. Spending time ineffectively on pursuing a goal is as problematic as not spending enough time on it. In this section, we will consider some issues that are relevant to the effectiveness of different study behaviours.

Multitasking and Taking Breaks

Compared to just 100 years ago, the choice of activities (work or play) in which humans can engage has increased exponentially, helped along greatly by technology. For example, one hundred years ago, the main forms of family entertainment were music making, playing physical or mental games, reading, or making things (yes, this was before even television!). Now, the choice of entertainment is vast and highly personalisable. For example, we can download music, movies, or television series onto almost any device, and watch anything, anytime, and any place.

Along with this technological explosion, the nature of work life has also changed dramatically. For example, most people in Western societies have significant choice in their careers, and their day-to-day roles are constantly changing. The demands on our personal and work lives have also increased significantly, and as a result we are expected to undertake multiple tasks simultaneously. We have gotten so used to talking on the phone, finishing our breakfast, and watching YouTube simultaneously that we unsurprisingly believe that we *can* effectively multitask. Indeed, in many cases this is true. If you do not really have to attend to what your mother is saying (Aunty June is at it again), then you can concentrate on chewing your toast while watching a cat try on mittens. However, there's a catch. Your brain can't actually do all those tasks simultaneously; you just think it can. If, for example, you're watching cat videos while reading an article for class tomorrow, you likely won't absorb much of either, making the in-class discussion the following day pretty awkward.

While you may think that you are an excellent multitasker and can study for an exam at the same time as watching a cat ride a dog, research tells us two things: (1) you can't really multitask; and (2) thinking you can might have negative consequences. The brain doesn't really do attention-demanding tasks simultaneously as we think it does, rather, it just switches between tasks quickly. Each time you move from watching those cats, to studying about Pavlov, there is a stop/start process in the brain, which takes time away from both tasks. So when you are 'multitasking', you are actually repeatedly interrupting the process of memory consolidation for the material you are studying. This means that tomorrow in the exam room, you will find less in your long-term memory than you had led yourself to believe was there (see Stephen Chew's study videos in *More Resources*). Thinking you can multitask is an easy trap to fall into, but you can't escape the limits of human memory! If there is hard work to be done in terms of memorising facts or working through challenging material for an assessment, then don't try to multitask. Eliminate distractions so that you can focus on one attention-demanding task at a time, the way your brain is designed to. *Turn off your phone, turn off Netflix, shut your door.*

What about breaks? Research has shown that taking brief breaks (e.g., 5 minutes) after a reasonable period of study (e.g., 25 minutes) can be beneficial. However, these breaks need to be low in cognitive and emotional effort. For example, making a snack, walking around the block, or just closing your eyes and resting. Intense cognitive or emotional activity (which may include checking your social media), could interfere with memory consolidation. Moreover, if you are really starting to get engaged in your assignment or study, keep going, because it is likely you are experiencing what Csikszentmihalyi termed 'flow' (see Chapter 6), which is the sense of total absorption that you sometimes feel when you are doing something that you find both interesting and challenging, but is not beyond your current resources.

Study Strategies

Myriad study strategies exist, each with thousands of students swearing by the effectiveness of their favoured one. However, although the time you spend on a task matters, it really is the *quality* of that time that makes a difference (i.e., work smarter, not necessarily longer, to obtain better grades). Before reading on, take a moment now to jot down all of the study strategies you use to prepare for tests or examinations.

You might be surprised to know that after examining a wide range of study strategies, probably including some of those you have identified above, psychological scientist John Dunlosky and colleagues found that only two study strategies are really effective: testing yourself and spacing your learning over time (rather than cramming it into a single block). Why? There are a number of theories, most of which point to the strengthening of memory networks that support both the consolidation of the long-term memories, as well as the retrieval of the memory in different contexts. Here are some suggestions for putting these findings into practice:

- Complete existing practice exams and/or make up possible questions and test yourself.

- Spacing out study over time has been found to lead to longer-lasting memory of that material than undertaking the same number of hours of study in a single block just prior to the exam. For example, within a week of being exposed to a lecture, ensure that you have complete notes on that lecture, then make up questions on the lecture material, test yourself, re-learn the answers, then test yourself again. Undertake these last three steps again at least twice before having a final study session.

You might find it difficult to believe that some of your favourite study strategies, such as highlighting, do not appear to be very effective. One reason may be that highlighting does not involve enough effort in actually learning the material, producing surface rather than deep learning, while giving you false reassurance that you have spent sufficient time on that task. Highlighting is also undertaken in one session (likely just before the exam?), rather than several. So try changing your study approach to include these evidence-based strategies, and if you need more help, try your university's learning support centre, or see *More Resources*.

Attention Training and Exam Performance

Memory for material is improved if you focus your attention on that material (surprise!). There are several ways to improve your attention, but we will mention just one here: **Mindfulness Meditation**. In a rigorously controlled experimental study, students who undertook standard training in mindfulness meditation (vs. training in improving diet) displayed superior performance on both a practice Graduate Record Examination, and an attention test. It was shown that these effects were due to reduced mind-wandering while undertaking these tasks.

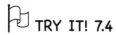 TRY IT! 7.4

Daily Mindfulness Tips*

Try these simple strategies for bringing mindfulness into your day:

- When you first wake up in the morning, while still in bed, bring your attention to your breathing. Observe five mindful breaths.

- When you hear a phone ring, a bird sing, a train pass, laughter, a car horn – use any sound as the bell of mindfulness. Really listen and be present and awake to your environment.

- Whenever you eat or drink something, take a minute and breathe. Pay attention as you eat, consciously consuming your food. Bring awareness to seeing, smelling, tasting, chewing, and swallowing your food.

- Notice your body while you walk or stand. Notice your posture and pay attention to the contact of the ground under your feet. Feel the air on your face, arms, and legs as you walk.

- Bring awareness to listening and talking. Can you listen without agreeing or disagreeing, or planning what you will say when it is your turn? When talking, can you just say what you need to say without overstating or understating? Notice how your mind and body feel.

- Whenever you wait in a line, notice your standing and breathing. Feel the contact of your feet with the floor and how your body feels standing there. Bring attention to the rise and fall of your abdomen. Notice whether you are feeling impatient, and where in your body you are experiencing this.

- Focus your attention on daily activities such as brushing your teeth, washing up, brushing your hair, putting on your shoes. Bring mindfulness to each activity.

- Before you go to sleep at night, take a few minutes and bring your attention to your breathing. Observe five mindful breaths.

See *More Resources* for more on Monash's mindful approach to academic success.

*adapted from Monash University

What About Exam Anxiety?

Many students experience high levels of physiological arousal (e.g., rapid heart rate, shortness of breath, sweating) as they go into an exam. How they interpret this arousal — in terms of positive challenge or negative distress — is determined by a number of different factors (see Chapter 5). Essentially, it is normal to feel 'hyped up' as you enter an exam — your capacity is being tested, and there are consequences for you. However, if these feelings are negatively framed in terms of exam anxiety, this can lead to a lack of focus, including 'mental blanks'— the inability to retrieve relevant information. Indeed, anxiety about exam performance can affect study effort prior to the exam, performance during the exam, and behaviour after the exam. So how do you avoid debilitating exam anxiety?

Before the Exam

- Develop your study skills and time management. Cramming before the exam is an ineffective way to learn. So forget cramming and give yourself enough time to prepare and understand the material.

- Sleep matters. Research has shown that students that have good sleep patterns perform 30% better than students who stay up late to study.

- Eat well — a healthy diet will improve your concentration. However, excessive amounts of energy drinks or caffeine may interfere with your ability to get a good night's sleep and may increase anxiety.

- Don't give up on exercise, as it will release feel-good hormones and improve your concentration.

- Take some (limited) time to do something fun, such as catching up with friends or family.

- Practice strategies to centre your mind such as identifying helpful (and unhelpful) self-talk (see Chapter 4). Use mindfulness to bring yourself to the present and refocus the mind on the task at hand.

- Be aware of your worries, but don't get caught up in them. Imagine that your thoughts are like the traffic on a busy highway. Watch the cars go by without having to know where they are going or trying to stop them. You choose not to take their journey, but to watch them pass you by. Thoughts are just thoughts — mindfulness practice encourages you to watch thoughts pass gently through your mind without chasing or dwelling on them. Learning to watch your thoughts, without reacting to them, will enable you to feel calm, and to study better.

During the Exam

- Acknowledge your anxious feelings ('I notice that I am experiencing feelings of nervousness') and try to manage your thoughts and feelings using tools from Chapter 4 (e.g., avoid catastrophising).

- If you struggle to focus just before or during the exam, try brief mindfulness strategies, such as noticing everything green in the exam room, or doing the 5-4-3-2-1 strategy of noticing 5 things you can see, 4 you can hear, 3 you can feel, 2 you can smell, and 1 you can taste. Both of these exercises will gently return your attention to the present moment.

After the Exam

*   To wind down and to reward yourself for completing the exam, do something that you enjoy — listen to music, meet a friend, or even watch Netflix.

*   MOVE! Your body may still be filled with adrenalin, so it is a good idea to work it out physically. Go to a gym class or go for a walk!

*   Practice mindfulness and just be in the moment rather than worrying about the past exam or the future result. Use an app to support your mindfulness practice before and after an exam.

Non-exam Assessments

In writing an essay, for example, there will be both specific and general resources and skills required. Firstly, you need to determine what your goal is for the assignment. Are you looking for just a C, or are you really aiming for an A? Clearly, for the latter, a higher quantity and quality of time is required. Use the tools outlined in this chapter to help you set and achieve your goal. Firstly, plan early. Try to work out what resources (e.g., essay writing skills, specific literature, marking rubric) are required. Then, break down the assessment into sub-goals and associated tasks, and assign deadlines and specific details (e.g., place, time, duration) to each task (see the Time Management section above). Attempt to keep your motivation high by occasionally reminding yourself of your aspirations (e.g., to do well in the subject and your degree, to get a good job and develop your chosen career), and/or by giving yourself a small, tangible reward for completing each sub-task. Reach out for help from your tutor or fellow students when needed (although be aware of academic integrity boundaries) and check Chapter 4 when you find yourself frozen by unhelpful thinking, such as catastrophising (e.g., 'I'm behind on my schedule — I'm going to fail!').

Study Groups

How useful are study groups? Stephen Chew (see *More Resources*) warns that unless these groups are run in a highly business-like manner, with specific intended outcomes (e.g., increased shared understanding of a particular chapter) and clear 'rules of engagement' (e.g., if you have not already read the chapter and constructed 5 potential exam questions and answers, do not show up), they may be less than effective in terms of positive learning outcomes. Of course, such study groups may serve other useful purposes, such as creating a sense of connectedness with your learning community, which usually increases general motivation to persist with studies (see the TV show *Community*). Nevertheless, the study group should be clear about its purpose. If social activity is important to the group, it is best to specifically schedule it, for example, at the end of the 'hard work' of the study session (e.g., getting food together; but try not to drink too much, as alcohol disrupts memory!).

Balancing your Needs

When studying for an exam or attempting to complete your assessments, it is important to ensure your basic physiological needs (e.g., sleep, healthy eating, exercise — remember Maslow!) are being met, even if you are only minimally satisfying other psychological needs (e.g., relatedness, autonomy). Research has shown that a decent night's sleep improves memory consolidation, and general academic functioning, yet studies consistently report that many university students are not getting enough sleep. See *More Resources* for some excellent resources on the subject of sleep, including internationally acclaimed online sleep programs.

The Paralysing P's: Procrastination and Perfectionism

Consider the following scenarios for students Kelly and Van:

Once again, Kelly finds herself in a living hell. She wrote the bulk of her assignment days ago and since then has been trying to finish it so that she can submit it. Kelly has this nagging feeling that her work isn't quite perfect, but it is due in one hour! Should she force herself to submit it now in its imperfect state, lest she endure the shame of a late penalty? Or should she spend another day attempting to perfect it, and hope that by tomorrow she will have shaken the fear that her work just isn't quite good enough?

It is 7pm on Sunday. Van has known for weeks that he has an assignment due at 5pm tomorrow and he even planned several blocks of time over the past two weeks to work on it. Yet when each scheduled time arose, he seemed to have more important (or fun) things to do. Now, Van has just 22 hours to write an entire essay, minus, of course, all the classes he has the following day. The spectre of failure scares Van into action and he spends the whole night researching and writing the first draft of the essay. He manages to snatch a few moments of sleep on the train, and then after his morning lab sessions, he spends another hour revising the draft and finishing the references. He submits it one hour before the deadline and immediately feels jubilant that he had 'made it' again!

Yes, this last-minute adrenalin-fuelled effort is becoming a habit. He goes home and crashes, exhausted, but with a smile on his face.

If you are finding it difficult to motivate yourself and/or if you only start a task in the 'last hour' (like Van) then you are likely procrastinating. Procrastination is when you delay completing a relevant or important task (e.g., an essay) by spending time on irrelevant tasks (e.g., putting hats on your dog and sending pics to your friends). There are many different reasons why people procrastinate. Some people find it difficult to focus on long-term goals in the face of short-term pleasurable activities. Humans tend to prefer activities (e.g., gaming) that deliver multiple immediate small rewards, rather than activities (e.g., effective study) that deliver one large but distant reward. Knowing this, it's tempting to think that you can just fix procrastination by spending all your time working towards future goals. But life can't be all long-term gain; you need some short-term pleasures too! If you make time for immediate rewards, you will find it easier to stay focused on those longer-term goals. For example, you could break up each study session in the following way:

- Temporarily shut off distractions (e.g., phones, notifications etc),

- work for 25 minutes on the essay research, then

- give yourself a 5-minute break during which you reward yourself with a snack, or with a chat with your flatmate, then

- return to (a) and so on, until the task is done.

Other people find it easy enough to focus on long-term goals, but important tasks bring up difficult thoughts or feelings that they would rather not deal with, so they delay or avoid the task itself. Some of these are:

- **Feeling Overwhelmed.** 'I've too much to do, I don't know where to begin.'

  Possible solutions: Clarify and prioritise your tasks using one of the tools in this chapter. For example, break down the top 3 tasks into steps, and then schedule time to work through those tasks, one step at a time. If you are finding some of the tasks difficult, seek help from friends or experts.

- **Boredom.** 'I am not interested in what I have to do.'

  Possible solutions: Make a list of the long-term reasons for doing it (e.g., finishing your degree and commencing your desired career);

find elements that interest you; set rewards for completing each step of the task.

- **Fear.** 'I'm afraid that I don't have what it takes to do this.'

  Possible Solutions: Break the task into small chunks or subtasks, take the first step; obtain guidance from your tutor; discuss with another student/colleague.

- **Perfectionism.** (like Kelly) 'What I'm doing is never good enough.'

  Perfectionism is the need to produce a perfect product. Sometimes you really do want things done 'perfectly' (e.g., open heart surgery), but most of the time it isn't necessary. At university, perfectionism can lead to: (a) fear of starting an assignment, because of anxiety about not being able to produce a perfect product; or (b) never handing in an assignment, because it is not quite perfect yet.

  Possible solutions: See *TRY IT! 7.5*; brainstorm the many upsides of obtaining a reasonable, rather than a perfect result; see *More Resources*; get professional help so you can learn the difference between high standards and impossible standards.

As you may be starting to realise, there are many different reasons for, and ways to handle, procrastination. See Chapter 4 for some ideas on how you can change your relationship with the difficult thoughts and feelings that can lead to procrastination and perfectionism.

TRY IT! 7.5

Strategies for Dealing with Perfectionism*

There are many different thoughts and beliefs that lead to perfectionism (as displayed by Kelly), so it can be useful to reflect on your own thinking and see if you can relate to some or all of these. As you read through the list below, identify whether you engage in any of these unhelpful ways of thinking, and consider whether and how you can change your thinking. Be aware, however, that these ways of thinking may be so ingrained that you may need assistance from a professional such as a psychologist, to move beyond perfectionism and get valued things done!

Increasingly demanding standards. 'Doing well isn't good enough, I have to do better.'

Set *realistic* goals and hold them lightly, knowing that sometimes you will achieve them; other times you won't. Ideally, goals are flexible, and if we fail to reach our original goal (e.g., getting an A for the essay) we can use this to make our subsequent goals more realistic (e.g., getting a B for the next essay). Once our goals are realistic and attainable, we stand a chance of achieving them. Even if we don't achieve our goals, remaining flexible and willing to learn can help us re-think things and possibly do better next time.

All-or-nothing thinking. 'If I don't get an A in this subject then I don't deserve to be doing this degree.'

There are many options between 'all' and 'nothing', some of which you might never have considered. Your place at university or college usually does not hinge on a single mark. Is an A grade realistic? It is *necessary*? You may have done well in other subjects, and realistically, that usually is good enough to graduate. Perhaps accepting a lower grade in one subject can allow you to do better in another subject. Try to be more flexible in how you think about your goals.

Fear of failure. 'If I get this wrong then others will criticise me.'

Success is rarely (if ever) achieved in the absence of failure. Making mistakes is human and can teach us a great deal (see Chapter 6: FAIL = First Attempt In Learning). The next time you fail, see how much you can learn from that failure. Even if people do criticise you, you can use their feedback to identify which behaviours you could change. See *More Resources* regarding Receiving Feedback.

Shoulds and musts. 'I must study for four hours every night.'

Very few things 'should' or 'must'; rather, try 'could', 'might' or 'prefer' (e.g., 'I would prefer to study for four hours tonight, and I'll see how it goes. I could study every night, but on Fridays I could let myself have a night off'). When you catch yourself saying 'I should', try replacing it with 'I'd prefer to...'. You will likely feel less pressure and guilt.

Excessive checking. 'I have to go over any work I do several times before I can show it to anyone else.'

Checking is time-consuming and anxiety producing, especially when it becomes excessive. If you want to use your attention to detail as a tool, schedule a finite amount of time before it is due to review and refine your work. Once your refinement time is up, hand it in (or ask a friend to!).

Rules About Self-control. 'I have to finish all my work before I can rest.'

Having self-control is about making healthy, realistic choices, not limiting your options with rigid rules! If you're fatigued, then rest is a necessary component of finishing your work. Sticking to the 'rule' will only reduce the quality of your work and make you feel awful. Try to soften those rules a bit. For example, you could have a goal of finishing all your work but be willing to take breaks as needed.

Beliefs About Control. 'I can't let anyone else do a task in case it does not get done exactly how I would do it.'

Aiming to control everything is unrealistic. Life involves risk and uncertainty. Practice giving up control in situations where lack of control does not really have any important consequences: Let a colleague complete part of a project that is not critical to success of the project; let your friend choose meals at a restaurant. See what happens.

See *More Resources* and Chapter 4 for different approaches.

*Adapted from https://student.unsw.edu.au/practice-safe-perfectionism.

Structured Problem-Solving and Psychological Flexibility

We are all faced with challenging problems to solve in our studies, work, and personal lives, so having some tools to help us effectively and systematically problem-solve can be very useful. Within the context of *getting motivated*, this tool is particularly relevant to preventing or dealing with obstacles. Effective problem solving can help you to recognise when to persist with a given approach, and when to adopt a different strategy. This requires psychological flexibility, which refers to the extent to which a person (a) adapts to fluctuating situational demands, (b) reconfigures mental resources, (c) shifts perspective, and (d) balances competing desires, needs, and life domains.

The following *TRY IT!* 7.6 activity is a problem-solving approach which includes thinking about what may have *caused* the problem (or what thinking (M) may have caused the problem!).

 TRY IT! 7.6

Problem Solving: What Caused the Problem in the First Place?

With some problems, you may be wasting your time brainstorming solutions if you are not fully aware of all of the important factors that caused the problem in the first place. If you are able to take the time, and if you are brave enough to consider that the causal factors may include your own faulty thinking such as confirmation bias (see Chapter 2), then this exercise will be worthwhile in terms of creating better solutions *and* building your psychological flexibility skills (see Chapter 4). Remember Kelly? She had issues with submitting her assignments on time. Along with Kelly, try the steps below after setting out the following table headings on a sheet of paper.

Causes	%	Supporting Evidence	Contradictory Evidence

Step 1. What is the problem you are trying to solve?

Consider who, what, when, where. For example, Kelly might think: 'I did not submit my Biology 101 report on time last week; I want to avoid the late penalty, and the stress, with future assignments'.

Step 2. What caused the problem?

List your immediate thoughts about all of the relevant causes in the first column. Use these 3 critical questions to help you:

• How did I contribute?

• What specific behaviours contributed to the problems?

• How did others or circumstances contribute?

You could ask someone else (who you trust to be honest with you) to help you identify the causes.

For example, Kelly might think: (a) 'I didn't have time to research it properly'; (b) 'my flatmate Tim had a crisis the day before it was due and helping him put me further behind'. When she pushed herself a little harder, Kelly added (c) 'I do not like to deliver work that is below my high work standard'.

Step 3. Apportioning Causality

Put a percentage of 'causality' next to each cause in the second column (e.g., *(a) 20%; (b) 50%, (c) 30%*). This should sum to 100%.

Step 4. What's the evidence that each factor contributed to the problem?

Fill in the rest of the table. Be fair — try to distance yourself from your beliefs, and note any thinking errors that might have reared their ugly heads. For example, Kelly might think: for (b) 'Although Tim did have a crisis and I wanted to help him, we were talking about his crisis while I was on the bus, and I usually don't work on the bus anyway' = contradictory evidence (so re-adjust 50% to 0%); for (c) 'In high school I had a tendency to want all my submissions to be as perfect as possible' = supporting evidence (so adjust 30% to 50%).

Step 5. What *really* caused the problem?

Assess the evidence and work out what were the most likely causal factors, changing the percentages to acknowledge that. For example, Kelly might think: *'Although I could always do more research (a), the crux of the problem is really my wanting things to be perfect (c), which was why I handed in my last assignment (and many before that) late'* (so adjust (c) from 50% to 80%). Thus, we end up with one primary cause: (c).

Step 6. What can you *do* about it?

Consider what factors you can control and influence (e.g., Kelly decides to seek out the free help available at her university's learning support centre, regarding how to better manage her perfectionist tendencies).

SMR Model and Motivation

How do these skills relate to our SMR model of Optimising Minds? The initiating situations (S) in the scenarios above are often the demands to complete assessments or to engage in required, desired, or healthy behaviours. The mind 'intervenes' with varying consequences. For example, Kelly's perfectionist beliefs (M_{SUB}) produce maladaptive procrastinating behaviours (R_{SUB}) with regard to finishing and submitting her assignment. In general, the tools we have presented here are designed to help you change maladaptive thoughts (M_{SUB}) by learning new skills (M_{OP}) that will result in more adaptive responses (R_{OP}), for example, producing high-quality work, on time.

As we come to the end of this chapter, let's see how Ruby is travelling. After a disappointing essay result, Ruby reflected on what had worked and what hadn't worked in her goal setting. She set herself a new goal to get a B in her favourite elective subject (tapping into the needs of competence and autonomy). Ruby managed to achieve her sub-goals of studying for each weekly quiz and used time management tools to ensure she spent sufficient time studying for the exam over an extended period (rather than her usual cramming), including testing herself. She also started practicing mindfulness meditation, especially before study sessions and exams, which helped her to focus and reduced her exam anxiety. Although she still sometimes procrastinated, Ruby became better at identifying the thoughts that were stopping her from getting started and finding strategies to get going. As Ruby travelled through her first year at university, she continued to be challenged with balancing the different demands on her time, which she managed by: revisiting her values, interests, and capabilities; prioritising goals and working on her time management; and seeking advice from experts (both online and face-to-face). In doing so, Ruby identified what is most important to her, and which goals she really wants to pursue. She also discovered that she had been holding tightly to the belief that 'If I can't do it all by myself, then I am a failure'. Ruby eventually realised that she would be much better off in the long run if she let others help teach her the skills she needed to achieve her meaningful goals.

Summary Points

- At the core of the concept of motivation is the impetus to act, however the concept is so much more than 'simply' that. In this chapter, we focused on intentional goal-pursuit behaviour.

- There are a number of motivational myths perpetuated by pseudoscience — which need to be busted.

- Motivation is about change: You want something that you currently do not have (you are in a state of *wanting*), and you need to make a change — engage in goal-pursuit behaviour — in order to obtain that desired outcome (state of *having*). In the domain of changing health-related behaviours, the Stages of Readiness for Behavioural Change Model provides a useful explanatory framework.

- The Simple Tools section provided approaches to effective goal pursuit: the GROW model and SMART goals. These supplement the Super tools identified in Getting Prepared and Getting It Done.

- The Super Tools section provides an overview of intentional goal pursuit, involving 8 steps for goal-planning, goal-pursuit and goal-review:

  The 5 steps for *goal-planning* are: (1) identifying 4–5 goals (including a consideration of Maslow's Hierarchy, and SDT's 3 psychological needs); (2) elaborating goals; (3) evaluating goals; (4) determining sub-goals, strategies, and milestones; (5) identifying obstacles and strategies for dealing with those obstacles.

  The 2 steps for *goal-pursuit* are: (1) implementing the strategy to attain the first sub-goal (getting going); (2) progressing your goal-pursuit plan, including monitoring and revising strategies (keeping it going).

  At the end of the process, Getting Goal Wise entails reviewing your goal-planning and goal-pursuit behaviour.

- The 'Additional Tools' section provides evidence-based tools for time-management, studying effectively, the 'paralysing P's' (procrastination and perfectionism), and general problem-solving.

- Research on evidence-based study strategies for examinations indicates that testing yourself, as well as spacing your learning, have strong evidence for effectiveness.

More Resources

- Goal setting and pursuit:
  https://vimeo.com/120112496
  www.thefridge.org.au
  https://www.thedesk.org.au/
  www.therubberbrain.com

- Effective Study Strategies, Multi-tasking, Study Groups:
  Stephen Chew, *How to get the most out of Studying*,
  https://www.youtube.com/watch?v=RH95h36NChI
  Studying at UNSW:
  https://student.unsw.edu.au/skills
  www.thefridge.org.au

- Attention Training and Mindfulness Meditation:
  https://www.monash.edu/health/mindfulness/resources

- Exam anxiety:
  https://student.unsw.edu.au/mindsmart

- Sleep:
  https://student.unsw.edu.au/mindsmart
  Evidence-based web program for improving sleep, SHUTi
  http://www.myshuti.com/

- Paralysing P's and receiving feedback:
  https://student.unsw.edu.au/mindsmart

- Excellent CBT program for procrastination:
  http://www.cci.health.wa.gov.au/resources/infopax.cfm?Info_ID=50

CHAPTER 8

Connecting and Communicating

Imagine that you have just won first prize in a meatball sub eating contest. This prize involves an all-expenses-paid week-long trip to a gorgeous island resort. There is (of course) one catch: there is no 'you and a friend' deal. You would be going alone to a place where you know no one, and the resort is too expensive for your friends to just 'tag along' at their own expense. Despite the luscious destination on offer (with its endless supply of meatball subs), would you still want to go by yourself? If you do decide to go, before you know it you will probably find yourself embroiled in some social interaction with others at the resort. For example, you may find yourself chatting to someone at the pool bar who may also be there alone (or at least, that's what they want you to think!). Or perhaps you don your most supportive swimming costume to join the water aerobics group and joke with the other participants about the instructor's creative contortions. You might even find yourself striking up a conversation with someone at the lunch buffet discussing the merits of ice vs. butter sculptures in the tropical heat. Despite initially knowing no one on your island, the fact is that we are social creatures: we seek out other people to talk to and be with.

In the words of the Dalai Lama 'We human beings are social beings. We come into the world as the result of others' actions. We survive here in depen-

191

dence on others. Whether we like it or not, there is hardly a moment of our lives when we do not benefit from others' activities. For this reason, it is hardly surprising that most of our happiness arises in the context of our relationships with others'. Psychological research (including that in the field of positive psychology) supports this Buddhist perspective that connections with 'other people' can be some of your most positive experiences and can lift you up when you are down. While we might vary in our level of socialness, all humans share a fundamental need to interact with others, and social connections contribute significantly to feelings of wellbeing.

It has even been suggested that a key function of our hugely complex brain is to solve social problems, for example what to say in an awkward situation, how to make someone laugh, how to convince others of your opinion, and sometimes all three simultaneously. Mostly without us being aware of it, the billions of neurons in our prefrontal cortex can run through alternative social scenarios and produce the most likely one to facilitate our relationships.

So far in this book you have been learning how to optimise how you think about (and for) yourself. This chapter is about optimising how you think about connecting with others.

Why is Connectedness so Important?

Decades of wellbeing research has shown that the quality and quantity of a person's social connections are closely related to wellbeing and happiness; from friendships, to familial relationships, to neighbourly relations over the back fence. Relationships might vary in terms of closeness, frequency of contact, longevity, how much we are prepared to share, and how much support we give and receive, but each meaningful relationship brings with it love, happiness, and companionship. As shown in Figure 8.1, you might have a 'pyramid' of relationships. This often begins at the top with a partner and/or best friends and moves downward through several close family members and friends, multiple broader friendships and extended family, and numerous acquaintances such as co-workers, team mates, friends of friends, or even social media 'friends' and 'followers'. Each level might contain more connections than the one above, but your lower-level connections are likely to be less intense, less intimate, and entail less contact than your higher-level relationships. Stronger relationships with those on lower levels can develop as you invest more time, get to know people, find things in common, and share more experiences.

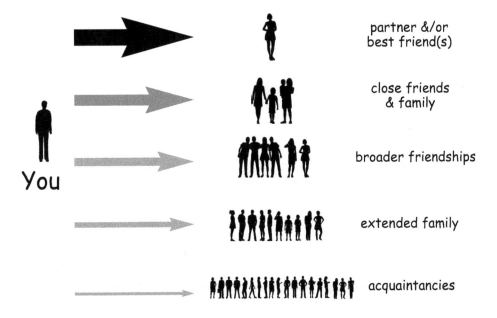

partner &/or
best friend(s)

close friends
& family

broader friendships

extended family

acquaintancies

Figure 8.1 A typical hierarchy of connections, with fewer deeper connections at the top, and numerous less intimate connections below. Arrow thickness denotes the strength of relationship with individuals at each level.

The higher the quality of your social connections, the less likely you are to experience loneliness, low self-esteem, sadness, and insomnia, as well as depression and anxiety. In addition to psychological wellbeing, connectedness is associated with a range of cardiovascular, endocrine, and immune benefits. For example, hand-holding can decrease levels of the stress hormone cortisol. Interestingly, it is not just connections with humans that can have positive benefits on our wellbeing — other animals can also provide social support. Moreover, as anyone who has ever taken a dog for a walk can tell you, they also serve as canine ice-breakers, increasing the number of social interactions with strangers or casual acquaintances.

Although your psychological health is certainly enhanced by having close relationships with people who truly care for you, even brief encounters like ordering coffee from your friendly barista can help combat loneliness and contribute to your wellbeing. This even extends to chatting with your classmates (gasp!). Studies have shown that students who interact more with their class-mates are happier and feel a stronger sense of belonging than those who don't.

🏳 **TRY IT! 8.1**

Connections

Brainstorm all of the different connections that you have with other people. These may be friends, family members, Facebook friends (actual friends; not your Mum's friend's dog), classmates who you know by name, sport teammates, people in a shared interest group (e.g., Meatball Sub-eaters) etc. Using the heading structure below, list down each different category and the approximate number of connections that you have in each. You might also think of what types of things in your life you would discuss with them (e.g., serious issues in your life, trivial flatmate troubles [more dishes to wash, seriously?], a movie you would recommend).

Connection type	Connection Number	What you would discuss

And more than simply being icing on your wellbeing cake (mmm, wellbeing cake), belonging and connectedness are considered critical psychological *needs*; they are crucial to your wellbeing (see Chapter 7). Most theories of human motivation describe some sort of innate drive to establish and maintain meaningful connections with others. The need to connect may even be as compelling as the need for food, since for a very long time in our evolutionary history, being part of a social group meant the difference between life and death. So, it makes sense that, over time, belonging became high on the list of human priorities. The importance of connectedness is illustrated by the fact that one of the most severe punishments someone can receive is social isolation.

In terms of our SMR model, the first step toward optimising how we think about connecting with others is to realise that other people actually matter to our own wellbeing.

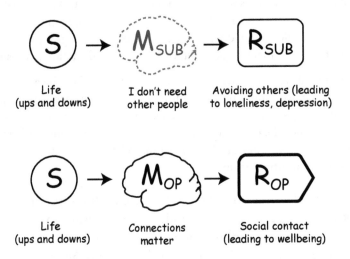

Figure 8.2   Having a suboptimal mindset (M_{SUB}) that "I don't need other people", especially when things get tough, can lead to suboptimal responding (R_{SUB}). Changing this mindset is an essential step to wellbeing.

DIVING DEEPER 8.1

Online vs. Face-to-Face Connectedness

Given that you're probably reading this while WhatsApping 5 people, you may be wondering if social connectedness differs between face-to-face versus online contact, and if this makes a difference to our wellbeing? Rachel Grieve and her colleagues set out to directly examine this by studying Facebook (old school, we know, but bear with us). They found that a higher level of Facebook connectedness was related to less depression, anxiety, and stress. In fact, higher Facebook connectedness was associated with a greater level of subjective wellbeing. Grieve and colleagues concluded that Facebook could provide an alternative to face-to-face connections in promoting a higher level of positive psychological wellbeing. Without underestimating the importance of connecting face-to-face, there is certainly a role for online social networking in building social relationships that enable positive wellbeing (so keep SnapChatting random pictures of your cat wearing ties).

Of course, there are some downsides to social media. While social media can certainly enhance belonging, psychological wellbeing, and identity development, and allow individuals to create and form online groups with ease, it can also have potentially negative outcomes such as alienation and ostracism.

Given that we don't have much research into social media and its impact on wellbeing, we should remain cautious about how much we engage in social media as opposed to face-to-face engagement. Face-to-face relationships are certainly not the only way to connect and develop a sense of belonging, but we need to be mindful of when online relationships are putting us down, rather than lifting us up.

Maybe you get that it is important to have connections, yet in the real world (as opposed to imaginary book world) it is not always so easy to connect. Although we may have optimal thoughts about other people in general, we may still have some niggling suboptimal thoughts about our own social prowess, or even our own social worthiness. This kind of thinking may result from negative social experiences, or times when we find ourselves temporarily alone. Consider Bailey, who found herself at an orientation for new students in her program, where she knew exactly no one. Bailey stood there for a few minutes pretending to text someone, but feeling completely alone. Instead of acknowledging that new social situations such as this can be hard for everybody, Bailey's suboptimal mind started telling her that her growing discomfort was just a symptom of her inescapable lameness (see the fundamental attribution error in Chapter 2 and pessimism in Chapter 6). Rather than gathering up her courage and approaching someone, Bailey felt that no-one wanted to talk to her, and so she slunk away from the orientation as quickly as she could, missing out on the opportunity to meet other people in her program (who were probably all feeling as uncomfortable as she was). When suboptimal thinking stops us from engaging with others, we can end up isolated, which can seriously impact our wellbeing (see Figure 8.3).

Unlike Bailey, who hasn't yet learned how to optimise her social thinking and boost her connectedness, Ben has a different story. Ben had just started his first year at university, and recently moved out of his parent's home and into an on-campus residential college. Ben was known as a nerd at high-school and found it hard to make friends. After years of eating lunch alone in the library, Ben ended up with the belief that he was unlikeable (M_{SUB}). Because of this suboptimal thinking, Ben tended to avoid meeting new

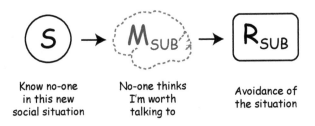

Figure 8.3   Having a suboptimal mindset (M_{SUB}) about yourself in a new social situation can lead to avoidance of social situations (R_{SUB}).

people, and during his first week at university, preferred to sit alone in his room meeting new pizzas (R_{SUB}).

On his first weekend away from home, Ben wandered his new neighbourhood and stumbled upon an obscure pizzeria, which as it turned out, served the best pizza of his life. As Ben mulled the intricacies of this gustatory symphony, he longed for a fellow pizza fanatic to share this moment with. Unfortunately, Ben had avoided his new classmates all week because he believed no one would want to be his friend. Surely, Ben thought, someone this good at finding amazing pizza can't be *totally* unlikeable? Ben decided that his pizza prowess was at least one thing that people would like about him (M_{OP}), so the next day he decided to share his gift with the world: Ben started a Pizza Club (R_{OP}).

Ben was trembling as he walked to the first club meeting, assuming no one would show up. But he was wrong. Three people had come along, each with their own love of deep-dish deliciousness. They ate, they laughed, and they argued the finer points of pecorino versus parmesan. As he finished his final slice, Ben realised that he had been wrong about two things. First, there *were* things to like about him. And second, friends can make anything better, even pizza (roll credits and cue inspiration ballad). After learning new things about himself and other people, Ben approached future social opportunities with a more optimal mindset, which in turn led to more constructive behaviour and greater wellbeing (see Figure 8.4).

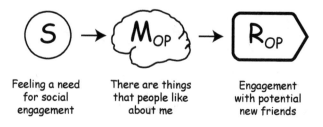

Figure 8.4   Having an optimal mindset (M_{OP}) that 'there are things that people like about me', can lead to optimal responding (R_{OP}).

How Do We Boost Our Connectedness?

Hopefully at this point you understand that social connectedness is not just nice to have; it is very important to your health and wellbeing. However, it's not enough to simply *have* relationships — the *quality* of our relationships also matters. Positive relationships entail genuine mutual liking, mutual disclosure and knowledge, pro-social behaviour, self-esteem support, loyalty, and intimacy. High quality connections occur when people engage in a reciprocal manner, meaning that that each party feels understood and accepted. By contrast, low quality interactions occur when one person lacks empathy, acts in a judgemental way, or doesn't even try to understand the perspective of the other.

The good news for you is that, just like everything to do with human behaviour, there are tools that can help you foster positive relationships, many of which involve communication. In this next section, we will provide evidence-based strategies for increasing your connectedness by developing and strengthening relationships with your family, friends, and colleagues. Specifically, we will consider the 3 'A's' of effective communication — **active listening, active-constructive responding**, and **assertive communication** — each of which can help turn a mediocre relationship into a great one.

Active Listening

In *The 7 Habits of Highly Effective People*, Stephen Covey makes the very important point that we spend years learning to write and speak, but very little time learning to listen and understand another person's frame of reference. Active listening means that we give our total and undivided attention to another person, and in doing so we show that person that we care about what they think and feel. While active listening can really help us communicate and connect with other people, it can be a very difficult skill to learn!

Sometimes when someone is talking, we are not *truly* listening. We may be distracted, or thinking about other things, but most often, we are thinking about what *we* are going to say next. Conversely, active listening requires the listener to *understand, interpret,* and *evaluate* what they hear, and to *reflect* that back to the speaker. It is a structured way of listening and responding to others that focuses attention on the speaker. Active listening means suspending our own frame of reference (sigh), avoiding judgment (double sigh), and suspending other mental activities (which reminds me, I must send Pete that hilarious dog video).

Think about an important person in your life. Looking at Figure 8.5, what level of listening do you most often use when you are talking with them?

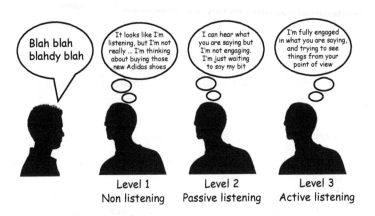

Figure 8.5   Levels of active listening (adapted from Mellish, Morris, and Do).

Active listening uses both verbal and non-verbal communication skills. Verbal communication skills include asking timely and thoughtful questions, paraphrasing, and using reflective language to show the speaker that you are paying attention. For example, your friend might be telling you a truly horrifying story about her cousin's wedding. After your friend has finished you might follow up with, 'You must have felt awful! I can't believe he tried to kiss you! What happened next?'. In just 5 seconds, you have reflected your friend's feelings, paraphrased the climactic moment, and asked her a thoughtful and timely question. Not only will your friend feel like you are listening, you're more likely to hear the rest of this wonderfully disgusting story!

Non-verbal skills on the other hand, include gestures and appropriate posture to indicate that you are engaged and interested in what the other person has to say. This may include appropriate eye contact, or engaging facial expressions and body movement or posture (e.g., leaning in slightly toward the person). In the previous example of your friend's tale of wedding horror, you might widen your eyes at shocking details, cover your mouth in disgust, or roll your eyes in disdain (just make sure it's genuine; this isn't an episode of *Real Housewives*). Here is an active listening checklist that you might want to use as you practice increasing your active listening skills (just don't read this list at the same time as you are trying to listen actively!).

Active Listening Checklist:

- Use inviting (but not creepy) body language.
- Try not to appear distracted or detached during the conversation (that vibrating alert from your phone can wait).
- Give the speaker time and space to talk, including allowing silence.
- Don't butt in.
- Encourage clarification, especially if you don't understand.
- Express understanding non-verbally (nodding, smiling, sympathetic eye contact).

A key part of active listening involves reflecting back to the speaker what you think you have heard and how they seem to be feeling. This helps you to clarify their message and tells the person that they are understood. Some reflective listening tools are shown in Table 8.1, all of which help you to better ensure that you understand what the speaker is trying to tell you, and send the message that what they have to say is important to you, thus building your connection with them.

Active-Constructive Responding

Once you have learned to listen actively, responding constructively can further foster positive relationships. Psychologist Shelly Gable has found that the way that we respond to someone sharing good news can either build a relationship

Table 8.1   Reflective listening skills (adapted from Mellish, Morris, & Do).

Tool	What	Why
Reflecting	A verbal response to the speaker's emotion	Helps respondent feel understood; express and manage emotions
Paraphrasing	Choosing the most important details said by the speaker, and reflecting them in your own words	Helps convey understanding, encourages elaboration, and allows you to check the accuracy of your perceptions
Summarising	Pulling together and restating key parts of what is being communicated (verbally and non-verbally)	Helps you to identify key ideas in what is being said

or undermine it and is a strong indicator of the quality or strength of our relationships. Imagine that a good friend of yours, Zoe, shares news that she did very well in her psychology exam. How do you react to her news? Are you engaged and interested, or aloof and disengaged? Do you probe to find out more about what she has done, or do you change the subject to something that interests you? Figure 8.6 shows the four different response types, which vary along the dimensions of active vs. passive, and destructive vs. constructive.

If you responded to Zoe in an **active** and **constructive** way, you would demonstrate real interest in her news, ask relevant questions, and comment on the likely way in which she achieved such a great outcome, 'I'm really proud of you Zoe! You must have worked really hard. Got any cool psychology tips for me?'. You would also maintain eye contact with her, and show her some displays of positive emotion like genuine smiling, hugging, and possibly laughing. Active-constructive responding not only makes the person sharing the news feel great, it also strengthens the relationship between the two people.

While active-constructive responding is an optimal way to bring you and Zoe closer, there are other ways of responding that aren't so optimal. For example, you may respond with a quiet, low-energy 'well done'. This is a **passive-constructive** response — still positive, but a lot less engaged. Even worse, you might respond in a destructive way to Zoe's success. **Active-destructive**

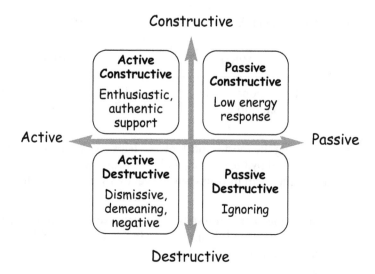

Figure 8.6 Ways of responding to another person's good news and achievements. Adapted from Gable et al. (2004).

responding is when you point out the downside of someone else's good news: 'It must have been tough for someone like you to try to get good grades in all your classes. I bet some of your other marks suffered'. This style of response can be dismissive or demeaning, and non-verbal aspects may include a harsh tone of voice or a disparaging facial expression. **Passive-destructive** responding is less overt but equally damaging, and often involves changing the subject. A passive-destructive response might be 'So what are we going to watch on Netflix tonight' — showing no interest whatsoever in Zoe's news.

TRY IT! 8.2

How do you Respond?

Think about your response when someone shares their good news with you.

Of the four types of responding, which one do you use most?

Does your mode of responding differ in different contexts? Think about significant others in your life such as your partner, your parents,

your colleague, or your employer. Note any variations in your responding to each of these people and think about why this may be.

Next, think of one recent interaction in which you did not use
active-constructive responding. What would be a more active-constructive response?

In terms of our SMR model, the situation (S) is Zoe telling you her good news.
Your thoughts will likely guide how you respond to Zoe's good news. Negative
thoughts that reflect resentment, jealousy, or disinterest (M_{SUB}) are likely to
lead to less optimal responding (R_{SUB}), which can adversely impact your relationship. On the other hand, reminding yourself of the value of friendships
(M_{OP}) can motivate you to engage with Zoe in more supportive ways, such as
active-constructive responding (R_{OP}).

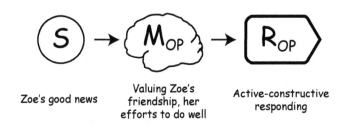

Zoe's good news	Valuing Zoe's friendship, her efforts to do well	Active-constructive responding

Figure 8.7   Having an optimal mindset (M_{OP}) that 'I value Zoe's efforts to do well',
can lead to optimal responding (R_{OP}).

By now you can (hopefully) see how active-constructive responding can help
you foster relationships by making others feel heard and understood. But you
can use active-constructive responding to make yourself feel good, too. For
example, active-constructive responding can super-charge the positive feelings
you experience. The first step is to vividly imagine a positive event that you
have recently experienced. Think deeply about the event and try to identify
your feelings at that time. Next, notice how you're feeling right now —
probably pretty positive. You could stop there, but if you share this positive
event with another person and they respond in an active-constructive way, this
actually causes additional positive feelings over and above the positive feelings
associated with the original event. This is known as **capitalisation**, and the

more capitalisation we engage in, the greater social resources and resilience we will cultivate. Psychologist Shelly Gable suggests that capitalisation occurs due to a number of factors:

- **Savouring:** Sharing a positive event with others requires retelling the event, creating an opportunity for reliving and re-experiencing the event.

- **Memory:** Talking about a positive experience causes us to think deeply about the event, which will strengthen our memory of the event and thus make it easier to recall.

- **Social Resources:** Sharing events with others may build social relationships by fostering positive social interactions.

- **Self-esteem:** Sharing good news may give other people the opportunity to show that they are happy for our success, which can boost our pride and self-esteem.

Usually, good news relates to a goal that has been achieved. In our example, this was Zoe's good mark on her psychology exam. By responding in an active-constructive manner, you are reinforcing Zoe's feelings of self-pride and self-efficacy, and you are rewarding the actions that helped Zoe achieve this positive outcome. Increasing self-efficacy can help Zoe get into an 'upward spiral'; that is, after achieving a good result, and being rewarded for it (with your very thoughtful praise), Zoe is more likely to work hard on her subjects in her next semester, leading to more good results (which, of course, will elicit more active-constructive responding from you!). Also, because Zoe feels that she has your support in achieving her goals, she is more likely to share all her news with you in the future, thus further building your relationship.

Assertive Communication

You may not consciously be aware of it but the way that you communicate reflects your beliefs about yourself and other people, and the extent to which you consider their (and your) rights and feelings, as shown in Figure 8.8.

Assertive communicators advocate for themselves while respecting the rights of others; they believe that all people matter (M_{OP}). This belief helps them respond to others with respect without sacrificing their own needs (R_{OP}). Assertive communication provides an optimal context to build a healthy relationship. Aggressive communicators advocate for their own needs at the expense of others, believing that they matter more than other people (M_{SUB}).

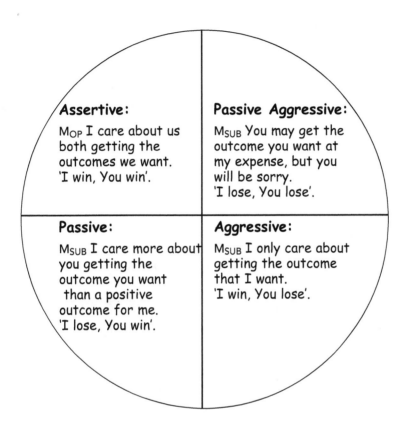

Figure 8.8 The four ways in which you may respond to a challenging interpersonal situation based on your beliefs about yourself and the other person (M)

Conversely, passive communicators believe that they matter less than other people (M_{SUB}), so they don't stand up for their own rights, and allow others' needs to come before their own (R_{SUB}). Over time, passive communicators can start to feel anxious or depressed, as life seems beyond their control. Finally, passive-aggressive communicators may appear outwardly passive, but allow anger and resentment towards others to fester, rather than tackling the issue. In each of the latter three cases, the communicator becomes alienated from those around them.

Assertive communication can be particularly useful when you are in a situation that requires you to express your opinion, ask for help, say 'no' when you don't want to do something, or stand firm when your view is challenged. Many such situations arise working in groups, whether on the job, at school, or even in social settings. It is therefore worth having some assertiveness tools up your sleeve for when these situations arise.

To begin, let's get a sense of what your typical communication style is. Imagine that you have been placed in a group in class and your tutor has asked you to complete a major assignment together. You have attended a few group meetings and your team leader has delegated the tasks evenly amongst you. A few days before the assignment is due, Karen, one of your team members, has contacted you to say that she has a family gathering on the weekend and asked if you would mind completing her section of the assignment in addition to your own. Which of the following responses best captures how you would you respond to Karen?

1. You quietly accept the extra workload without making any kind of fuss. Although you are annoyed, you keep your feelings of resentment to yourself.

2. You tell her you would be happy to do the work; however what you don't tell her is that you really feel taken advantage of and complain to other group members behind Karen's back.

3. You start abusing Karen for having the gall to ask for this huge favour and for letting the rest of your team down.

4. You tell Karen that what she is asking is unfair, particularly as she is asking this favour so late in the game. You tell her that you understand that she would want to be with her family, but she still needs to meet her commitments. You suggest that the two of you brainstorm options about how to best complete her section, and then let the others know what is happening.

To understand assertive responding, let's see what your other team members might have done when Karen approached them. First, take Lily. As an assertive communicator, Lily tends to believe that 'people can be trusted' or 'I need to give people a chance to be reasonable'. When talking through a difficult issue, Lily maintains eye contact, respects both her and her colleague's personal space, and tries to express her opinion firmly, but kindly. Lily benefits from assertive communication by gaining self-confidence and self-esteem, understanding and recognising her own feelings, earning respect from others, improving communication, creating win-win situations, improving her decision-making skills, creating honest relationships and gaining more job satisfaction.

In terms of our SMR model, Lily is a living, breathing example of optimised thinking. When faced with a difficult conversation (S), Lily draws on her trust of others and her belief that she should give them a chance to be reasonable (M_{OP}), allowing her to respond assertively (R_{OP}). In the teamwork situation above, Lily would have gone with response 'd', which allows her to take care of herself while respecting Karen's rights and beliefs, which is fundamental to a healthy relationship. Some people think of being assertive as being demanding or pushy, but assertive responding involves communicating in a way that is clear, controlled, and respectful (especially in a challenging situation like the one above). In assertive communication, you are sending the message that your own beliefs, opinions, and feelings are as important as the other person's. It is an effective and diplomatic communication style that honours your right to have a say in issues that affect you.

But not all of Lily's team members are as assertive as she is. First, meet Jeremy. Jeremy is all about Passive Communication and would have gone with response 'a' above. Jeremy likely holds a belief like 'it's wrong to complain' (M_{SUB}) so he tends to avoid conflict (R_{SUB}). As a result, Jeremy may seem shy or easy-going, and he probably genuinely believes that this approach helps to keep the peace. When he is talking to others, Jeremy would likely avoid eye contact, stand in a withdrawn posture, and use his quietest possible voice (R_{SUB}). Jeremy might be a great peacekeeper, but his passive behaviour usually results in internal conflict because Jeremy's needs are not being met, leading to feelings of stress, resentment, anger, or a desire to exact revenge.

Across from Jeremy sits George — a classic Aggressive Communicator — who would have chosen response 'c' above. George comes across as self-righteous and superior; a bully who disregards the needs, feelings, and opinions of others. George likely believes that 'I must be dominant in every situation' or 'things should always go my way' (M_{SUB}). In a conversation, George likes to give the impression of controlling the other person, so he stands over them, invades their personal space, stares at them intensely, and sometimes makes aggressive physical contact with the other person (R_{SUB}). George's needs are often met, but often at a cost to the needs of others, and thus at a cost to his relationships with them.

Just behind George (and slightly to the left) sits Kirstin, our Passive-Aggressive Communicator. Kirstin would have gone with option 'b' above. Kirstin likely holds the belief that 'some people are just jerks and you have to put up with them, but not quietly' (M_{SUB}). Kirstin often says 'yes' when her colleagues ask her to take on additional responsibilities, but behind closed doors she complains about them. She constantly makes sarcastic comments, but always follows them up immediately with 'just joking!' (R_{SUB}). Over time, Kirstin's behaviour damages her relationships, which makes it difficult for her to get her needs met.

After reading about Jeremy, George, and Kirstin, it is not too hard to appreciate that assertive communication is the most effective way to communicate in this, and many other, situations. But if you're just not assertive by nature, how can you learn to communicate more effectively? Fortunately for you (and us), psychologist Karen Reivich and colleagues devised a five-step model to do just that:

1. Identify and work towards understanding the situation (e.g., identify your core beliefs and values relevant to the situation).

2. Describe the situation as accurately and objectively as you can.

3. Express why the situation is important to you and how it affects you.

4. Ask the other person for his/her perspective and work together towards an acceptable change.

5. Once change has been implemented, list the benefits to the situation and the relationship.

TRY IT! 8.3

Practical Tips for Being Assertive

Here are some practical tips to try to learn to be more assertive. Think of some recent communication episodes and see if you can apply some that you might use in future to improve your assertiveness.

Assess your communication style.

How do you respond to a given situation? Do you remain quiet? Do you stand up for your convictions? In the above group project example, would you accept additional workload when you feel it is unfair to do so? You might also want to ask your family or friends to provide feedback as to what type of communicator you tend to be. Be sure to understand your communication style before you go about making changes.

Be aware of your body language.

Because communicating with others doesn't only involve speech, make sure to also include appropriate body language. Make regular eye contact and try to act confidently even if you don't feel confident. Try to soften your facial expression as much as you can. Avoid using dramatic gestures with your arms. You can practice these behaviours with a friend or even in front of a mirror.

Use the first person ('I' statements).

When you express your point of view using 'I' statements, it lets the other person know how you are feeling about the situation without being judgmental or accusatory. For example, say, 'I don't see it that way', rather than, 'You are wrong'.

Practice practice practice!

If you find confrontation difficult, perhaps write down what you want to say, say it out aloud in front of a mirror or to a friend, and ask for feedback.

Practice saying 'no'.

If you tend towards the passive communication style and have a difficult time saying 'no', try saying 'I'm sorry but I can't do that right now'. Try to be direct — don't avoid the situation.

Keep your emotions in check.

Confronting someone about something important is difficult for many people. Feeling as if you want to get angry or want to cry are all normal emotions but they can get in the way of resolving a conflict. If it is too overwhelming, perhaps take some time to get yourself together before confronting that person. Try to remain calm and listen to your breathing.

Begin in low-risk situations.

Try rehearsing your assertive communication with someone you can trust before tackling a difficult situation. Get feedback from your friend as to how you went and if necessary, try to improve your technique.

Connecting and Communicating in Teams

So far we have focused on how building new connecting and communicating skills can help you build better relationships with family and friends, primarily as these are the most important relationships in your life. However, these skills are also useful when working in teams. You probably have some mixed experiences of teamwork (we can hear you groaning from here), and you will certainly find yourself as a part of many teams as you go through life: in your workplace, at university, in shared accommodation etc. In an ideal world, teamwork would always help us accomplish more outcomes to higher standards, but not all team experiences are that effective.

Effective teams need to work as a cohesive unit. This cohesion depends on strong relationships between team members, which (*drumroll*) relies on effective connections and communication. Effective team members need to listen actively and reflectively, respond in an active and constructive manner to one another, and be assertive. With strong communication skills, a team is most likely to share good ideas without fear of being criticised, appreciate each other's perspectives, avoid misunderstandings, and manage conflict effectively.

In order to perform well, group members each need to work on perspective taking, empathy, and psychological flexibility. There is evidence that mindfulness is associated with higher levels of perspective taking, increased empathy, and lower levels of distress in the workplace — so, in a nutshell, mindfulness is great for enhancing teamwork! (See Chapters 4 and 7 for more on mindfulness).

A common stumbling block in teamwork is a tendency to avoid the uncomfortable emotions that can arise during negotiation or conflict. Although you now know how to communicate assertively, managing uncomfortable emotions may not come easily as you begin to put your new assertiveness skills into practice. Accepting uncomfortable emotions that arise during conflict can help us move toward desired goals and is a key component of Acceptance and Commitment Training (ACT). You may recognise this ACT technique from Chapter 4. Using ACT, you can make space for your negative emotions in the short term, helping you to focus on agreed teamwork guidelines and ultimately to achieve the team goal.

Connecting and Communicating Across Cultures

You've just read a bit about communicating within groups, but what about communicating between groups? Look at the news and before long you will see evidence that we humans don't always communicate well between groups. This is often due to how differently our groups have developed across the course of history (see Chapter 9 for more on in-groups and out-groups). The different ways in which individuals connect and communicate is highly influenced by **cultural differences**. Cultural differences usually refer to ethnic or national differences in the way in which people think about the world, including preferred or acceptable ways of communicating and forming relationships. However, 'culture' can also refer to the values and behaviours that are shared within organisations or groups, such as your sporting club, the company you work for, or your particular social group. Cultural differences can be reflected in everything including humour, language, religion, gender roles, and so on. As our world becomes increasingly globalised, the need for cultural responsivity — the capacity to appreciate, respect, and learn more about cultural diversity — is increasingly valued in employment and other social contexts.

TRY IT! 8.4

Diversity and Intercultural Awareness: How do I Differ From Others?

Many beliefs and behaviours differ across cultural contexts. List all of the ways in which you differ in your beliefs and behaviours from others you know (e.g., in your work or study contexts) who are (a) from a foreign country with a non-English speaking background, and/or (b) raised in a family that is very different from yours in terms of systems of beliefs and behaviours, such as religion. Hint: you might need to strike up a conversation and ask them!

Unfortunately, cultural responsivity is too complex an issue to cover thoroughly in this chapter, but it is worth mentioning because the strategies discussed in this chapter are largely from a Western point of view. We know, for example, that assertive communication is valued in most Western cultures, however how people show their assertiveness may differ significantly between different cultures. For example, Indian students seem to display lower levels of assertiveness than Serbian students. This may be due to national personality differences, but it also may reflect cultural, religious, and socio-demographic differences. Furthermore, the ability to differentiate assertiveness from passive or aggressive behaviours may be affected by the prevailing culture, so your newly discovered assertiveness may come across as something else entirely in other parts of the world. In sum, although the connecting and communicating tools you have learned in this chapter should help you foster better relationships in a Western society, keep in mind that as you meet people from other cultures, you may need to be flexible and sensitive in your approach. You might like to discuss the main tools we have outlined in this chapter with friends from different cultures and get their first-hand perspective on whether these tools work in their cultures, or indeed, whether they have other tools which they think could work well in your culture. Your reciprocally respectful consideration of these cultural differences should lead to a deepening of your relationships, and should help you to develop cultural responsivity.

Summary Points

- Quality relationships with other human beings are essential to our survival and to our wellbeing, and suboptimal thoughts often get in the way of initiating and maintaining these relationships.

- Active listening is a structured way of listening and responding to others that focuses attention on the speaker. It requires the listener to put aside his or her own frame of reference, avoid judgment, and suspend other mental activities in order to accurately *understand* what they are hearing, and to reflect that understanding back to the speaker.

- Active-constructive responding results from valuing the person talking and the good news they are conveying. It involves verbally and nonverbally demonstrating real interest in their news, asking thoughtful questions, and commenting on the likely way in which they achieved such a great outcome.

- Assertive communicators are strong advocates for themselves while being very respectful of the rights of others. They believe that other people matter, and this provides an optimal context to work on building a healthy relationship.

- In order for a team to perform well, team members each need to work on perspective taking, empathy, and psychological flexibility (see Chapter 4), with a key skill being able to mindfully accept negative emotions during uncomfortable interactions in order to achieve shared goals.

- Cultural responsivity involves continually learning about, appreciating, and respecting cultural differences in 'the way we do things around here' and coming to shared understandings of how to achieve common goals.

CHAPTER 9

The Moral Mind

David was standing in a Subway® queue, patiently waiting to buy a cheese-covered meatball sub, when some guy shoved into the queue ahead of him. David almost choked on his moral outrage at this blatant disregard of a fundamental tenet of civilised societies: waiting your turn! When David tapped the guy on the shoulder and pointed out his grievous transgression, the guy started yelling at David, which was ill-advised given David's 'hangry' state of meatball deprivation! But why did waiting just a few more minutes for his lunch upset David so much? Why do we care about issues of right and wrong? And, how do we know if the view we hold is actually 'right'?

David's minor but relatable example highlights how often we evaluate our behaviour (and that of others) in terms of morals. Our 'moral mind' can impact many areas of our daily life, from the frustration of queue-jumping, to private moral challenges such as whether we return a cash-filled wallet, to public moral challenges such as whether we defend someone who is being abused by another passenger on our bus. How we think and act in each of these situations can affect our relationships and our wellbeing.

If our moral mind can have such an impact on our lives, it might be worth considering optimising it! By doing so, we can enhance our capacity to cooperate with others, and improve our close personal and work relationships that we strengthened using the skills in Chapter 8.

Morals or Ethics?

First, let's clarify some key terms. Morals and ethics both refer to 'rightness' (or goodness) in relation to **intentions** (what you want to do), **behaviour** (what you actually do), and their **outcomes** (what happens as a result). While 'morals' and 'ethics' are often used interchangeably, they are actually different things. Morals focus on both universal principles or laws of rightness (so-called 'objective' morality) and on our personal sense of 'rightness' ('subjective' morality). In contrast, ethics are the standards or principles set by a group, organisation, or professional society, which serve to guide behaviour. Ethical codes of conduct are often based on moral perspectives. For example, Belinda may be personally disgusted by the actions of a sex offender (according to her subjective moral belief system), yet she continues to provide evidenced-based psychological treatment to the sex offender, thus upholding the ethical principle of respect (according to her professional code of ethics).

Discovering our Moral Mind

This chapter will provide tools to help you identify where your moral beliefs came from, and how they guide your decision-making and behaviour. Because of the complexity of moral beliefs and morally relevant situations, some of these tools may initially seem more complicated than the tools we have discussed so far in this book. However, our old friend the SMR model can help us understand the complexities of our moral mind.

As shown in Figure 9.1, M_{SUB} reflects the belief that something is right or wrong, and we can hold this belief without understanding the reasons why we hold the belief. Unsurprisingly, at first beliefs tend to reflect our family's beliefs, and are later influenced by the media, teachers, friends, partners, work colleagues, and so on. For most people, during adolescence we begin to challenge our family's beliefs (especially Mum's belief that a bedroom must always be tidy). Knowing where our beliefs came from and examining the credibility of our beliefs is a critical part of optimising our moral mind. This can help us make sure that our beliefs are not based entirely on social media or blogs, where the credibility of information may be questionable to say the least (we're looking at you, *Buzzfeed*).

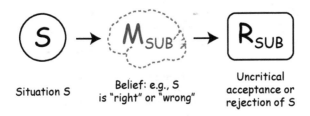

Figure 9.1   Having a belief that something is 'right' or 'wrong', but not being fully aware of why you believe that (hence the 'unaware' M), makes that belief suboptimal (M$_{SUB}$). Thus, the 'suboptimal' aspect is not necessarily in reference to the content of the belief itself, but the fact that you are not fully aware of the reasons that you hold that belief, and in particular, you may not have fully examined the credibility of information leading to your belief. Consequently, your response may be suboptimal.

The suboptimal-ness of our moral mind, then, isn't necessarily about the moral position that we hold. Instead, our moral mind can become suboptimal if we aren't aware of how our moral position developed, and how it affects us (and others) in the present. Unsurprisingly, suboptimal moral thinking leads to suboptimal responses! For a start, most people accept or reject another's view without critically evaluating it. When we reject people's views, we can easily get into arguments about what is the 'right' moral position. At best, we express our opinions on the 'right' moral position by changing our profile picture for a righteous cause, or sharing a meme criticising a political view different from our own. At worst, we can find ourselves in the murky depth of trolling people we don't know, or filling entire comments sections with vicious remarks about others without really considering why. These kinds of arguments can break apart friendships, families, and even communities, so it's important that we understand the moral thinking behind them and consider optimising that thinking!

As shown in Figure 9.2, optimising our moral mind can help us to understand the similarities and differences between people's perspectives on what is 'right' and 'wrong', and forms the basis for compromise, collaboration, and even harmony (aww). Clearly this is relevant to global and national politics, but it is also relevant to whether you can 'get on' with your neighbours, your colleagues, your classmates, even your family.

It is worth reiterating that we are not saying that the content of your moral mind is 'right' or 'wrong'. Far be it from us to judge! Rather, this chapter is

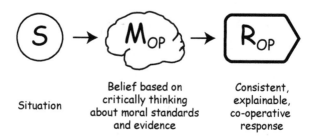

| Situation | Belief based on critically thinking about moral standards and evidence | Consistent, explainable, co-operative response |

Figure 9.2 M~OP~ reflects beliefs about a particular stimulus or situation founded on intentional critical examination of the relevant evidence, behavioural standards, and moral standards. With optimised beliefs, you can be more confident your responses are explainable in relation to relevant evidence/standards, and consistent with your moral beliefs (i.e., optimised responding; R~OP~). Further, given your critical thinking mindset, you will re-examine and adjust your beliefs when you become aware of new evidence or of different behavioural or moral standards (e.g., if you are in a different culture).

about giving you some tools to determine yourself *where* your sense of right and wrong comes from, and whether that sense is optimal.

 Diving Deeper 9.1

The Evolutionary Basis of Moral Behaviour

One theory of particular relevance for considering the 'wiring' behind moral behaviour is **evolution by natural selection**. Evolutionarily, attributes that enhance our chance of survival provide more opportunities for reproduction and passing on those quality genes, so our offspring tend to inherit these attributes from us. Humans have long lived in groups (tribes) for survival, because there is power in numbers. Thus, over our history, group members have needed to cooperate effectively to collect and share food, build shelter, defend themselves from ferocious predators, and defend their tribe from the even more ferocious tribe from down the road. This effective cooperation required a group mindset: less selfish thinking ('me') and more selfless thinking ('us'). However, it has also been important to cooperate only with in-group members, and be distrusting of other groups that may pose a threat (like that tribe from down the road; 'them'). Basically, a moral mind may have been advantageous for our survival because it encourages in-group cooperation, which has been the key to the success of our species.

216

Evolving to have a group mindset has implications for today's societies. Despite the fact that most of us no longer live in tribes, humans remain social creatures creating varied and often fluid groups based on any categorical affiliation we may be lucky enough to choose (e.g., personal friendships, work, sporting team, political affiliation). For example, we could establish an in-group with strangers over our shared love of Manchester United football club and shared dislike of Liverpool FC. Although Liverpool FC supporters are out-group members, this doesn't always need to be this way. We can create a super-ordinate group to increase cohesion — by reminding both Manchester and Liverpool supporters that they both love English football, and should join forces in supporting the English national team when they play Germany (the new out-group).

As we can see, these 'us vs. them' group-categorisations can be positive or even funny (e.g., cultural peculiarities or sporting rivalries), but they can also be divisive when out-group members are discriminated against (e.g., racism). Perhaps if aliens attacked our planet we would unite as humans, putting aside the negative aspects of group categorisations to fight these intergalactic out-group members. Until then, we might have to try to just optimise our thinking.

To start thinking about how our moral mind can affect us, let's meet Aisha. Aisha always believed that homosexuality is wrong, regardless of the laws of the land. Then one day, Aisha's best friend, Sally, told Aisha she is a lesbian. Sally said she had wanted to tell Aisha for a long time but was aware of Aisha's views and did not want to risk their friendship. Now, Sally could not live the lie any longer, and needed to be true to herself. She asked Aisha to think about where she had acquired her beliefs about homosexuality, and told her that she would give her a call next week. Aisha was shocked, angry, and even disgusted. She felt betrayed, and wondered if she would ever be able to talk to Sally again.

We can begin to understand Aisha's response of shock, anger, and disgust at being confronted with a lesbian, who she had previously assumed was her best heterosexual friend, if we consider Aisha's moral mind – her thinking about what is 'right' and 'wrong'— as depicted in Figure 9.3.

Aisha might have some sense of where her moral belief about homosexuality came from (family or religion), but what we (and Sally) are asking her to do is to examine the broader foundations of her moral mind. Perhaps Aisha could consider the relative nature of religious belief systems, and the very different views that some religions have of homosexuality (e.g., apparent acceptance vs. punishment by death). Aisha could also challenge some of the views (accurate

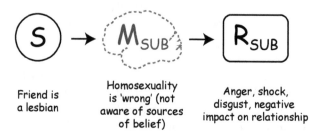

Friend is a lesbian | Homosexuality is 'wrong' (not aware of sources of belief) | Anger, shock, disgust, negative impact on relationship

Figure 9.3   Having a belief that homosexuality is 'wrong', but not being fully aware of the basis of that belief makes that belief suboptimal (M$_{SUB}$). Consequently, the response to a friend may be suboptimal, involving anger, shock, and even disgust, leading to a weakening or breaking of social bonds.

or otherwise) that 'support' her belief, such as a 'higher rate of child sexual abuse perpetrated by homosexuals compared to heterosexuals', by actually looking at crime statistics.

So what did Aisha do, once she had calmed down enough to think? Aisha had two older sisters, Yasmine and Fatima. She spoke to Fatima first, who informed Aisha that she no longer held their parents' belief that homosexuality is wrong, and that she personally had many gay friends, including Adam. Fatima invited her to discuss these issues anytime, although best not in front of their parents — not worth rocking the boat! Again, Aisha was shocked, partly by Fatima's proclamation, and partly by the new knowledge that Adam is gay. Aisha really liked Adam!

Reeling from these new revelations, Aisha anxiously sought out her oldest sister, Yasmine. Yasmine was damning of both Sally and Adam, telling Aisha that Fatima was careless in her thinking and with her friendships, that their parents were correct in their beliefs, and that Aisha should very carefully think about the whole picture. Yasmine warned of the dire consequences of accepting homosexuality. Aisha immediately felt some relief from having her beliefs supported by her oldest sister, but she still felt a bit uncomfortable for some reason.

At this point in time, can we say that Aisha's beliefs about homosexuality are 'right' or 'wrong'? No, and as we've mentioned, that's not up to us! What's more important is for us to consider if Aisha has **critically examined** the sources of her beliefs about homosexuality, and the answer to that is also 'no'. Critically examining her beliefs will require substantial effort from Aisha, and some people struggle to find the motivation for this process, instead preferring to tread the easy path of supporting their existing beliefs. In this instance, Aisha preferred to listen to Yasmine and ignore Fatima, which is a great example of the confirmation bias discussed in Chapter 2.

But what about that uncomfortable feeling that still bothered Aisha? If Aisha's ongoing discomfort drove her to attempt to identify and evaluate the sources of her beliefs about homosexuality, how could she go about it? One approach is to compare her moral belief system to that of others and try to understand the basis of their different beliefs. Aisha could examine her general beliefs, and her specific beliefs regarding homosexuality, through the lens of different moral perspectives.

The rest of this chapter will describe several established moral perspectives in the moral philosophy literature. As we go along, you should think about how *your* moral mind aligns with these philosophical perspectives. Spoiler alert for you (and Aisha): for the most part, this comparison exercise does not produce 'the answer', as these philosophical perspectives have different strengths and weaknesses. Instead, this comparison process can help you to:

(a) become more aware of your 'moral' beliefs,

(b) find where you sit in the moral landscape of possible beliefs others hold, and in doing so,

(c) realise the variance in moral beliefs held by others.

Remember, our goal is not to reveal the ultimate 'right' and 'wrong' (other than *our* belief that it is ultimately right to fully examine the nature and genesis of one's beliefs, and to fairly weigh the evidence!).

The next two sections, **moral foundations** and **philosophical perspectives**, will deliver many 'tools' by which you can examine your own moral beliefs. To help you consider these tools, try to think of a moral challenge that you have faced in the past, or indeed, that you are facing now. To help even more, you might also like to think about two moral challenges that we have already encountered:

- **Chris** (from Chapter 3). Chris has already cheated in his exams once, and this has made him sick to the stomach (visceral responses are common in morally challenging situations, and have consequences for decisions and behaviours — but unfortunately we don't have time to dig into that). Although he has been talking with Eva about how to move forward with his studies and career, he is now faced with another situation where he needs to do well in an exam. Will he cheat again, just as many of his fellow students still do, or will he stay honest even if it means getting a poorer grade?

- **Aisha.** What will she do when Sally contacts her in a week to talk about the future of their friendship? How will Aisha deal with the moral challenge of the clash between her negative beliefs about homosexuality and the fact that her best friend is a lesbian?

Moral Foundations

Many of us share a common goal of wanting to improve society, but we often have different conceptions of what constitutes 'improvement'. For example, what government structure is ideal: democracy, capitalism, communism, socialism, fascism, or feudalism? And what policies advance society or degrade it: same-sex marriage, abortion, euthanasia, unconstrained free speech? It can be challenging to find a common definition of social improvement with so many moral minds involved!

Moral concerns can be categorised into at least one of six foundations (see Figure 9.4), These foundations include loyalty to one's in-group (vs. betrayal), respecting tradition and legitimate authority (vs. subversion), sanctity and avoidance of disgusting things (vs. degradation), care and protection of others (vs. harm), fairness and justice (vs. cheating), and fighting for liberty (vs. oppression).

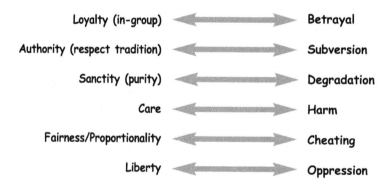

Figure 9.4 Moral foundations.

TRY IT! 9.1

Your Moral Foundations

Find out what you own moral foundations are by completing the test at http://www.celebritytypes.com/morality/6/test.php

These moral foundations likely gave us a survival advantage and served us well when we functioned as small tribes. However, in an increasingly globalised society these foundations can cause problems.

Consider asylum seekers. We may be conflicted between thoughts of wanting to help other people survive and/or not live under a repressive regime (care and liberty) on the one hand, with thoughts that these individuals are non-citizens (out-group members) who could have a negative effect on our existing way of life by not respecting our culture (authority and sanctity vs. degradation of values, beliefs, attitudes, and behaviour), on the other. Furthermore, asylum seekers aren't going through the usual channels of immigration and might even be taking advantage of others' kindness (cheating).

If you're concerned that these values are too ingrained for anyone to change, there is some good news. Our evolved group thinking mentality (us vs. them) and these six moral foundations simply describe the current state of human moral development — they don't prescribe what moral foundations you *should* hold. If you remain flexible, you can use these six moral foundations to consider where your moral views fit in the moral landscape. You can also use these foundations to help you see the variance of moral belief systems between people and the capacity to change their beliefs over time. For example, people who identify with conservative politics seem to place high value on all six factors equally. In contrast, those who identify with more liberal politics place high value on care, fairness, and liberty; however, they tend to place lower value on in-group loyalty, authority, and sanctity.

TRY IT! 9.2

Applying Moral Foundations to Chris, Aisha, and Yourself

Below we have filled in what we think are the answers for Chris (you may disagree). Read through those answers, then use the same approach for

Aisha. Then, most importantly, think of a moral challenge that you currently face, or that you have faced in the past, and fill in the answers for your own moral challenge.

- **Chris — cheating:**

Care / Harm	Chris cares about helping his future clients, which is why he desperately needs to succeed in the course (even if it means cheating).
Fairness / Cheating	Some students do not have a 'cheating advantage' in the exam. Thus, it is not fair to them. However, other students *are* cheating — so in that sense, it is perhaps unfair if Chris cannot?
Liberty / Oppression	(not applicable)
Loyalty / Betrayal	Betrayal of the academic integrity system (thus breaking the Student Code of Conduct)
Authority / Subversion	Cheating is subverting the system of fair assessment, and going against the authority of the examiners.
Purity / Degradation	Chris would like to see himself as a virtuous person. Cheating is degrading that image.

- **Aisha — rejecting her friendship with Sally:**

_____

- *Your* **action given your moral challenge:**

_____

Moral Philosophical Perspectives

To help us think more deeply about morality, we can dip our toes into the vast oceans of moral philosophy. There are multiple philosophical perspectives, each providing a different take on how someone might think and act in a given situation. Morals can be assessed in terms of the resulting outcomes from a situation (consequentialism), the intentions and behaviour of those involved (deontology), the emotional experience invoked (ethical emotivism), and from examining the personal characteristics of those involved (virtue ethics).

We will discuss each of these perspectives in more detail in the coming sections, and we will encourage you to consider your own moral challenges within each. Again, we can't guarantee that you will come up with the 'right' answer, but by considering your moral challenges within each philosophical perspective, you may begin to optimise your own moral reasoning.

Let's begin with an exercise (because you know how we love those). Try to vividly imagine that you are facing the following ethical dilemma. As we go along, you will get to consider how each moral perspective might guide your thoughts and behaviours in this situation:

> You work casually in a fast-food outlet where you notice that one of the supervisors behaves in an overly familiar fashion with some casual employees from ethnic minority backgrounds. The employees who grin and bear the advances seem to get extra shifts. As a fellow employee whom they respect, you hear their dissatisfaction with the supervisor's conduct but, at the same time, you need the work and do not wish to rock the boat (adapted from Davidson & Morrissey, 2010, p. 41).

Consequentialism (focuses on outcome)

Consequentialism suggests that what is 'right' can be determined based on the consequences of our actions. The most popular consequentialist perspective is **utilitarianism**, whose leading proponents were Jeremy Bentham and John Stuart Mill. According to utilitarianism, we can tell if someone's behaviour is moral by looking at how much wellbeing it produces (i.e., utility), and for how many people; basically, *the greatest good for the greatest number*. Specifically, if we were to add up all the pleasant experiences and deduct all the suffering, whatever results in the highest positive value would be considered the most moral course of action to undertake. Utilitarianism gives us a scale (see Figure 9.5) whereby at one end we have the most suffering for the most people, and at the other end we have the most wellbeing for the most people. Actions that move society toward an outcome of suffering (i.e., wars and famines) are considered immoral, whereas actions that move society toward an outcome of wellbeing (i.e., social cohesion, equality, happiness) are considered moral.

In terms of our fast-food worker scenario, how do you think a utilitarian perspective would influence moral reasoning, decision-making, and action? Here is one possible answer: You would likely wish to maximise the benefit for

Figure 9.5 The utilitarianism morality scale.

as many of your co-workers as possible. Thus, your first step would be to discuss the issue with your co-workers. They may decide to keep quiet and put up with the supervisor's behaviour, or they may work out a plan of action to do something about the supervisor's behaviour (which may, or may not, involve you.) So, what about Chris's decision whether to cheat or not? Or Aisha's decision about whether to cut-off her friendship with Sally? What about your own moral dilemma?

Are you starting to think that utilitarianism might be right for you? Let's take utilitarianism for a test drive as we consider the famous 'trolley cart dilemma':

> **Dilemma A:** There is a runaway trolley barrelling down the railway tracks. Ahead, on the tracks, there are five people tied up and unable to move. The trolley is headed straight for them. You are standing some distance off in the train yard, next to a lever. If you pull this lever, the trolley will switch to a different set of tracks. However, you notice that there is one person on the side-track. You have two options:
>
> (1) Do nothing, and the trolley kills the five people on the main track.
>
> (2) Pull the lever, diverting the trolley onto the side-track where it will kill one person.

Which is the 'right' choice? According to utilitarianism, the second option is the moral course of action. When given this version of the trolley dilemma, most people's responses to this question are in alignment with utilitarianism.

However, consider the same scenario, except, rather than pulling a lever to stop the trolley, you must physically push a rather large man onto the tracks in front of the trolley, thus stopping it (but ending messily for the man in question). Would you push him? Most people won't push the man even though the outcome (lives saved) is exactly the same as pulling a lever. Similarly, people are less likely to divert the trolley if it would kill a family member or friend.

Let's assume for the moment that utilitarianism represents 'objective' morality; morality that is always true no matter what the circumstances. It does then seem rather selfish that we wouldn't always choose to push one person to their death to save 5 others, regardless of whether they are some random guy or family member. But is our own selfishness the only reason why we might not want to act in a utilitarian manner? Consider the next moral dilemma:

> **Dilemma B:** A brilliant transplant surgeon has five patients, each in need of a different organ, each of whom will die without that organ. Unfortunately, there are no organs available to perform any of these five transplant operations. A healthy young traveller comes in for a routine check-up. In the course of doing the check-up, the doctor discovers that his organs are compatible with all five of his dying patients. Suppose further that if the young man were to disappear, no one would suspect the doctor. Do you support the decision of the doctor to kill that tourist and provide his healthy organs to those five dying patients, to save their lives?

If utilitarianism is measured solely by lives saved, then the traveller should be sacrificed to save the five patients, but do *you* agree with this practice? Interestingly, most people do not agree. If we focus solely on 'lives saved' as an index of wellbeing or utility, there will be additional societal costs. Imagine living in a society where, at any moment, you could be sacrificed for the greater good without your consent! It would be fair to say most people in that society would have a sense of anxiety and distrust (and travel insurance would cost a fortune). Would saving more lives be worth living in such a society? If utilitarianism is the best moral system for a society, then wellbeing might need to be reconceptualised not merely in terms of lives saved, but also in terms of other important factors like consent.

These dilemmas raise the question of why, and in what ways, human life and consent are valued. They also raise some criticisms of utilitarianism, such as considering the *intentions* of the individual rather than just the outcome, as well as the rights of individuals as entities deserving of respect (instead of treating them merely as numbers). Finally, in the real world, we cannot foresee all possible outcomes of an action, nor discern unambiguously who constitutes the 'greater good'. In the fast-food example above, it could be argued that the upheaval that would result from confronting the supervisor might jeopardise the local clientele's access to fried chicken, which might outweigh any impact on the significantly smaller number of employees!* Some of these criticisms are addressed by the Deontological perspective, which we consider next.

Deontology (focuses on behaviour and intentions)

Deontology — or **duty-based morality** — proposes that morality is based on one's actions, regardless of the consequences. People have a duty to uphold certain principles or rules (e.g., to not lie) regardless of whether the outcome is more negative or positive (e.g., greater suffering from hearing the truth). Immanuel Kant was the most prominent philosopher of this perspective. He argued that *people have an imperative to do good things*, not because doing so will reap reward or mitigate adversity (i.e., as a means to an end), but because it is the *right thing to do, in and of itself* (i.e., as an end). He called this the **categorical imperative.**

According to the categorical imperative, we can determine moral imperatives based on reasoning. Only humans are capable of pure reason, and as such, deserve to be treated with respect and dignity. To ensure we treat people with this respect and dignity, it is an imperative to not use or manipulate them for our own benefit (means to an end), by removing their opportunity to use their rational capacity, or free will. Thus we can see why Kant was against utilitarianism, because he felt that doing what appeared to be best for the greatest number of people would lead to violations of the rights, respect, and dignity of others (e.g., taking 1 healthy person's organs without consent to save 5 others).

> 'Act in such a way that you treat humanity, whether in your own person or in the person of any other, never merely as a means to an end, but always at the same time as an end.'

Kant provided an evaluation tool for determining what other moral imperatives we should follow. In essence, he rephrased the 'golden rule': *treat others how you would like to be treated.*

> 'Act only according to that maxim whereby you can at the same time will that it should become a universal law without contradiction'.

That is, our moral reasoning should not be relative, or tied to particular circumstances or people, but must be uniform or universal.

Consider lying (as a concept, not a course of action). Most of us would hate to live in a world where we couldn't believe anything other people said! According to Kant, if we don't want other people to lie, then *we* shouldn't lie

---

* We are grateful to a 3rd-year Psychology student for drawing this interesting perspective to our attention.

either, regardless of the consequences (as consequences render the moral behaviour as the means to an end, rather than as an end in and of itself). According to Kant, then, if a murderer appears on your doorstep and asks you where your father is, you are duty-bound not to lie, as lying violates the categorical imperative, thus is never permissible (understandably, many of Kant's friends began to decline his dinner invitations). You could either tell the truth, tell the murderer that you refuse to disclose this information, or try and convince him not to follow through with his dastardly plans (good luck!). There is, however, a loophole — if you tell the murderer that you don't know where your father is, technically that may not actually be a lie, as for all you know, he may have just a second ago run from the back of the house (run, Dad, run!). This loophole is sometimes generously applied, most notably by politicians ('I never had sexual relations with that woman'!).

We can consider the application of the categorical imperative in areas such as sales and marketing. When selling a product or service, the categorical imperative suggests that any sale would only be a moral transaction if the customer acted autonomously in their purchasing choice. If the customer was coerced, the salesperson would be using the customer merely to obtain money (i.e., using them as a means to an end), rather than additionally providing the customer with something they needed or wanted based on rational choice. If you think about sales and marketing today, you might notice some subtle (or huge) differences between the categorical imperative and reality.

Now, think back to the trolley dilemma. The categorical imperative would conclude that pushing a man onto the tracks is 'wrong', as it would be using him only as a means to an end.

Remembering our fast-food worker scenario, how do you think a categorical imperative perspective would influence moral reasoning, decision-making, and action? The supervisor's wrongness is based on his attempt to use staff as a means to an end (i.e., to get what *he* wants through unwanted and non-consensual advances). Moreover, doing the 'right' thing is absolutely necessary, regardless of the consequences to yourself or others.

So, you might make it clear to the co-workers and supervisor (separately) about what is 'wrong' about the supervisor's overly familiar behaviour, and you would report the supervisor to authorities. But what about Chris's decision whether to cheat or not? Or Aisha's decision about whether to end her friendship with Sally? What about your own moral dilemma?

Ethical Emotivism (focuses on emotion)

Ethical emotivism focuses on your *feelings* about the rightness or wrongness of an intention, behaviour, or outcome. This position is subjective and is based on Hume's notion that 'reason is, and ought to only be the slave of the passions'. As such, something you think is immoral may be neutral or even moral to someone else. For example, for different people, abortion may evoke feelings of disgust, anger, indifference, or empowerment. Some interesting research has revealed that certain emotions are closely linked with our sense of morality. Disgust is often tied to notions of impurity or contamination, and anger may be linked to violations or harm. For example, many Western societies would feel some disgust at the thought of eating rats and may consider such behaviour as immoral. Historically, rats are associated with impurity, given their perceived capacity to carry disease (e.g., many thought they were responsible for bubonic plague — they were not). However, other cultures consider rat meat to be a delicacy. In contrast, some individuals find rats to be wonderful pets, even better than dogs, and would be just as upset as many dog-lovers about the thought of eating family pets — whether rat or dog.

In terms of our fast-food worker scenario, how do you think an ethical emotivism perspective would influence moral reasoning, decision-making, and action? You may be disgusted by the employer's behaviour, and ethical emotivism suggests that this should guide your judgment of immorality. However, you may also wish to consider not just your own reaction, but whether others are similarly disgusted. If you feel particularly strongly, you may take action. If most people feel that something is wrong, then it is likely that someone will take action. So, what about Chris's decision whether to cheat or not? Or Aisha's decision about whether to end her friendship with Sally? What about your own moral dilemma?

The main (and substantive) criticism of ethical emotivism is its relativism — in terms of individuals, cultures, and even times. For example, there was a period when buying and keeping another human being as property, to work in horrific conditions for no pay, did not evoke the revulsion that it does for most people in most places today (but don't get us started on child labour conditions in some countries). *No opinion can be definitively correct or incorrect*, according to ethical emotivism. To give an extreme example: ethical emotivism can't really say there is anything wrong with a psychopath's manipulative behaviour, or the murder of innocent people. Some people may *feel* it is immoral, whilst the psychopath or murderer may *feel* indifference or pleasure.

Thinking about ethical emotivism does, however, have the practical benefit of drawing attention to our emotions when making moral evaluations. Reflecting on our emotions during moral evaluations can help us optimise our moral mind — do you have an emotional or gut reaction to a moral situation? Is this the driving cause of your belief in the rightness or wrongness of that situation, or is it based on another criterion (wellbeing — utilitarianism; or reason — categorical imperative?).

Virtues (infers character based on behaviour and intentions)

Virtue ethics is mainly concerned with character development. There are many philosophical conceptions of what a virtuous character is, and how we can build one. While this chapter will focus mainly on the Greek philosopher Aristotle, we acknowledge similarities with other dominant influences including Christianity, Islam, Judaism, Buddhism, and Confucianism.

Aristotle spent many a Sunday afternoon pondering a wide range of topics including biology, morals, and government, and how they are all linked by the concept of **teleology** — the idea that everything has a purpose. An acorn's purpose (its *telos*) is to become an oak tree, a human's purpose is to live a good life, and a government's purpose is to put in place the mechanisms allowing us to achieve this good life (ideally, anyhow). According to Aristotle, the 'good life' encompasses a type of happiness called **eudemonia**, in which you seek to fulfil your purpose, leading to contentment and flourishing. This is a different type of happiness to **hedonism**, in which you merely seek and enjoy pleasure, rather than purpose.

Aristotle argued that the 'good life' could be developed through **intellectual virtues**, such as learning, science, and reflecting, together with **moral virtues**, character traits that make you a better person. Aristotle considered moral behaviour as that which a 'virtuous' person would do. To help define moral behaviour, Aristotle proposed the **golden mean** — the idea that moral (or virtuous) behaviour sits between two vices; one of deficiency and one of excess (see Table 9.1). For example, courage can be considered the mean or middle ground between the vices of cowardliness on the one hand, and foolishness or rashness, on the other. Having vices either side of each virtue might be one reason it is easier to give into vices, and not stick to virtuous behaviour — vices outnumber virtues, 2-to-1!

Table 9.1   Aristotle's golden mean: virtuous behaviour sits between two vices, one of deficiency and one of excess.

Sphere of action or feeling	Excess	Golden Mean	Deficiency
Fear and confidence	Rashness	Courage	Cowardice
Pleasure and pain	Gluttony	Temperance	Indifference
Getting and spending	Vulgarity	Humility	Pettiness
Honour and dishonour	Self-centredness	Generosity	Timidity
Anger	Irascibility	Patience	Lack of spirit
Self-expression	Boastfulness	Truthfulness	Understatement
Conversation	Buffoonery	Wittiness	Boorishness
Social conduct	Fawning	Friendliness	Surliness
Shame	Shyness	Modesty	Shamelessness
Indignation	Envy	Righteous indignation	Malicious enjoyment

We can use these virtues as a template as we optimise our moral mind. Where do you fall on the spectrum of virtue or vice, and in which domains of your life (romantic relationships, family, career, etc.)?

Getting back to our fast-food worker scenario, how do you think a virtue perspective would influence moral reasoning, decision-making, and action? Here is one possible answer: Do what a virtuous person would do, that is, be courageous and just, rather than selfish and cowardly. Confront the matter regardless of your loss or gain. So, what about Chris's decision whether to cheat or not? Or Aisha's decision about whether to end her friendship with Sally? What about your own moral dilemma?

Sometimes, of course, the situation does not necessarily yield a straight-forward answer. Consider Jane. She lied to her current girlfriend, Kai about speaking with her ex-girlfriend, Mika. A virtuous person would have been truthful, so Jane is not behaving as a virtuous person would. If Jane lied because she was intending on cheating, then this would be a reflection of Jane's character as untruthful and unfaithful. However, if Mika reached out to Jane because she was going through a difficult time, as her mum had just died and she had nobody else to talk to, then Jane may still be thought of as untruthful, but perhaps also with the virtue of friendliness. As a result, Jane's character may be considered less negatively, and her behaviour less immoral. If Jane's reason for lying to Kai was because Kai might react very negatively, then this may also suggest something about Kai's character.

 DIVING DEEPER 9.2

The Subjective vs. 'Objective' Nature of Morality

Discussing whether morality is subjective or 'objective' is a sensitive issue due to the consequences that are implied. If morals are subjective, it allows individuals to shed responsibility for questionable behaviour. For example, female circumcision may be defended based on cultural relativism. You could never say that certain actions are absolutely wrong; it would just be your opinion or, perhaps, a cultural peculiarity that others just don't understand. This was the criticism against ethical emotivism, in which your feelings towards an event determined whether it was moral or immoral. This kind of moral subjectivity may make you feel uncomfortable. If so, you would be in good company. Dostoevsky also felt there was a need for 'objective' morality. His basis for this objectivity was of divine origins: 'If God does not exist, then everything is permitted'.

Religion is one avenue by which an 'objective' basis for morality is proposed. In this case, a god sets the moral standards. However, this means you need to decide which god to follow and, whether a god is truly objective. Also, if such morals are indeed 'objective', one potential consequence is the authority provided to an individual to praise or denounce the behaviour of others. For example, an individual may condemn abortion using authority (e.g., religious) as an 'objective' basis for its 'immorality' (i.e., 'wrongness').

Religion is not the only basis for 'objective' morality that has been proposed. You have already read about attempts to define morality 'objectively' by equating morality with wellbeing (utility; utilitarianism), appealing to reason (categorical imperative), or seeing morality at a tool for human flourishing (virtue ethics). For example, utilitarianism might consider female circumcision immoral because it causes pain and reduces subsequent pleasurable experiences. The categorical imperative might consider it immoral if the individual did not consent, as it took away their free will. As female circumcision leaves a woman deficient for certain types of sexual experiences, virtue ethics could deem it as immoral by denying someone the opportunity to develop their own sexual self-restraint. That is, Aristotle would view 'proper' sexual activity as the mean between a deficient sexual character (abstinence) and excessive sexual character (promiscuity).

⚑ TRY IT! 9.3

Can Self-driving Cars make Moral Decisions?

With technological advances, we are moving to an era of artificial intelligence requiring a moral framework. While self-driving cars will reduce the number of accidents, there will be situations where the car must decide whether to protect the driver or prevent a collision at the cost of the driver (e.g., crashing into a wall to save a group of pedestrians). What moral framework would you want your car (and others) to hold?

Developing Your Own Moral Beliefs

Our aim in discussing these moral perspectives was to provide you with tools to raise your awareness and understanding of your own moral beliefs, so that you could optimise your moral mind and make the best possible decisions in morally challenging situations (moving from Figure 9.1 to 9.2). As you become more aware of your moral beliefs, you may notice they are based partially on your parents' or friends' beliefs and values (such as in Aisha's case). Your parents' or friends' beliefs may contain 'virtuous' characteristics, such as integrity and courage, which most of us readily embrace to guide our behaviour.

However, there may be other aspects of your parents' or friends' moral beliefs that you are considering challenging or even discarding now that you have examined them more closely. As you continue optimising your moral mind in this way, you will hopefully begin to start thinking and acting in a way that feels more authentic, and ultimately makes you happier and healthier. An additional benefit to this effortful, but liberating process is that we can start to identify others' (often implicit) moral beliefs, and understand where and why we differ.

Remember, we are not advocating any one moral perspective over another. You may find that you favour just one philosophical perspective, or you may adopt different perspectives for different domains of your life, or different situations you encounter. For example, you may be more consequentialist at work (e.g., embellish achievements in a job interview) but more deontological with your friends or partner (e.g., not lie to one another). If you're feeling brave, you could even try combining perspectives, for example, utilitarianism bounded by the categorical imperative: behaviours that seek to increase well-being would be considered moral only if they did not, at the same time, take away someone's free will, respect, and dignity. In this case, utility would be defined as maximum wellbeing without taking away individual rights (you may want to read further into rule-based and act-based utilitarianism).

Additional Tools to Identify and Evaluate Moral Beliefs

In addition to determining which moral perspective your belief aligns with, there are approaches that you can take to understand the basis of your beliefs, and to think more critically about your moral position. As shown in Chapter 2, rather than seeing a situation objectively, the confirmation bias suggests that when you want something to be true, you gather information to support your ideas. This is true of moral positions, where we tend to seek out information and individuals with the same views as ours, to reinforce the 'rightness' of our position. Take Aisha's views about homosexuality — the following strategies can assist her to evaluate the sources of her beliefs.

- **Seek out evidence both for and against your belief.** Any beliefs that Aisha has about homosexuality could be critically examined by finding credible sources of evidence, such as government statistics, or better still, scientific studies using rigorous methodology (see Chapter 2). Another approach might be for Aisha to compare the characteristics of her two homosexual friends (Sally and Adam) to her negative beliefs about homosexual people. If she found mismatches, then she may start to question the validity of those beliefs!

- **Critically compare relevant laws and policies.** Aisha could compare how different governments are treating homosexuality in terms of laws and policies, and consider which governments are truly progressive on the basis of other criteria she values, such as laws and policies regarding how women are treated, and regarding religious tolerance. These laws and policies reflect expected moral and behavioural standards, influenced by social customs and expectations.

- **Critically compare relevant codes of ethics** (see below). Aisha could examine the codes of ethics of organisations that she admires (such as the professional organisation she intends to join after she finishes her training), to see if they make any statements about membership criteria or professional behaviour standards regarding clients, that are relevant to homosexuality (see, for example, the American Psychological Association's documents on homosexuality).

Morals, Ethics, and the Law in Our Personal and Professional Life

'It takes 20 years to build a reputation, and 5 minutes to ruin it. If you think about that, you will do things differently' (Warren Buffet)

As we mentioned earlier, ethics are standards of behaviour set by a group, organisation, or professional society. It is important that we conduct ourselves to a high standard both for our moral development and to cooperate effectively with others — getting along to get ahead.

Most ethical standards have common underlying principles such as respect for autonomy and dignity, equality, beneficence and harm minimisation, justice, and integrity. These are further refined within different professional ethical codes, which may include more contextualised principles such as confidentiality, professional responsibility, and consent.

Sometimes our moral beliefs don't align with the ethical standards of an organisation, or even with the law. In these cases, some individuals choose to behave in accordance with their moral perspective. For example, when same-sex marriage was legalised in the United States, a clerk denied a same-sex couple their marriage certificate because she disagreed with the practice, even though her workplace ethics would have asked that she treat people with respect and according to the law. At times and in places where laws have denied particular groups the right to vote in democratic elections (e.g., women, Indigenous peoples), many thousands have followed their moral compass in protest against such laws. While sometimes we feel that our morals must be expressed, we want to be careful not to simply heap our subjective moral beliefs onto others. With this in mind, defining the ethical standards for a group can be somewhat challenging.

We can use a thought experiment called the **veil of ignorance** to help us consider what ethical principles we should uphold. Imagine being born into a society with an equal chance of becoming any of its members. We could be born on any spectrum of wealth, racial identity, sex, sexual preference, physical attractiveness, ability, or status. Before we lift the veil and see how we turn out, what moral and ethical principles would we like the society to uphold? It is likely that you would want certain principles in place to protect you, should you be less fortunate in that society. Many progressive societies try to provide individuals with equal rights where there is general agreement (e.g., education, careers, voting) while they take more time to nut out more complex areas of moral disagreement (e.g., euthanasia).

Conclusion

What we consider 'right' and 'wrong' is often determined by our moral mind. We may have never previously examined our moral mind in detail, particularly in terms of how it developed, and how it compares to objective evidence, laws, codes of conduct, and established moral perspectives and standards. When the origins of our sense of 'right' and 'wrong' remain buried deep within our mind, we can't always be confident that this sense is optimal, or even appropriate in our rapidly changing world. If we take the time to evaluate and optimise our moral mind, we can engage in more helpful decision-making and behaviour in the face of moral challenges. We can also become capable of helping others deal with their personal and interpersonal moral challenges.

Summary Points

- We are often not aware of where our moral beliefs come from, or where they sit in the vast and historical 'moral landscape'.

- Given that 'moral indignation' can lead to frustration (e.g., from queue-jumping), or even bloodshed (e.g., from religious wars), it seems rational to put in the effort to identify and evaluate our moral beliefs and determine whether they are optimal in terms of guiding our behaviour.

- Tools or approaches that can be used to examine our moral beliefs include: gathering all the available quality evidence (not just that which confirms our beliefs!); comparing our beliefs to laws (which represent the moral beliefs of the majority of people in democracies — not always perfectly!, or, the current political party in power); comparing our beliefs to the ethical codes of organisations that we admire (e.g., professional codes of conduct — again, not always perfect); and testing our beliefs against established moral perspectives.

- The bulk of this chapter presents different moral philosophical perspectives — none perfect for every situation — so you need to think carefully about what you feel most comfortable with (and why). Examining, and if necessary, revising your moral beliefs can help you to optimise how you respond to morally challenging situations, to appreciate where other people are coming from in their moral beliefs, and even to lead others in optimal moral decision-making and behaviour.

CHAPTER 10

Optimising Minds

'Life is not meant to be easy, my child, but take
courage: it can be delightful'
— George Bernard Shaw

Remember Liam from the first chapter? He had been suffering as a result of his dysfunctional beliefs about what *should* happen in the aftermath of a first date... and he almost blew the beginning of his relationship with Bec (as well as his job — thankfully he had a somewhat forgiving boss). He and Bec are still enjoying the 'honeymoon' period of their relationship, sharing their interests and their friends, trying new things. Because Liam really is keen on Bec, he is putting a lot of work into discovering and assessing his 'should' and 'must' beliefs, then deciding which need to be changed to more optimal ways of thinking, allowing him to move toward his goal of building a long-lasting relationship with Bec. He does not want to make the same mistakes he made with his previous relationships, and so is willing to swallow his pride and make constructive change. Now, he feels comfortable enough with himself and his relationship with Bec that he has decided to tell Bec what he is up to. He is hopeful that she'll see why he is putting in the effort, and support him in doing so.

If you are an imperfect human being like Liam (wait — that's all of us), we are hoping that this book is useful to you in examining your ways of thinking, and then deciding what is optimal versus suboptimal thinking in striving toward your valued goals. If some of your thinking is unhelpful, then hopefully you will find some of the tools in this book useful in working out what is changeable, and what is not. If you cannot change (for whatever reason), then we hope that some of the tools in this book help you find ways of minimising the negative impact of those suboptimal ways of thinking. If it is possible to change, then we hope that the tools in this book serve you well in optimising those aspects of your thinking. Of course, this all takes quite a bit of courage and effort on your part. Nevertheless, remember that your brain has a natural rubber tendency, and is capable of supporting changes to ways of thinking.

The journey you take to rubberising your brain starts with understanding the imperfectness of your mind, and takes you through the process of shining a light on your M_{SUBS}, whether to do with stress or perfectionism, icebergs or procrastination. Along the way you can discover myriad tools for optimising your mind and becoming more positive, more connected, more mindful, and more motivated. Some of you may be content for now with just shining a light to become aware of your M_{SUB}'s. Others of you may pick up the tools on offer and try to optimise your thinking (remember Figure 1.4). Whichever steps you take on this journey, you are moving along the path of becoming aware of and optimising your thinking, which is a stellar achievement (sound of thunderous Oscar-worthy applause).

So, congratulations on getting to the last chapter of this book! Particularly because we know that life happens, and life is full of ups and downs (all of which can get in the way of reading this book). Bad things *do* happen, and often these things ('S' in our SMR model) are out of our control (yes, fellow control freaks, it really is impossible to control everything). Fortunately, *how we respond* to both good and bad situations can become predominantly within our control, because it is possible to learn new and better ways of thinking that lead to more optimal responses, and thus better outcomes. We hope that you have found the optimising tools in this book to be helpful to you personally.

There are, however, some caveats. Firstly, just as most of us cannot fix our own broken leg, and need the assistance of professionals (e.g., a surgeon), you may find yourself in a really deep psychological hole that you cannot dig yourself out of — even with the wonderful tools in this book. At that point, you need to have enough courage and psychological flexibility to throw out that 'I need to do this by myself' iceberg belief (see Chapter 3) and get the expert help you need (see *More Resources* for some leads). No-one can do it alone (human society has progressed because we are social animals, not hermits), and you might be surprised by how supportive your friends and family are when they see that you are trying to change from sub-optimised to optimised.

Secondly, as complex as your mind and behaviour is, we wanted to keep this book as light as possible, so that you could easily carry it with you to read on the bus and share with your friends. Thus, the book just 'scratches the surface' on many topics. We could have Dived Deeper on many topics, but we did not want you to trade in your suboptimal thinking for back problems as you lugged this tome of wisdom wherever you went. Thus, our approach was to have *More Resources* sections in most chapters, so that you can follow up ideas that you find helpful or that interest you. You can also look at our related website (therubberbrain.com) for more activities and resources.

Thirdly, the tools in this book are science-based — meaning they will work for the majority of people most of the time. That is, not all tools will work for you at all times. Using the tools is an iterative process, depending on your current needs and capacity. You may have skimmed over some sections because you do not need those tools now. But remember that as things change (they usually do), you may want to come back to some of those tools. Hopefully, though, you will have taken on some of the tools in this book, such that you have improved significant aspects of your life, as depicted in Figure 10.1.

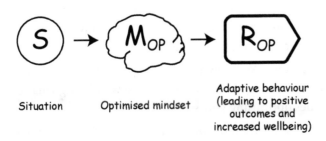

Situation   Optimised mindset   Adaptive behaviour
(leading to positive
outcomes and
increased wellbeing)

Figure 10.1 Learning to use the various mind-optimising tools can lead to well-practiced optimised ways of thinking (M_{OP}) in different life situations (S) that
will lead to adaptive behaviour (R_{OP}) in that particular situation, and thus
positive outcomes. [An additional caveat for the SMR model is that, for
the sake of simplicity, we do not separately emphasise the outcomes,
which would normally reinforce the behaviours — for more information
see the 'Learning' chapter of any first-year psychology textbook.]

239

Fourthly, we have deliberately skimmed over the point of conscious vs. unconscious thinking (i.e., aware vs. unaware) that underpins behaviour. Optimising thinking requires you, in the first instance, to become aware of your suboptimal thinking — that is, your M_{SUB}'s that may have become so automated that they are below consciousness ('unthinking'). Some of the tools in this book should help you 'shine a light' on these thoughts that sit below your awareness, so that you are now aware of them. Of course, a high proportion of your thinking is optimal, whether you are aware (conscious) of those thoughts, or not. And, as you change your M_{SUB}'s to M_{OP}'s, these M_{OP}'s may become habits and slip below our awareness. This is adaptive, because even the best of us do not have enough brain power to be thinking about our thinking ALL of the time! We'd never get anything done! However, having gone through the process of 'shining a light' on those thought processes, when you again need to reflect on the underlying M, it will not be difficult to understand the basis for your 'unthinking' behaviour. Before we leave this topic, however, we acknowledge that sometimes thoughts are *inaccessible* to simple introspection, even with our tools — this is a fact that many psychological scientists have addressed at great length, and we acknowledge this limitation to the power of the tools presented here.

If you were not looking to change yourself — yes, we know a rarefied few of you are perfect — but rather, you were attempting to understand the imperfect people you are forced to interact with every day (so tiring), then we hope that this book has been of some use to you in that regard. You might even want to buy them a copy of this book to help them to see the error of their ways. For others of you, this may have been a textbook, so remember to refer to the study tips to help ensure that you blitz the exam.

So where to now? We know that reading about (let alone enacting) optimising minds can be tiring, and you might be wondering what other benefits are there besides optimising yourself and thus increasing your own wellbeing?

If you are able to use tools that optimise your behaviour and thus create positive outcomes for yourself, it is likely you will create a ripple effect of wellbeing — that is, the wellbeing will 'spread' to those around you. How? Firstly, if a particular tool worked for you, then it is likely that you will tell others, and so others may also benefit. Secondly, you are likely to possess more psychological resources (e.g., you will not be wasting your emotional energy on fruitless worry), and thus you are more likely to have the capacity to be able to lend a hand to others when needed (e.g., social or physical support). As such, they benefit (and there may also be reciprocal effects for you, thus building relationships and community)*.

Our unified vision has been that of 'giving psychology away' to those who have the most potential — you — because you are interested enough in optimising yourself that you got to the end of this book. Years spent working with young adults has convinced us that (1) everyone, even you, can do with some help to improve self-management skills to become the best version of yourself, and (2) people like you have the power to have a positive impact on the world around you, and this power is increased when you use the tools in this book to optimise yourself. A key concept underlying the intent of this book is 'psychological literacy'— the capacity to intentionally use psychological science to meet personal, professional, and societal needs. Just as language literacy was the 'prime mover' of human advancement in the 20th Century, we argue (without any bias, of course) that psychological literacy is the 'prime mover' in the 21st Century. Having 'conquered' nature in the last century, we now need to turn our attention toward 'conquering' (i.e., managing) ourselves, in order to increase the possibility of preserving ourselves, and our world. The first step is right here — the tools in this book. We are optimistic that the more people (like you) who spend time and energy to optimise your thinking, the greater the amount of wellbeing generated, and the better the world will be (aw, shucks! No, really).

We wish you the best in this delightful adventure!

More Resources

• Professional Help:
For immediate help, call your national emergency number (in Australia, 000), or your national helpline (e.g., in Australia, LifeLine 131114). Online resources are listed at http://www.emhprac.org.au/, and at unistudentsuccess.com/studentlanding. Your national psychological society will have a listing of registered psychologists (Australia: http://www.believeinchange.com/Home/Become-the-Change/Find-A-Psychologist), and you can ask your general practitioner for a referral.

---

* Of course, there are ethical limits to how much you can effectively help others. For example, if they have severe psychological problems, the best you can do is to convince them that they need to find good professional help (and you should refrain from playing novice counselor, as it might get in the way of them getting expert help).

Bibilography

Chapter 2

Naïve and flawed reasoning practices:
Halpern, D. F. (1998). Teaching critical thinking for transfer across domains: Disposition, skills, structure training, and metacognitive monitoring. *American Psychologist, 53*, 449-455. http://dx.doi.org/10.1037/0003-066X.53.4.449

Confirmation Bias:
Nickerson, R.S. (1998). Confirmation bias: A ubiquitous phenomenon in many guises. Review of General Psychology, 2, 175-220. https://pdfs.semantic-scholar.org/70c9/3e5e38a8176590f69c0491fd63ab2a9e67c4.pdf

Self-fulfilling prophecy:
Rosenthal, R. (2002). The Pygmalion effect and its mediating mechanisms. In J. Aronson (Ed). *Improving academic achievement: Impact of psychological factors on education*, (pp. 25-36). San Diego, CA: Academic Press.

Availability Heuristic:
Tversky, A., & Kahneman, D. (1973). Availability: A heuristic for judging frequency and probability. *Cognitive Psychology, 5(1)*, 207-233.

Death Odds, 1990, September 24, cited in
https://courses.eller.arizona.edu/mgmt/delaney/p_chapter11.pdf.

National Safety Council US: http://www.nsc.org/learn/safety-knowledge/Pages/injury-facts-chart.aspx

Representativeness heuristic:

Tversky, A., & Kahneman, D. (1974). Judgment under uncertainty: Heuristics and biases. *Science, 185 (4157)*, 1124–1131.

The Just World Hypothesis:

Rubin, Z., & Peplau, A. (1973). Belief in a just world and reactions to another's lot: A study of participants in the national draft lottery. *Journal of Social Issues, 29*, 1–11.

Halo Effect:

Chandon, P., & Wansink, B. (2007). The Biasing Health Halos of Fast-Food Restaurant Health Claims: Lower Calorie Estimates and Higher Side-Dish Consumption Intentions. *Journal of Consumer Research, 34*, 301-314.

Fundamental Attribution Error:

Berry, Z., & Frederickson, J. (2015). Explanations and implications of the Fundamental Attribution Error: A review and proposal. *Journal of Integrated Social Sciences, 5 (1)*, 44-57. Retrieved from

http://www.jiss.org/documents/volume_5/issue_1/JISS%202015%205(1)%2044-57%20FAE.pdf

Logical fallacies:

https://yourlogicalfallacyis.com/

Correlation proves causation:

Stanovich, K.E. (2013). *How to think straight about Psychology* (10th edn). Boston: Pearson.

Aknin, L.B., Dunn, E.W., and Norton, M.I. (2012). Happiness runs in a circular motion: Evidence for a positive feedback loop between prosocial spending and happiness. *Journal of Happiness Studies, 13*, 347-355.

www.happify.com

Logic of flawed experimentation and Principle of converging evidence:

Stanovich, K.E. (2013). *How to think straight about Psychology* (10th ed). Boston: Pearson.

Chapter 3

Self-knowledge:

Wilson, T. D. (2009). Know thyself. *Perspectives on Psychological Science, 4,* 384–389.

Psychological Literacy:

Cranney, J. & Morris, S. (2011). Adaptive cognition and psychological literacy. In J. Cranney and D.S. Dunn (Eds.), *The psychologically literate citizen: Foundations and global perspectives* (pp. 251-268). New York: Oxford University Press.

Metacognitive knowledge:

Krathwohl, D. R. (2002). A revision of Bloom's Taxonomy: An overview. *Theory into Practice, 41 (4),* 212-218.

Knowledge we store about ourselves:

Mayer, J,D. (2014). Know thyself. *Psychology Today,* accessed from https://www.psychologytoday.com/articles/201403/know-thyself

Diehl, M, & Hay, E.L. (2011) Self-concept differentiation and self-concept clarity across adulthood: Associations with age and psychological well-being. *International Journal of Aging and Human Development, 73,* 125-152.

Accuracy and sources of self-knowledge:

Wilson, T. D. (2009). Know thyself. *Perspectives on Psychological Science, 4,* 384–389.

Nisbett, R.E., & Wilson, T.D. (1977). Telling more than we can know: Verbal reports on mental processes. *Psychological Review, 84 (3),* 231-259.

Kinch, J.W. (1963). A Formalized Theory of the Self-Concept. *American Journal of Sociology, 68 (4),* 481-486.

Social comparison:

Festinger, L. (1954). A theory of social comparison processes. *Human Relations, 7,* 117-140.

Helgeson, V. S., & Mickelson, K. D. (1995). Motives for social comparison. *Personality and Social Psychology Bulletin, 21,* 1200-1209.

Wills, T. A. (1981). Downward comparison principles in social psychology. *Psychological Bulletin, 90,* 245-271.

Henderson-King, D., Henderson-King, E., & Hoffman, L. (2001). Media images and women's self-evaluations: Social context and importance of attractiveness as moderators. *Personality and Social Psychology Bulletin, 27,* 1407-1416.

Dittmar, H., Halliwell, E., & Ive, S. (2006). Does Barbie make girls want to be thin? The effect of experimental exposure to images of dolls on the body image of 5- to 8-year-old girls. *Developmental Psychology, 42*, 283-292.

Diving Deeper 3.1 — How well do people know themselves?

Carlson, E. N., Vazire, S., & Furr, R. M. (2011). Meta-insight: Do people really know how others see them? *Journal of Personality and Social Psychology, 101*, 831–846.

Dunning, D., Heath, C., & Suls, J. M. (2004). Flawed self-assessment: Implications for health, education, and the workplace. *Psychological Science in the Public Interest, 5*, 69–106.

Nisbett, R.E., & Wilson, T.D. (1977). Telling more than we can know: Verbal reports on mental processes. *Psychological Review, 84* (3), 231-259.

Carlson, E.N. (2013). Overcoming the barriers to self-knowledge: Mindfulness as a path to seeing yourself as you really are. *Perspectives on Psychological Science, 8*, 173-186

Wilson, T. D. (2009). Know thyself. *Perspectives on Psychological Science, 4*, 384–389.

Icebergs/Core Beliefs:

Reivich, K., & Shatte, A. (2002). *The Resilience Factor: 7 Keys To Finding Your Inner Strength And Overcome Life's Hurdles.* New York: Broadway Books.

Know thy Values:

Hayes, S. C., Luoma, J., Bond, F., Masuda, A., & Lillis, J. (2006). Acceptance and Commitment Therapy: Model, processes, and outcomes. *Behaviour Research and Therapy, 44(1)*, 1-25.

Wilson, K. G., & Murrell, A. R. (2004). Values work in Acceptance and Commitment Therapy: Setting a Course for Behavioral Treatment. In Hayes, S. C., Follette, V. M., & Linehan, M. (Eds.), *Mindfulness & Acceptance: Expanding the cognitive-behavioral tradition* (pp. 120-151). New York: Guilford Press.

Identifying your values:

Cranney, J. & Nithy, V. (2015). Academic Self-management Program Manual Retrieved from http://unistudentsuccess.com/the-fridge/

Character Strengths:

Peterson, C., & Seligman, M.E.P. (2004). *Character strengths and virtues: A handbook and classification.* Oxford: Oxford University Press.

Proyer, R.T., Gander, F., Wellenzohn, S., & Ruch, W. (2015). Strengths-based positive psychology interventions: A randomized placebo-controlled online trial on long-term effects for a signature strengths-vs. a lesser strengths intervention. *Frontiers in Psychology, 6,* Article 456.

Forest, J., Mageau, G. V. A., Crevier-Braud, L., Bergeron, L., Dubreuil, P., & Lavigne, G. V. L. (2012). Harmonious passion as an explanation of the relation between signature strengths' use and well-being at work: Test of an intervention program. *Human Relations, 65(9),* 1233-1252.

Linley, P. A., Nielsen, K. M., Gillett, R., & Biswas-Diener, R. (2010). Using signature strengths in pursuit of goals: Effects on goal progress, need satisfaction, and well-being, and implications for coaching psychologists. *International Coaching Psychology Review, 5(1),* 6-15.

Madden, W., Green, S., & Grant, A. M. (2011). A pilot study evaluating strengths-based coaching for primary school students: Enhancing engagement and hope. *International Coaching Psychology Review, 6(1),* 71-83.

Seligman, M. E. P., Steen, T. A., Park, N., & Peterson C. (2005). Positive psychology in progress. Empirical validation of interventions. *American Psychologist, 60,* 410–421.

Know thy personality:

Bernstein, D.A., Pooley, J.A., Cohen, L., Gouldthorp, B., Provost, S., & Cranney, J. (2013). *Psychology: An international discipline in context: Australian and New Zealand Edition.* Melbourne: Cengage.

McCrae, R. R., & Costa, P. T. Jr. (1997). Personality trait structure as a human universal. *American Psychologist, 52,* 509-516.

Diving Deeper 3.3 — Identity:

Szubanski, M. (2016). *Reckoning: A memoir. Melbourne:* Text Publishing.

Sheldon, K.M. & Houser-Marko, L. (2001). Self-concordance, goal- attainment, and the pursuit of happiness: Can there be an upward spiral? *Journal of Personality and Social Psychology, 80,* 152-165.

Thinking about Desired Futures:

Morisano, D., Hirsh, J. B, Peterson, J. B., Pihl, R. O., & Shore, B. M. (2010). Setting, elaborating, and reflecting on personal goals improves academic performance. *Journal of Applied Psychology, 95,* 255-264.

Your journey to self-knowledge:

Zimmerman, B. (1995). Self-regulation involves more than metacognition: A social cognitive perspective. *Educational Psychologist, 30,* 217-221.

4

Chapter 4

Equivalence of ACT and CBT:

Ruiz, F. J. (2012). Acceptance and Commitment Therapy versus Traditional Cognitive Behavioral Therapy: A Systematic Review and Meta-analysis of Current Empirical Evidence. *International Journal of Psychology & Psychological Therapy, 12*, 333–357.

Mindfulness and its Benefits:

Grossman, P., Niemann, L., Schmidt, S., & Walach, H. (2004). Mindfulness-based stress reduction and health benefits. *Journal of Psychosomatic Research, 57*, 35–43. http://doi.org/10.1016/S0022-3999(03)00573-7

Jha, A. P., Krompinger, J., & Baime, M. J. (2007). Mindfulness training modifies subsystems of attention. *Cognitive Affective & Behavioral Neuroscience, 7*, 109–119. http://doi.org/10.3758/CABN.7.2.109

Chiesa, A., & Serretti, A. (2009). Mindfulness-based stress reduction for stress management in healthy people: A review and meta-analysis. *The Journal of Alternative and Complementary Medicine, 15*, 593–600.

Hölzel, B. K., Carmody, J., Vangel, M., Congleton, C., Yerramsetti, S. M., Gard, T., & Lazar, S. W. (2011). Mindfulness practice leads to increases in regional brain gray matter density. *Psychiatry Research: Neuroimaging, 191*, 36–43. http://doi.org/10.1016/j.pscychresns.2010.08.006

Ivanovski, B., & Malhi, G. S. (2007). The psychological and neurophysiological concomitants of mindfulness forms of meditation. *Acta Neuropsychiatrica, 19*, 76–91. http://doi.org/10.1111/j.1601-5215.2007.00175.x

Acceptance and Commitment Therapy (ACT) and its Benefits:

Powers, M. B., Vorde Sive Vording, Zum, M. B., & Emmelkamp, P. M. G. (2009). Acceptance and Commitment Therapy: A Meta-Analytic Review. *Psychotherapy and Psychosomatics, 78(2)*, 73–80. http://doi.org/10.1159/000190790

Cognitive Behaviour Therapy (CBT) and its Benefits:

Beck, J. S. (2011). *Cognitive Behavior Therapy, Second Edition: Basics and Beyond.* New York: Guilford Publications.

Butler, A. C., Chapman, J. E., Forman, E. M., & Beck, A. T. (2006). The empirical status of cognitive-behavioral therapy: A review of meta-analyses. *Clinical Psychology Review, 26(1)*, 17–31. http://doi.org/10.1016/j.cpr.2005.07.003

Disputing Thoughts:

Ellis, A. (2003). Cognitive Restructuring of the Disputing of Irrational Beliefs. In W. T. O'Donohue, J. E. Fisher, & S. C. Hayes (Eds.), *Cognitive behavior therapy: Applying empirically supported techniques in your practice.* NJ: USA: John Wiley & Sons, Inc.

Edelman, S. (2013). *Change your thinking* (3rd edn).Harper Collins Australia.

Behavioural Experiments:

Bennett-Levy, J. (2004). *Oxford Guide to Behavioural Experiments in Cognitive Therapy.* Oxford University Press.

Jacobson, N. S., Dobson, K. S., Truax, P. A., Addis, M. E., Koerner, K., Gollan, J. K., et al. (1996). A Component Analysis of Cognitive-Behavioral Treatment for Depression. *Journal of Consulting and Clinical Psychology, 64,* 295–304.

Longmore, R. J., & Worrell, M. (2007). Do we need to challenge thoughts in cognitive behavior therapy? *Clinical Psychology Review, 27*(2), 173–187. http://doi.org/10.1016/j.cpr.2006.08.001

Diving Deeper 4.1 — The Birth of the Cognitive Model and Cognitive Behaviour Therapies

Alloy, L. B., Abramson, L. Y., & Whitehouse, W. G. (1999). Depressogenic cognitive styles: Predictive validity, information processing and personality characteristics, and developmental origins. *Behaviour Research and Therapy, 37,* 503–531.

Beck, A. T. (1970). Cognitive therapy: Nature and relation to behavior therapy. *Behavior Therapy, 1,* 184–200.

Beck, A. T. (1974). The development of depression: A cognitive model. In R. J. Friedman & M. M. Katz (Eds.), *The psychology of depression: Contemporary theory and research.* Oxford, England.

Chapter 5

Diving Deeper 5.1 — The Stress Response:

Selye H. (1956). *The stress of life.* New York: McGraw-Hill Book Co.

Chronic stressors and health:

Kiecolt-Glaser, J. K., McGuire, L., Robles, T. F., & Glaser, R. (2002). Psychoneuroimmunology: Psychological influences on immune function and health. *Journal of Consulting and Clinical Psychology, 70*(3), 537-547.

Kiecolt-Glaser, J. K., (1999). Stress, Personal Relationships, and Immune Function: Health Implications. *Brain, Behavior, and Immunity 13*, 61–72

Segerstrom, S.C., & Miller, G.E. (2004). Psychological stress and the human immune system: a meta-analytic study of 30 years of inquiry. *Psychological Bulletin, 130 (4)*, 601-630.

Primary & Secondary Stress Appraisal:

Lazarus, R., & Folkman, S. (1984). *Stress, appraisal, and coping.* New York: Springer Publishing.

Folkman, S., & Lazarus, R. S. (1985). If it changes it must be a process: Study of emotion and coping during three stages of a college examination. *Journal of Personality and Social Psychology, 48(1)*, 150-170.

Stress as a Performance enhancer:

Yerkes R.M., & Dodson, J.D. (1908). The relation of strength of stimulus to rapidity of habit-formation. *Journal of Comparative Neurology and Psychology, 18*, 459–482.

Stress can be your friend:

McGonigal, K. (2015). *The Upside of Stress: Why Stress Is Good for You, and How to Get Good at It.* Avery.

Tend and Befriend response:

Taylor, S.E., Cousino Klein, L., Lewis, B.P., Gruenewald, T.L., Gurung, R.A.R., & Updegraff, J.A. (2000). Biobehavioral Responses to Stress in Females: Tend-and-Befriend, Not Fight-or-Flight. *Psychological Review, 107 (3)*, 411-429.

Try-It! 5.2 — Positive Mindset:

Crum, A. & Lyddy, C. (2014). De-stressing stress: The power of mindsets and the art of stressing mindfully. In A. Ie, C.T. Ngnoumen, & E. J. Langer (Eds.) *The Wiley Blackwell Handbook of Mindfulness.* New Jersey: Wiley-Blackwell.

Crum, A., Salovey, P., & Achor, S. (2013). Rethinking Stress: The role of mindsets in determining the stress response. *Journal of Personality and Social Psychology, 104 (4)*, 716-733.

Lieberman, M. D., Eisenberger, N. I., Crockett, M. J., Tom, S. M., Pfeifer, J. H., & Way, B. M. (2007). Putting feelings into words. *Psychological Science*, 18(5), 421.

McGonigal, K. (2015). *The Upside of Stress: Why Stress Is Good for You, and How to Get Good at It.* Avery.

Pennebaker, J.W. (1997). Writing About Emotional Experiences as a Therapeutic Process. *Psychological Science, 8(3)*, 162-166

Approach and Avoidance Coping strategies:

Carver, C. S. & Connor-Smith, J. (2010). Personality and coping. *Annual Review of Psychology*, 61, 679-704.

Higgins, J. E. & Endler, N. S. (1995). Coping, life stress, and psychological and somatic distress. *European Journal of Personality*, 9, 253-270.

Problem- and emotion-focused coping strategies:

Folkman, S., Lazarus, R.S., Gruen, R. J., & DeLongis, A. (1986). Appraisal, coping, health status, and psychological symptoms. *Journal of Personality and Social Psychology, 50(3)*, 571-579.

Brenes, G.A., Rapp, S.R., Rejeski, W.J., & Miller, M.E. (2002). Do optimism and pessimism predict physical functioning? *Journal of Behavioural Medicine, 25 (3)*, 291-231.

Hölzel, B. K., J. Carmody, M. Vangel, C. Congleton, S. M. Yerramsetti, T. Gard & S. W. Lazar (2011). Mindfulness practice leads to increases in regional brain gray matter density. *Neuroimaging, 191*, 36-43.

Effect of laughter:

Cousins, N. (1979). *Anatomy of an illness as perceived by the patient: Reflections on healing and regeneration.* New York: Norton.

Fry, W. (1979). *Mirth and the Human Cardiovascular System: The Study of Humor.* Los Angeles: Antioch University Press.

Effect of music:

Thoma, M.V., La Marca, R., Bronnimann, R., Finkel, L., Ehlert, U., Nater, U.M. (2013). The effect of music on the human stress response. *PLOS One, 8* (8).

Chapter 6

Diving Deeper 6.1 — Positive Psychology and flourishing:

Lyubomirsky, S. (2008). *The how of happiness: A scientific approach to getting the life you want.* New York: Penguin Press.

Seligman, M. E. P., & Csikszentmihalyi, M. (2000). *Positive psychology: An introduction*. American Psychologist, 55, 5-14.

Hefferon, K., & Boniwell, I. (2011). *Positive psychology: Theory, research, and applications*. New York: Open University Press.

Howell, A.J. (2009). Flourishing: Achievement-related correlates of students' wellbeing. *The Journal of Positive Psychology, 4*, 1-13.

Lyubomirsky, S., King, L. A., & Diener, E. (2005). The benefits of frequent positive affect. *Psychological Bulletin, 131*, 803-855.

Diener, E., & Biswas-Diener, R. (2002). Will money increase subjective well being? A literature review and guide to needed research. *Social Indicators Research, 57*, 119–169.

Diener, E., Nickerson, C., Lucas, R.E., & Sandvik, E. (2002). Dispositional affect and job outcomes. *Social Indicators Research, 59*, 229-259.

Harker, L. & Keltner, D. (2001). Expressions of positive emotions in women's college yearbook pictures and their relationship to personality and life outcomes across adulthood. *Journal of Personality and Social Psychology, 80*, 112-124.

Carver, C.S., Scheier, M.F., Segerstrom, S.C. (2010). Optimism. Clinical Psychology Review, 30, 879-889.

Giltay, E. J., Geleijnse, J. M., Zitman, F. G., Hoekstra, T., & Schouten, E. G. (2004). Dispositional optimism and all-cause and cardiovascular mortality in a prospective cohort of elderly Dutch men and women. *Archives of General Psychiatry, 61*, 1126–1135.

PERMA:

Seligman, M.E.P. (2011). *Flourish: A visionary new understanding of happiness and wellbeing*. New York: Free Press.

Seligman, M. E P, Steen, T., Park, N., & Peterson, C. (2005). Positive psychology progress: Empirical validation of interventions. *American Psychologist, 60*, 410-421.

Peterson, C., Park, N., & Seligman, M. E. P. (2005). Assessment of character strengths. In G. P. Koocher, J. C. Norcross, & S. S. Hill, III (Eds.) *Psychologists' desk reference* (2nd ed.), pp. 93-98. New York: Oxford University Press.

Fredrickson, B. L. (1998). What good are positive emotions? *Review of General Psychology, 2*, 300-319.

Fredrickson, B. L. (2001). The role of positive emotions in positive psychology. *American Psychologist, 56*, 218 –226.

Csikzentmihalyi, M., & Larson, R. (1984). *Being Adolescent: Conflict and growth in the teenage years*. New York: Basic Books.

Csikzentmihalyi, M. (2009). *Flow: The psychology of optimal experience*. Harper Collins.

Frankl, V. E. (1963). *Man's search for meaning: An introduction to logotherapy.* New York: Washington Square Press.

Happiness baseline:

Brickman, P., Coates, D., & Janoff-Bulman, R. (1978). Lottery winners and accident victims: Is happiness relative? *Journal of Personality and Social Psychology, 36,* 917–927

Brickman, P., & Campbell, D. T. (1971). Hedonic relativism and planning the good society. In M. H. Appley (Ed.), *Adaptation-level theory* (pp. 287– 302). New York: Academic Press.

Lykken, D., & Tellegen, A. (1996). Happiness is a stochastic phenomenon. *Psychological Science, 7,* 186–189

Happiness determined by circumstances:

Lyubomirsky, S., Sheldon, K. M., & Schkade, D. (2005). Pursuing happiness: The architecture of sustainable change. *Review of General Psychology, 9,* 111-131.

Diving Deeper 6.2 — Broaden and Build:

Fredrickson, B. L. (1998). What good are positive emotions? *Review of General Psychology, 2,* 300-319.

Fredrickson, B. L. (2001). The role of positive emotions in positive psychology: The broaden-and-build theory of positive emotions. *American Psychologist, 56,* 218–226.

Estrada, C., Isen, A.M., & Young, M.J. (1994). Positive affect influences creative problem solving and reported source of practice satisfaction in physicians. *Motivation and Emotion, 18,* 285-299.

Fredrickson, B. L., & Branigan, C. (2005). Positive emotions broaden the scope of attention and thought-action repertoires. *Cognition and Emotion, 19,* 313-332.

Isen, A. M., Daubman, K. A., & Nowicki, G. P. (1987). Positive affect facilitates creative problem solving. *Journal of Personality and Social Psychology, 52,* 1122-1131.

Isen, A. M., Johnson, M. M. S., Mertz, E., & Robinson, G. F. (1985). The influence of positive affect on the unusualness of word associations. *Journal of Personality and Social Psychology, 48,* 1413-1426.

Isen, A. M., Rosenzweig, A. S., & Young, M. J. (1991). The influence of positive affect on clinical problem solving. *Medical Decision Making, II,* 221-227.

Johnson, K. J., & Fredrickson, B. L. (2005). "We all look the same to me": Positive emotions eliminate the own-race bias in face recognition. *Psychological Science, 16,* 875-881.

Positive emotion improves cardiovascular health:

Fredrickson, B.L. (2009). *Positivity*. New York: Three Rivers Press.

Tugade, M. M., & Fredrickson, B. L. (2004). Resilient individuals use positive emotions to bounce back from negative emotional experiences. *Journal of Personality and Social Psychology, 86*, 320-333.

Positive emotions buffer against stress and anxiety:

Folkman, S., & Moskowitz, J. T. (2000). Positive affect and the other side of coping. *American Psychologist, 55*, 647-654.

Positive emotions improve memory and compassion towards different races:

Johnson, K. J., & Fredrickson, B. L. (2005). "We all look the same to me": Positive emotions eliminate the own-race bias in face recognition. *Psychological Science, 16*, 875-881.

Nelson, D.W. (2009). Feeling good and open-minded: The impact of positive affect of cross cultural empathic responding. *Journal of Positive Psychology, 3 (4)*, 253-265.

Upward spiral:

Garland, E. L., Fredrickson, B. L., Kring, A. M., Johnson, D. P., Meyer, P. S., & Penn, D. L. (2010). Upward spirals of positive emotions counter downward spirals of negativity: Insights from the broaden-and-build theory and affective neuro-science on the treatment of emotion dysfunctions and deficits psychopathology. *Clinical Psychology Review, 30*, 849-864.

Growth Mindset:

Dweck, C.S. (2008). *Mindset: The new psychology of success*. New York : Ballantine Books.

Growth Mindset scale:

De Castella, K., Byrne, D. (2015). My intelligence may be more malleable than yours: The revised implicit theories of intelligence (self-theory) scale is a better predictor of achievement, motivation, and student disengagement. *European Journal of Psychology of Education, 30*, 245-267.

Diving Deeper 6.3 — Optimism:

Seligman, M. E. P. (1991). *Learned optimism*. New York: Alfred A. Knopf.

Carver, C.S., Scheier, M.F., Miller, C.J., & Fulford, D. (2009). Optimism. In S.J. Lopez & C.R. Snyder (Eds.), *Oxford Handbook of Positive Psychology*, 2nd Edition (pp. 303-311). Oxford: Oxford University Press.

Seligman, M.E.P., Kamen, L.P., and Nolen-Hoeksema, S. (1988). Explanatory style across the life-span: Achievement and health. In E.M. Hetherington, R.M. Lerner and M. Perlmutter (Eds.), *Child Development in Life-Span Perspective*, Hillsdale, N.J.: Erlbaum, 91-114.

Peterson, C., & Barrett, L. (1987). Explanatory style and academic performance among university freshmen. *Journal of Personality and Social Psychology, 53,* 603–607.

Positive Activity Interventions:

Sin, N. L., & Lyubomirsky, S. (2009). Enhancing well-being and alleviating depressive symptoms with positive psychology interventions: A practice-friendly meta-analysis. *Journal of Clinical Psychology: In Session, 65,* 467-487.

Lyubomirsky, S., & Layous, K. (2013). How do simple positive activities increase well-being? *Current Directions in Psychological Science, 22,* 57-62.

Emmons, R. A., & McCullough, M. E. (2003). Counting blessings versus burdens: An experimental investigation of gratitude and subjective wellbeing in daily life. *Journal of Personality and Social Psychology, 84,* 377–389.

Lyubomirsky, S., Sheldon, K.M., & Schkade, D. (2005). Pursuing happiness: The architecture of sustainable change. *Review of General Psychology, 9,* 111-131.

Seligman, Steen, Park, & Peterson, (2005). Positive psychology progress: Empirical validation of interventions. *American Psychologist, 60,* 5, 410-421.

Sheldon, K. M., Boehm, J. K., & Lyubomirsky, S. (2012). Variety is the spice of happiness: The hedonic adaptation prevention (HAP) model. In I. Boniwell & S. David (Eds.), *Oxford handbook of happiness* (pp. 901-914). Oxford: Oxford University Press.

Lyubomirsky, S., Dickerhoof, R., Boehm, J. K. , & Sheldon, K. M. (2011). Becoming happier takes both a will and a proper way: An experimental longitudinal intervention to boost well-being. *Emotion, 11,* 391–402.

Quoidbach, J., Berry, E.V., Hansenne, M. , Mikolajczak, M. (2010). Positive emotion regulation and well-being: Comparing the impact of eight savoring and dampening strategies. *Personality and Individual Differences, 49,* 368–373.

Gratitude:

Fredrickson, B. L. (2004). Gratitude, like other positive emotions, broadens and builds. In R. A. Emmons & M. E. McCullough (Eds.), *The psychology of gratitude* (pp. 145–166). New York, NY: Oxford University Press.

Character strengths:

Peterson, C., & Seligman, M. E. P. (2004). *Character strengths and virtues: A handbook and classification*. New York: Oxford University Press and Washington, DC: American Psychological Association.

Park, N., Peterson, C., & Seligman, M.E.P. (2004). Strengths of character and well-being. *Journal of Social and Clinical Psychology, 23*, 603-619

Proyer, R. T., Gander, F., Wellenzohn, S., & Ruch, W. (2015). Strengths-based positive psychology interventions: a randomized placebo-controlled online trial on long-term effects for a signature strengths- vs. a lesser strengths-intervention. *Frontiers in Psychology, 6*, 456.

Savouring:

Gable, S. L., Reis, H.T., Impett, E.A., Asher, E.R.(2004). What Do You Do When Things Go Right? The Intrapersonal and Interpersonal Benefits of Sharing Positive Events. *Journal of Personality and Social Psychology, 87(2)*, 228-245.

Gable, S. L., Gonzaga, G., & Strachman, A. (2006). Will you be there for me when things go right? Social Support for Positive Events. *Journal of Personality and Social Psychology, 91*, 904-917.

Chapter 7

The Stages of Readiness for Behavioural Change Model:

Prochaska, J.O., DiClemente, C.C., & Norcross, J.C. (1992). In search of how people change: Applications to the addictive behaviors. *American Psychologist, 47*, 1102-1114. PMID: 1329589.

Maslow's Hierarchy of Needs Model:

Maslow, A. H. (1970). *Motivation and personality*. New York: Harper & Row.

Self-determination Theory:

Deci, E. L., & Ryan, R. M. (2000). The "what" and "why" of goal pursuits: Human needs and the self-determination of behavior. *Psychological Inquiry, 11*, 227-268. doi: 10.1207/s15327965pli1104_01

Sheldon, K. M., Abad, N., Ferguson, Y., Gunz, A., Houser-Marko, L., Nichols, C. P., & Lyubomirsky, S. (2010). Persistent pursuit of need-satisfying goals leads to increased happiness: A 6-month experimental longitudinal study. *Motivation and Emotion, 34*, 39-48.

GROW Model:

Whitmore, J. (2002). *Coaching for performance: Growing people, performance and purpose.* London: Nicholas Brealey.

SMART Goals:

Bahrami, Z., & Cranney, J. (2018). A Self-concordant SMART Goal Intervention Leads to Greater Goal Attainment, Need Satisfaction and Eudaimonic Well-being. *Manuscript under review.*

SUPER Tools (in general):

Morisano, D., Hirsh, J. B., Peterson, J. B., Pihl, R. O., & Shore, B. M. (2010). Setting, elaborating, and reflecting on personal goals improves academic performance. *Journal of Applied Psychology, 95,* 255-264.

Oettingen, G. (2014). *Rethinking positive thinking: Inside the new science of motivation.* New York, NY: Penguin Random House.

SUPER Tools Step 1:

Bahrami, Z., & Cranney, J. (2018). A Self-concordant SMART Goal Intervention Leads to Greater Goal Attainment, Need Satisfaction and Eudaimonic Well-being. *Manuscript under review.*

SUPER Tools Step 2:

Bandura, A. (1977). Self-efficacy: Toward a unifying theory of behavioral change. *Psychological Review, 84,* 191-215

SUPER Tools Step 3:

Covey, S. (2004). *The 7 habits of highly effective people.* New York, NY: Free Press.

Green, P., & Skinner, D. (2005). Does time management training work? An evaluation. *International Journal of Training and Development, 9,* 124–139.

Time Management:

Claessens, B.J.C., van Eerde, W., Rutte, C.G. and Roe, R.A. (2007). A review of the time management literature. *Personnel Review, 36,* 255–276.

Liu, O. L., Rijmen, F., MacCann, C., & Roberts, R. D. (2009). The assessment of time management in middle-school students. *Personality and Individual Differences, 47,* 174-179.

Scheduling Time:

UNSW (n.d.) Support with time management. Retrieved from
https://student.unsw.edu.au/support-time-management

Multitasking:

Chew, S. (n.d.) How to get the most out of studying. Retrieved from
https://www.samford.edu/departments/files/Academic_Success_Center/How-to-
Study-Teaching_Resources.pdf

Studying effectively, taking breaks, study strategies:

Dewar, M., Alber, J., Butler, C., Cowan, N., Della Sala, S. (2012) Brief wakeful resting
boosts new memories over the long term. *Psychological Science, 23*, 955–960.

Dunlosky, J., Rawson, K. A., Marsh, E. J., Nathan, M. J., & Willingham, D. T. (2013).
Improving students' learning with effective learning techniques: Promising
directions from cognitive and educational psychology. *Psychological Science in the
Public Interest, 14(1),* 4–58

Cranney J., Ahn M., McKinnon R., Morris S., Watts K. (2009). The testing effect,
collaborative learning, and retrieval-induced facilitation in a classroom setting.
European Journal of Cognitive Psychology, 21, 919-940.
doi:10.1080/09541440802413505

Attention Training/Mindfulness Meditation:

Mrazek, M.D., Franklin, M.S., Phillips, D.T., Baird, B., Schooler, J.W. (2013).
Mindfulness training improves working memory capacity and GRE performance while reducing mind wandering. *Psychological Science, 24,* 776-781

Monash University (n.d.). Mindfulness resources. Retrieved from
https://www.monash.edu/health/mindfulness/resources

Exam Anxiety:

UNSW (n.d.). Understanding exam stress. Retrieved from
https://student.unsw.edu.au/exams-stress

The Paralysing P's:

UNSW (n.d.). Procrastination. Retrieved from https://student.unsw.edu.au/procras-
tination

Problem solving and psychological flexibility:

Kashdan, T. B., & Rottenberg, J. (2010). Psychological flexibility as a fundamental
aspect of health. *Clinical Psychology Review, 30,* 865-878.

Chapter 8

Human beings are social beings:

Ferrazzi,K. & Raz, T (2014). *Never eat alone and other secrets to success, one relationship at a time.* New York: Crown Business.

Why is Connectedness So Important?

Seligman, M.E.P. (2011) Flourish. A visionary new understanding of happiness and well-being. New York: Free Press.

Global Council on Brain Health (2017). 'The Brain and Social Connectedness: GCBH Recommendations on Social Engagement and Brain Health.' Retrieved from:
http://www.aarp.org/content/dam/aarp/health/brain_health/2017/02/gcbh-social-engagement-report.pdf

Sandstrom, G.M. & Dunn, E.W. (2014). Social interactions and well-being: The surprising power of weak ties. *Personality and Social Psychology Bulletin, 40(7),* 910-922.

Baumeister, R.F. & Leary, M.R. (1995). The need to belong: Desire for interpersonal attachments as a fundamental human motivation. *Psychological Bulletin, 117(3),* 497-529.

Face to face vs online connections:

Grieve R., Indian M., Witteveen K., Tolan G. A., & Marrington J. (2013). Face-to-face or facebook: Can social connectedness be derived online? *Computers in Human Behavior, 29,* 605–609.

Bourgeois, A., Bower, J., and Carroll, A. (2014). Social networking and the social and emotional wellbeing of adolescents in Australia. *Australian Journal of Guidance and Counselling, 242,* 167-182.

Allen, K.A., Ryan, T., Gray, D.L. McInerney, D.M., & Waters, L. (2014). Social media use and social connectedness in adolescents: The positives and the potential pitfalls. *The Australian Educational and Developmental Psychologist, 31(1),* 18-31.

Positive relationships:

Berndt, T.J., & Keefe, K. (1995). Friends' influence on adolescents' adjustment to school. *Child development, 66,*1312-1329.

Reis, H. T., & Shaver, P. (1988). Intimacy as an interpersonal process. In S. Duck (Ed.), *Handbook of personal relationships* (pp. 367-389). Chichester, England: Wiley.

Hojjat, M., & Moyer, A. (2016). *The psychology of friendship.* Oxford University Press.

Active Listening:

Covey, S. (2004). *The 7 habits of highly effective people.* New York, NY: Free Press.

Rogers, C.R., & Farson, R.E. (2015). *Active listening.* Martino Publishing.

Mellish, L., Morris, S., & Do, M. (2014). Psychology Interviewing Skills Interviewing Skills for Psychology Undergraduate Students. *Unpublished document.*

Active Constructive Responding:

Gable, S. L., Reis, H. T., Impett, E. A., & Asher, E. R. (2004). What do you do when things go right? The intrapersonal and interpersonal benefits of sharing positive events. *Journal of Personality and Social Psychology, 87*(2), 228-245.

Magyar-Moe, J.L., Owens, R.L., Conoley, C.W. (2015). Positive Psychological Interventions in Counseling: What Every Counseling Psychologist Should Know. *The Counselling Psychologist, 43,* 508-557.

Capitalisation:

Gable, S. L., & Reis, H. T. (2001). Appetitive and aversive social interaction. In J. Harvey & A. Wenzel (Eds.), *Close romantic relationships: Maintenance and enhancement* (pp. 169–194). Mahwah, NJ: Erlbaum.

Beach, S. R. H., & Tesser, A. (1995). Self-esteem and the extended self-evaluation maintenance model: The self in social context. In M. H. Kernis (Ed.), *Efficacy, agency, and self-esteem* (pp. 145–170). New York: Plenum Press.

Tesser, A., Millar, M., & Moore, J. (1988). Some affective consequences of social comparison and reflection processes: The pain and pleasure of being close. *Journal of Personality and Social Psychology, 54,* 49–61.

Assertive Communication:

Leaper, C. & Ayres, M.M. (2007). A meta-analytic review of gender variations in adults' language use: Talkativeness, affiliative speech, and assertive speech. *Personality and Social Psychology Review, 11(4),* 328-363

Five step model for effective communication:

Reivich, K.J., Seligman, M.E.P., & McBride, S. (2011). Master Resilience Training in the U.S. Army. *American Psychologist, 66(1),* 25-34.

Perspective taking, empathy and psychological flexibility:

Ciarrochi, J., Atkins, P., Hayes, L., Sahdra, B., Parker, P. (2016). Contextual positive psychology: Policy recommendations for implementing positive psychology into schools. *Frontiers of Psychology, 7,* 1561.

Mindfulness and teamwork:

Atkins, P. W & Parker, S.K. (2012). Understanding individual compassion in organizations: The role of appraisals and psychological flexibility. *Academy of Management Review, 37(4),* 524-546.

Cross cultural differences in assertiveness:

Tripathi, N., Nongmaithem, S., Mitkovic, M., Ristic, L. & Zdravkovic, J. (2010). Assertiveness and personality: Cross-cultural dfferences in Indian and Serbian male students. *Psychological Studies, 55(4),* 330-338.

Chapter 9

Moral foundations:

Haidt, J. (2012) The righteous mind: Why good people are divided by politics and religion. Retrieved from http://righteousmind.com/wp-content/uploads/2013/08/ch07.RighteousMind.final_.pdf

Moral foundations (2017) retrieved from http://www.moralfoundations.org/

Moral dilemma: Overly familiar work supervisor:

Davidson, G. R., & Morrissey, S. A. (2011). Enhancing ethical literacy of psychologically literate citizens. In J. Cranney & D. Dunn (Eds.), *The psychologically literate citizen: Founations and global perspectives* (pp. 41-55). New York: Oxford University Press.

Utilitarianism:

Habibi D. A. (2001). John Stuart Mill and the Ethic of Human Growth. In Floridi, L., & Mariorosaria, T. (Eds), *Philosophical Studies Series* (Vol. 85, pp 62-116) Retrieved from https://link.springer.com/chapter/10.1007/978-94-017-2010-6_3

Dilemma A (trolley problem) and B (transplant patient):

Jarvis Thomson, J. (1985). The trolley problem. *The Yale Law Journal, 94,* 1395-1415. Retrieved from http://philosophyfaculty.ucsd.edu/faculty/rarneson/Courses/thomsonTROLLEY.pdf

Thomas, B. C., Croft, K. E., & Tranel, D. (2011). Harming kin to save strangers: Further evidence for abnormally utilitarian moral judgements after ventromedial prefrontal damage. *Journal of Cognitive Neuroscience, 23,*2186-96.

Categorical imperative:

Immanuel, K. (1993) [1785]. Grounding for the metaphysics of morals. In Ellington, J. W. (Eds), *Kant Immanuel*, (pp. 30). Hackett. ISBN 0-87220-166-X.

Sandel M. (2009). Justice. Retrieved from https://www.youtube.com/watch?v=kBdfcR-8hEY&list=PL30C13C91CFFEFEA6

Ethical emotivism:

Hume D. (1986) *A treatise of human nature*. Selby-Bigge, L.A. (Eds). Oxford: Clarendon Press retrieved from http://oll.libertyfund.org/titles/342

Horberg, E. J. Oveis, C.; Keltner, D. & Cohen, A. B. (2009). Disgust and the moralization of purity. *Journal of Personality and Social Psychology*, 97, 963–976.

Anger and harm:

Cannon, P. R., Schnall, S. & White, M. (2011). Transgressions and expressions Affective facial muscle activity predicts moral judgments. *Social Psychological and Personality Science*, 2, 325–331.

Virtues:

Georgescu, A. (2017). *Artistotle and the benefits of moderation: Virtues and vice in the age of populism*. Retrieved from http://www.themarketforideas.com/aristotle-and-the-benefits-of-moderation-virtue-and-vice-in-the-age-of-populism-a126/

Aristotle (1955). *The ethics of Aristotle: The Nichomachaen ethics*. (rev. ed.) (J. K. Thomson, trans.). New York: Viking. p. 104. Retrieved from https://www.cwu.edu/~warren/Unit1/aristotles_virtues_and_vices.htm

Dostoevsky on religion:

Philosophy and philosophers (2012). If god does not exist everything is permitted – Dostoevsky. Retrieved from: http://www.the-philosophy.com/god-exist-permitted-dostoevsky

Morals and Ethics in our Personal and Professional Life:

The Telegraph (2013). Warren Buffett: His best quotes. Retrieved from: http://www.telegraph.co.uk/finance/newsbysector/banksandfinance/8381363/Warren-Buffett-his-best-quotes.html

Blinder, A., Perez-Pena. R. (2015). Clerk denying same-sex marriage certificates. Retrieved from https://www.nytimes.com/2015/09/02/us/same-sex-marriage-kentucky-kim-davis.html?_r=0

Chapter 10

George Bernard Shaw. Retrieved from http://izquotes.com/quote/266399

Giving psychology away:

Miller, G. (1969) Psychology as a means of promoting human welfare. *American Psychologist, 24,* 1063-75.

Psychological literacy:

Cranney, J., & Dunn, D. (Eds.) (2011). *The psychologically literate citizen: Foundations and global perspectives.* New York: Oxford University Press.

NOTES

NOTES

NOTES